MEDICAL SPANISH:
The Instant Survival Guide

"This book will fill a great need for medical personnel. It is concise, convenient to use, and provides rapid access to essential information."

George Sternbach, M.D., F.A.C.E.P.
Deputy Director, Emergency Services
Stanford University Hospital

"As an emergency department nurse, I am particularly impressed with the assessment section, which simultaneously sorts out both chief complaints and pertinent information."

Melinda S. Alves, R.N.
Clinical Nursing Coordinator,
Emergency Department
Stanford University Hospital

MEDICAL SPANISH:
The Instant Survival Guide

Susan Lister

Foothill College
Los Altos Hills, California
   and
West Valley College
Saratoga, California

Cynthia J. Wilber

ADDISON-WESLEY PUBLISHING COMPANY
Medical/Nursing Division • Menlo Park, California
Reading, Massachusetts • London • Amsterdam
Don Mills, Ontario • Sydney

Acquisition Editor: Richard W. Mixter
Production Coordinators: Karen Bierstedt, Margaret Moore
Copy Editor: Linnea Dayton

ISBN: 0-201-05950-9
BCDEFGHIJ-HA-89876543

DEDICATIONS

To my husband Tony, a man who is dedicated to helping others. He is a kind and understanding person who is always willing to listen to my problems. He has been patient and encouraging throughout the production of this book.

Susan Lister

To Bill, Matthew, and Simon, with thanks for their patience.

Cynthia Wilber

ACKNOWLEDGMENTS

It is with sincere gratitude that we thank all those who have been part of the writing, revision, and production of *Medical Spanish: The Instant Survival Guide*. Their names are too numerous to mention, but their contributions have been invaluable in making this book the practical tool that we hope it will be for those who use it. In particular, we thank Sister Inez Hernandez, P.B.V.M. for her painstaking care in helping to revise the manuscript.

 Addison-Wesley Publishing Company □ Medical/Nursing Division □ 2725 Sand Hill Road, Menlo Park, California 94025

FOREWORD

I am a family physician who is a Spanish language novice. As such, I might be regarded as lacking the epaulets that usually qualify one to write a foreword to a new book. I believe I do have a special perspective, however, that qualifies me to introduce *Medical Spanish: The Instant Survival Guide.* I care for Spanish-speaking patients and I am acutely aware of the need for improved communication with them.

In addition to being a provider of primary care medical services, I have the pleasure of being a teacher of young health care providers. These include family practice residents, medical students and budding social workers and physicians' assistants. Approximately half of the patients in the practice in which we work are Hispanic. Many of them speak Spanish as their first language. Our practice is located in an inner city in California, and though California has the largest Spanish speaking cohort of any state, there are 20 states in the country that have Spanish language populations exceeding 4% of their total. New York, Florida, and Texas all have substantial Spanish speaking populations. It is estimated that approximately 10,000,000 in the United States consider Spanish their preferred language.

In my office I find it imperative to have bilingual office personnel constantly in attendance. In spite of this assistance, my improving Spanish language skills are a real boon to my ability to deliver health care. As I understand more, I am better able to work with my patients and interpreters. Furthermore, my rapport with my patients—so important in optimizing care—is improved greatly because they perceive my efforts to communicate with them in their own language. Even simple greetings are appreciated.

I have read both early and final drafts of this text: *Medical Spanish: The Instant Survival Guide* by Susan Lister and Cynthia Wilber. This work will be a real boon to providers on the front line. The book also has much to offer the hospital-based caregiver in dealing with Spanish speaking patients. Despite its pocket size, this is a veritable encyclopedia, offering specific questions or instructions for every major hospital function or group, including special services such as labor and delivery, dialysis, or CAT scans. The emphasis in this book is always on what is practical and important. The language is simple, designed to elicit simple answers to medically appropriate questions. As well as covering diagnostic and therapeutic procedures, this book will help in obtaining informed consent. Furthermore, there is a large section of patient information and follow-up instructions that will greatly facilitate compliance and self-care.

The text is arranged in such a manner that most organizational health care units, such as an emergency room, a physician's office, or a poison control center, will find appropriate vocabulary, instructions, and forms conveniently available for immediate use. *Medical Spanish: The Instant Survival Guide* will be a great asset to all personnel and institutions caring for individuals who speak Spanish.

William C. Fowkes, Jr., M.D.
Head, Division of Family Medicine
Stanford University School of Medicine

PREFAÇE

Medical Spanish: The Instant Survival Guide evolved directly from observations and personal experiences in the medical field. We have worked for many years with and among health-care providers in the San Francisco Bay Area and have become aware of the need for an adequate medical language guide to assist in meeting the needs of the Spanish-speaking patient.

Illustrations of the language problem range from humorous to tragic. For example, the Spanish word for years, **años** (ăhn yōs), is very similar to the Spanish word for anus, **ano** (ăhn nō) and if the health professional interchanges the two words, he or she may unwittingly ask how many anuses the patient has.

A few years ago a diabetic baby was born to a Hispanic-American mother at a major West Coast hospital. Vital information and literature on dietary and medical management of diabetes was presented to the mother in English only. A short time after discharge the baby was brought back to the hospital in a diabetic coma and subsequently died.

In another case a man was diagnosed as needing a colostomy. The only interpreter available was a janitor, who attempted to relay the information to the patient. The custodial employee, unwilling to disclose that he did not understand in English what the physicians were asking him to translate, simply told an entirely different and false story to the patient, who signed the surgical consent form.

Unlike the examples presented so far, many language problems occur in day-to-day routine care situations, where the health-care professional and the Spanish-speaking patient experience not tragedy but great difficulty and frustration in making themselves understood. In such situations simple hospital functions may be confusing.

Every day in hospitals, clinics, and medical offices throughout the country, the health-care provider carries out such simple procedures as starting an intravenous line, explaining a call button, or giving medication. The patient has a basic right to understand and consent to what is occurring. We have sought to provide in this source book assistance with communication in as many facets of health care as possible. Responding to the needs of health professionals, we have written a book that provides simple, useful medical conversation for many general medical situations and medical subspecialities. We believe adequate communication and comprehension are vitally important to the effectiveness of all health-care personnel—physicians, nurses, paramedics, orderlies, and medical social workers. We hope this book will help improve communication between the medical professional and the Spanish-speaking patient seeking health care.

Cynthia J. Wilber and Susan Lister

CONTENTS

SECTION C

Patient Information   147

INTRODUCTION

This book has been designed as a language guide to be used "on the spot" with Spanish-speaking people in medical situations. The medical person using the book *does not have to be skilled in understanding Spanish*. We have designed most of the questions to elicit yes or no answers. For other questions, we have provided a list of likely responses in Spanish.

To facilitate Spanish use for English-speaking medical personnel, expressions have been purposely shortened and designed for easier pronunciation without sacrificing meaning. The Spanish used is correct, but we endeavored to maintain everyday language rather than literate Spanish to reach patients of all education levels.

HOW TO USE THIS BOOK
We suggest the reader become familiar with the book and its structure before using it on the job. Locate and read those sections that you are likely to use the most; underline phrases and statements you feel you might need in a hurry.

In Section C, "Patient Information," there are many sets of patient instructions. Instructions are cross-referenced in the text and footnotes of other sections, in which their particular subject matter is presented. These instructions are designed to be sent home with the patient. However, you, the health-care provider, should thoroughly review instructions with the patient, adapting the instructions, if necessary, to each individual situation.

Most importantly, remember that Spanish-speaking patients will be very grateful and pleased that you are making an effort to communicate with them. Do not be afraid of mispronouncing words. Far more important than pronunciation is the effort you make to communicate and understand. If you feel that pronunciation will be a problem for you, read the section on language necessities at the end of the book and mark or underline those parts that are particularly useful to you. Good luck/**Buena suerte**.

CULTURAL NOTES

There is more to transcultural health care than bridging language differences. It is important that the medical professional have some understanding of folk medicine and health beliefs of Hispanic Americans and of the origins and history of these beliefs. Such understanding may foster a more sensitive practitioner-patient relationship.

Religion is generally the most pervasive force in Hispanic-American culture. Religious beliefs are a mixture of Catholicism and, in the case of the Mexican-American, of the Maya/Aztec beliefs of pre-Hispanic Mexico. The attitude that results from this mixture of beliefs is an accepting, somewhat fatalistic belief that life is predetermined and controlled by God. It is very important that health-care personnel be aware of the prevalent concept that body, mind, and religion are inseparable; therefore if something is wrong with the body, it may be the result of such causes as sin, a curse, a hex, or exposure to bad winds. For example, **mal de ojo** ("evil eye"), whether transmitted with or without evil intent, is thought to cause a multitude of real symptoms and pathology from miscarriage and madness to fallen fontanels. **Empacho,** a common ailment probably best described as acute constipation and gastrointestinal pain, is said to be derived from certain foods that produce balls of food in the stomach and intestines, which are impossible to pass and stick to the stomach walls, causing extreme pain in the navel area. The traditional cure for **Empacho** is massage and manipulation to free the balls of food and administration of herbs to purge the body. Another disorder seen frequently is **Susto,** which is severe paranoid depression believed to be caused by a bad experience or a curse on the individual.

Many folk cures involve maintaining or regaining balance in the body. This stems probably from a simplified form of Greek humoral pathology. The body is believed to be regulated by its four forces or humors—hot, cold, wet, and dry—and health is maintained by balancing these four forces. Traditionally, blood, which is said to be the life force, is hot and wet; the other bodily forces counterbalance it. Illnesses are diagnosed as hot or cold and wet or dry (or some combination) and are treated with foods and medicines believed to be opposites of the illnesses and therefore able to restore balance and health.

It is our hope that the few sociocultural points presented will serve to illustrate the way that some facets of Hispanic-American life styles interact with medicine.

Generally speaking, the Spanish-speaking American has strong feelings about family, religion, and causes of some illness and death. Practically speaking, in the hospital situation, understanding these feelings may help the health-care professional assist patients and their families and develop a health-care program agreeable to both practitioner and patient.

RIGHTS OF PATIENTS

Each person voluntarily admitted or involuntarily detained for evaluation or treatment shall have the following rights:

a. To wear his own clothes; to keep and use his own personal posessions including his toilet articles; and to keep and be allowed to spend a reasonable sum of his own money for canteen expenses and small purchases.

b. To have access to individual storage space for his private use.

c. To see visitors each day.

d. To have reasonable access to telephones, both to make and receive confidential calls.

e. To have ready access to letter writing materials, including stamps, and to mail and receive unopened correspondence.

f. To refuse shock treatment.

g. To refuse lobotomy.

h. Other rights as specified by regulation.

FROM:
Section 5325
Welfare and Institutions
Code
State of California

DERECHOS DE PACIENTES

Cada persona admitida voluntariamente o detenida involuntariamente para evaluación o tratamiento tendrá los siguientes derechos:

a. De llevar su propia ropa; de guardar y usar sus artículos personales incluyendo los artículos de tocador; y de guardar y permitírsele gastar una suma módica de su dinero para artículos de uso o consumo personal.

b. De tener disponible espacio para guardar sus objetos de uso personal.

c. De recibir visitas cada día.

d. De tener acceso razonable al uso del teléfono para hacer y recibir llamadas confidenciales.

e. De tener a mano lo necesario para escribir cartas, incluyendo estampillas, y de enviar y recibir correspondencia sin abrir.

f. De rehusar tratamiento de choques eléctricos.

g. De rehusar operación del cerebro.

h. Otros derechos especificados por regla.

DE:
Sección 5325
Código de Bienestar
e Instituciones
Estado de California

MEDICAL SPANISH:
The Instant Survival Guide

SECTION A

Emergency Information

PARAMEDICS

Level of Consciousness

1. What is your name?

2. Do you know where you are?
3. Do you know who you are?
4. Do you know the day/date?

5. How many fingers am I holding up?
6. What were you doing when the pain started?
7. Is there anything that makes it feel better or go away?
8. What type of pain is it?
   a. sharp?
   b. dull?
   c. tightness?
   d. pressure?
   e. heaviness?
   f. stabbing?
   g. ripping?
   h. tearing?
9. Where is the pain?
10. Can you point with one finger to it?
11. Does the pain travel anywhere? To the jaw, arm, or back?

PARAMÉDICOS

Nivel de Conocimiento

1. ¿Cómo se llama usted?
   (¿Cuál es su nombre?)

2. ¿Sabe usted dónde está?
3. ¿Sabe quién es usted?
4. ¿Sabe qué día es hoy?
   ¿Sabe la fecha?

5. ¿Cuántos dedos le estoy mostrando?
6. ¿Qué hacía usted cuando le comenzó el dolor?
7. ¿Hay algo que le alivia el dolor? ¿O que se lo quite?
8. ¿Qué tipo de dolor tiene?
   a. agudo?
   b. sordo?
   c. tirantez?
   d. de presión?
   e. pesado?
   f. punzante?
   g. rasgante?
   h. desgarrante?
9. ¿Dónde está el dolor?
10. ¿Puede enseñarme con un dedo?
11. ¿Le corre el dolor? ¿A la quijada, al brazo, a la espalda?

12. How severe is the pain? Mild, moderate, or severe?

13. On a scale of one to ten (ten being the worst) how would you rate it?

14. Does the pain increase with a deep breath?

15. How long have you had the pain?

16. Does it come and go or is it constant?

17. Have you ever had this pain before?

18. Is it the same as before?

19. Do you feel nauseated?

20. Did you break out in a sweat?

21. Are you allergic to any medications?

22. Do you take any medications?

23. Do you have a history of
    a. heart disease?
    b. diabetes?
    c. epilepsy?
    d. bronchitis?
    e. emphysema?
    f. asthma?

12. ¿Qué tan fuerte es el dolor? ¿Ligero, simple, moderado, agudo, severo?

13. ¿En una escala de uno a diez (diez es el peor) cómo lo calificaría?

14. ¿Le aumenta el dolor al respirar profundo?

15. ¿Desde cuándo tiene el dolor?

16. ¿Se va y viene o es constante?

17. ¿Ha tenido este dolor antes? (Ha sido siempre así?)

18. ¿Es semejante como antes?

19. ¿Tiene náuseas?

20. ¿Sudó usted cuando vino el dolor?

21. ¿Es usted alérgico a alguna medicina?

22. ¿Toma usted algunas medicinas?

23. ¿Padece
    a. del corazón?
    b. de diabetes?
    c. de epilepsia?
    d. de bronquitis?
    e. de enfisema?
    f. de asma?

BASIC EMERGENCY ADMISSION QUESTIONS

Allergies _____

    antibiotics? _____ which ones? _____

    aspirin? _____

    sulfa drugs? _____

    pain medications? _____ which ones? _____

    others? _____

Required medications   _____

Medical problems   _____

Blood type   _____

Religion   _____

Referral physician   _____

EMERGENCY ROOM

Administration

1. Are you the patient? Are you related to the patient?
2. What is your name?
3. What is your last name, first name, middle initial?
4. What is your telephone number? address? zip code?
5. What is the name of your nearest relative?

PREGUNTAS BÁSICAS PARA UNA EMERGENCIA O INGRESO

Alergias _____

    ¿antibióticos? _____ ¿cuáles? _____

    ¿aspirina? _____

    ¿drogas de azufre ("sulfa")? _____

    ¿pastillas para dolor? _____ ¿cuáles? _____

    ¿otras? _____

Medicamentos requeridos   _____

Problemas médicos   _____

Grupo sanguíneo   _____

Religión   _____

Médico que le mandó   _____

SALA DE EMERGENCIA

Administración

1. ¿Es usted el/la paciente? ¿Es usted pariente del/de la pacien
2. ¿Cuál es su nombre?
3. ¿Cuál es su apellido, primer nombre, inicial?
4. ¿Cuál es su número de teléfono, dirección, zona postal?
5. ¿Cuál es el nombre de su pariente más cercano?

6. How are you related? Relative's address? Telephone number?

7. How old are you? What is your date of birth? Place of birth?

8. What is your marital status?
   a. married?
   b. divorced?
   c. single?
   d. separated?
   e. widowed?

9. When were you hurt?

10. What happened?

11. What is your employer's
    a. name?
    b. telephone?
    c. address?
    d. zip code?

12. What is your Blue Cross Number? Kaiser?

13. What type of medical insurance do you have?

14. Do you have a Medicare card?

15. Do you have your Medi-Cal stickers?

16. What is the number of your green card?

17. Fill out this form, please.

18. Sign here, please.

19. This is an authorization form. Please read it and then sign here.

6. ¿Cuál es el parentezco? ¿Dirección de sus parientes? ¿Número de teléfono?

7. ¿Cuántos años tiene usted? ¿Cuál es la fecha de su nacimiento? ¿Lugar de nacimiento?

8. ¿Cuál es su estado civil?
   a. casado(a)?
   b. divorciado(a)?
   c. soltero(a)?
   d. separado(a)?
   e. viudo(a)?

9. ¿Cuándo fue lastimado?

10. ¿Qué pasó?

11. ¿Cuál es
    a. el nombre de su empleado?
    b. el número de teléfono?
    c. la dirección?
    d. la zona postal?

12. ¿Cuál es su número de Cruz Azul? ¿de Kaiser?

13. ¿Qué clase de seguro médico tiene usted?

14. ¿Tiene usted una tarjeta de Medicare?

15. ¿Tiene usted los sellos de Medi-Cal?

16. ¿Cuál es el número de su tarjeta verde?

17. Llene esta forma, por favor.

18. Firme aquí, por favor.

19. Esta es una forma de autorización. Favor de leerla y firmarla aquí.

Assessment

1. Who is the patient?
2. What is wrong?
3. Where is the pain? How long have you had it? Have you had it before?
4. How did the accident happen?
5. How did this happen? How long ago?
6. Did you injure yourself?
7. Do you know where you are?
8. Do you have identification to get you registered/signed in?
9. Have you been here before?
Perhaps in the clinics?
10. Are you still living at this address?
11. What is your phone number?
12. Where do you work? What do you do?

13. Do you have a private doctor we should call?
14. Have you seen another doctor about this problem?
15. What medicines are you taking now? Do you have
a. diabetes?
b. high blood pressure?
16. Have you had a tetanus shot in the last five years?

Reconocimiento

1. ¿Quién es el paciente?
2. ¿Cuál es el problema?
3. ¿Dónde siente el dolor? ¿Desde cuándo lo tiene? ¿Ha tenido este dolor antes?
4. ¿Cómo sucedió el accidente?
5. ¿Cómo sucedió esto? ¿Cuánto tiempo hace?
6. ¿Se lastimó?
7. ¿Sabe dónde se encuentra usted?
8. ¿Tiene la identificación para registrarse/firmar?
9. ¿Ha estado aquí antes?
¿Tal vez en las clínicas?
10. ¿Todavía vive en esta dirección?
11. ¿Cuál es su número de teléfono?
12. ¿Dónde trabaja? ¿Cuál es su profesión o trabajo? (¿Qué hace Ud?)

13. ¿Tiene algún doctor particular que debemos llamar?
14. ¿Ha visto a algún otro médico con este problema?
15. ¿Qué medicinas está Ud. tomando ahora? ¿Tiene Ud.
a. diabetes?
b. presión alta?
16. ¿Ha recibido una inyección para tétano en los últimos cinco años?

17. When was your last tetanus shot?

18. Do you have allergies to any medicines?

19. Did you lose consciousness? For how long?

20. Does anything hurt? Does it hurt much?

21. Where? Show me.

22. Does it hurt when I press here?

23. When does it hurt more—during the morning or evening?

24. Have you ever injured your foot?

25. Can you feel me touching you here?

26. Tell me, when I touch you, is it sharp or dull?

27. Can you move your arms? legs? fingers? toes?

28. Does it hurt when you breathe?

29. Does it hurt when you move?

30. It is necessary to inject anesthetic to make the area numb. You will be O.K.

31. You need to call this number for an appointment in the clinic.

32. You have an appointment in the _____ clinic on _____(date)_____ at _____(time)_____.

33. Here is your prescription.

34. Please come back in _____ hours.

35. You will need blood and urine tests.

17. ¿Cuándo recibió su última inyección para tétano?

18. ¿Tiene alergias a algunas medicinas?

19. ¿Perdió su conocimiento? ¿Por cuánto tiempo?

20. ¿Le duele algo? ¿Le duele mucho?

21. ¿Dónde? Enséñeme.

22. ¿Le duele cuando le aprieto aquí?

23. ¿Cuándo le duele más—por la mañana o por la noche?

24. ¿Alguna vez se ha lastimado un pie?

25. ¿Me siente cuando lo/la toco aquí?

26. Dígame, cuando lo/la toco, lo siente agudo o sordo?

27. ¿Puede mover los brazos, piernas, dedos, dedos del pie?

28. ¿Le duele al respirar?

29. ¿Le duele al moverse?

30. Es necesario inyectarle anestesia para dormirle la parte afectada. Ud. estará bien.

31. Ud. necesita llamar a este número para una cita en la clínica.

32. Ud. tiene una cita en la Clínica _____ el _____(fecha)_____ a la(s) _____(hora)_____.

33. Aquí tiene su receta.

34. Favor de regresar en _____ horas.

35. Ud. va a necesitar pruebas de sangre y de orina.

36. I am calling the specialist to see you.

37. You will be admitted to the hospital.

36. Voy a llamar al especialista para que lo(la) examine.

37. Ud. será ingresado al hospital.

Injuries

Fractures, Sprains

1. You have broken _____ (a bone) _____.

   You have fractured _____ (a bone) _____.

2. You have dislocated _____ (a joint) _____.

3. You have pulled _____ (a muscle) _____.

4. You have twisted (sprained) (a muscle)/(a ligament) _____.

5. You will need a cast for your broken _____.

6. Return at once if your fingers (toes) become numb or blue or if you cannot move them.

Wounds, Cuts

1. You have been
   a. wounded.
   b. cut.

2. You have a
   a. laceration.
   b. gash.
   c. puncture wound.

Lastimadas

Fracturas, Torceduras

1. Ud. se ha quebrado/roto _____ (un hueso) _____.

   Ud. se ha fracturado _____ (un hueso) _____.

2. Ud. se ha dislocado _____ (una coyuntura) _____.

3. Ud. se ha distendido _____ (un músculo) _____.

4. Ud. se ha torcido (un músculo)/(un ligamento) _____.

5. Necesita un yeso para su _____ quebrado.

6. Regrese en seguida si los dedos/los dedos del pie se le entumecen, se le azulan o si no puede moverlos.

Heridas, Cortadas

1. Ud. se ha
   a. herido.
   b. cortado.

2. Ud. tiene una
   a. laceración.
   b. cuchillada.
   c. herida punturada.

3. You won't need stitches.

4. I will put on medicine to make the pain go away.

5. It will not hurt.

6. You will need stitches for your cut.

7. You must keep the stitches dry.

8. Return in _____ days to have the stitches removed.

9. Do not get the bandage wet.

10. Return at once if the wound becomes painful, red, or swollen.

Burns

1. How did you burn yourself?
   a. lard? oil?
   b. stove?
   c. oven?
   d. hot water?
   e. fire?
   f. lye?
   g. acid?

2. Tell me if this hurts.

3. You must keep the wound clean at all times.

4. I want to check it again in 5 days.

3. **Ud. no necesitará puntos.**

4. **Le voy a aplicar medicina para quitarle el dolor.**

5. **No le va a doler.**

6. **Necesita puntos para su cortadura.**

7. **Debe mantener los puntos secos.**

8. **Regrese en _____ días para que se le quiten los puntos.**

9. **No se moje la venda.**

10. **Regrese en seguida si la herida le duele, o si se le enroja o se le hincha.**

Quemaduras

1. **¿Cómo se quemó?**
   a. **¿manteca? ¿aceite?**
   b. **¿estufa?**
   c. **¿horno?**
   d. **¿agua caliente?**
   e. **¿fuego?**
   f. **¿lejía?**
   g. **¿ácido?**

2. **Dígame si le duele esto.**

3. **Ud. debe mantener la herida limpia todo el tiempo.**

4. **Quiero examinarla otra vez en <u>cinco</u> (5) días.**

Unconscious Patient

1. What happened to him/her?
2. Has he fainted?
3. He complained of pain and fell to the floor.
4. He choked on food.
5. He got drunk.
6. Does he have
   a. heart disease?
   b. diabetes?
   c. emphysema?
   d. bronchitis?
   e. breathing problems?
7. Is he taking any medications? What kind? For the heart, for the lungs? Insulin?
8. Can you bring me the medicines he takes?
9. Has he had a recent head injury?
10. Has he vomited?
11. Has he been treated in this hospital before?
12. Has he been ill before?
13. Is she pregnant?
14. Does he have allergies?
15. Has he been stung by a bee/wasp?
16. Was he bitten by a snake? What kind?

El Paciente Inconsciente

1. ¿Qué le pasó? (¿Qué le sucedió?)
2. ¿Se ha desmayado?
3. El se quejó de dolor y se cayó al suelo.
4. El se atragantó con la comida.
5. Se emborrachó.
6. ¿Padece
   a. ¿del corazón?
   b. ¿de diabetes?
   c. ¿de enfisema?
   d. ¿de bronquitis?
   e. ¿de problemas al respirar?
7. ¿Está tomando algunas medicinas? ¿De qué clase? ¿Para el corazón, para los pulmones, insulina?
8. ¿Puede traerme las medicinas que él toma?
9. ¿Ha sufrido recientemente un daño a la cabeza?
10. ¿Ha vomitado?
11. ¿Ha sido tratado en este hospital antes?
12. ¿Ha estado enfermo antes?
13. ¿Está embarazada?
14. ¿Tiene alergias?
15. ¿Ha sido picado(a) por una abeja/avispa?
16. ¿Fue mordido(a) por una culebra? ¿De qué clase?

Pediatrics

1. Why did you bring your child to the hospital?
2. Tell me, can the baby sit up? Put him on the table for the examination.
3. Was he crying a lot?
4. Does he eat well?
5. Did he vomit?
6. Does he have diarrhea? What color is it?
7. Has he had a rash recently?

8. Did you take his temperature? Can you tell me how high it was? Did you take it by rectum?
9. Does your child have fever, a cough, vomiting, diarrhea, trouble breathing?
10. Has you child had
    a. mumps?
    b. measles?
    c. chickenpox?
    d. convulsions?
11. How much did your child weigh at birth?
12. In general, what does your child eat?

Pediatría

1. Por qué trajo a su niño(a) al hospital?
2. Dígame, ¿se puede sentar su niño(a)? Póngalo/la en la mesa para el examen.
3. ¿Estaba llorando mucho?
4. ¿Come bien?
5. ¿Vomitó?
6. ¿Tiene diarrea? ¿De qué color es?
7. ¿Recientemente ha tenido salpullido (o erupción de la piel)?
8. ¿Le ha tomado la temperatura? ¿Me puede decir qué de alta estaba? ¿La tomó por recto?
9. ¿Su niño(a) tiene fiebre, tos, vómitos, diarrea o problemas al respirar?
10. ¿Ha tenido su niño(a)
    a. paperas?
    b. sarampión (rubéola)?
    c. varicela (viruela loca)?
    d. convulsiones?
11. ¿Cuánto pesó su niño(a) al nacer?
12. Por lo general, ¿qué come su niño(a)? (¿Qué le da de comer a su niño(a)?)

13. I want you to put him to bed. Give him water and juice to drink. Here is a prescription for medicine. You must give it to him every 4 hours.

14. How was your child hurt?

15. Did he lose consciousness?

16. Has he been unusually sleepy?

17. Does he speak coherently?

18. Does he hurt in any other place?

Parents, Family, Patients

1. When did the pain start? When did the accident happen?

2. Would you like a cup of coffee? Black coffee, with cream, or with sugar?

3. Please sit down. The nurse will call you shortly.

4. Your husband/wife would like to see you.

5. Do you need a taxi?

13. Quiero que lo/la ponga en cama. Déle a beber agua o jugos. Aquí está una receta para medicina. Debe dársela cada <u>cuatro</u> (4) horas.

14. ¿En qué forma fue dañado(a) su hijo(a)?

15. ¿Perdió conocimiento?

16. ¿Ha tenido mucho sueño? (¿Ha tenido muchas ganas de dormir?)

17. ¿Habla coherentemente?

18. ¿Le duele en algún otro lugar?

Padres, Familia, Pacientes

1. ¿Cuándo empezó el dolor? ¿Cuándo pasó (ocurrió) el accidente?

2. ¿Gusta una taza de café? ¿Café solo, o con crema o con azúcar?

3. Favor de sentarse. La enfermera le llamará dentro de poco.

4. Su esposo(a) quisiera verlo(la).

5. ¿Necesita un taxi?

POISON CONTROL

Use of Syrup of Ipecac in Toxic Ingestions

Ipecac syrup is used to induce vomiting in the early management of acute oral poisonings. The drug produces emesis in 80% to 99% of patients with a mean recovery of 28% (range 0% to 78%) of the gastrointestinal contents. Because emesis may not evacuate all of the toxic material, patients should be followed carefully for signs of increasing intoxication.

Ipecac syrup should <u>not</u> be used if the patient is unconscious, semicomatose, severely inebriated, convulsing, or in shock, or has lost the gag reflex.

Ordinarily, the drug should <u>not</u> be used after ingestion of strychnine or other convulsant poisons, caustics or corrosives including acids and alkalies, or volatile oils.

Telephone Instructions in Case of Ingestion

1. What was swallowed?
2. Please spell the name of the product for me.

CONTROL DE VENENO

Uso del Jarabe de Ipecacuana en Casos de Ingestiones Tóxicas

El Jarabe de Ipecacuana se usa para inducir vómitos en el tratamiento pronto de envenenamiento bucal grave. La droga produce émesis en ochenta por ciento (80%) a noventa y nueve por ciento (99%) de los pacientes con término medio de recobro de veintiocho por ciento (28%)—rango cero por ciento (0%) a setenta y ocho por ciento (78%)—del contenido gastrointestinal. Porque es posible que la émesis no evacúe todo el material tóxico, los pacientes se deben vigilar cuidadosamente para señales del aumento del envenenamiento.

El Jarabe de Ipecacuana <u>no</u> debe usarse si el paciente está inconsciente, semicomatoso, severamente embriagado, en convulsiones, en choque o si ha perdido el reflejo de vomitar.

Ordinariamente, la medicina <u>no</u> se debe usar después de una ingestión de estricnina o de otros venenos que producen convulsiones, o de venenos cáusticos o corrosivos, incluyendo los ácidos y álcalis o de aceites volátiles.

Direcciones Telefónicas en Caso de Ingestión

1. ¿Qué se tragó?
2. ¿Favor de deletrear el nombre del producto?

3. How old is the person who swallowed this? What is his/her age?

4. How much does the person weigh?

5. Is the person breathing all right?

6. Is the person complaining of any pain or other difficulty?

7. How long ago did the person swallow the product?

Advise the caller to administer Ipecac and water according to the following table. The water is quite important initially and following each emesis to assure a thorough washing of the Ipecac and toxin from the stomach.

1–2 Years

1. Give 1 measuring tablespoon of the Ipecac and a small glass of water.

2. This medicine will make the child vomit in 20–30 minutes.

3. He/she will vomit a total of three to four times.

4. Each time the child vomits, give another small glass of water.

5. If the child gets tired from vomiting and wants to rest, be sure the child lies face down.

2–10 Years

1. Give 1 measuring tablespoon and 1 measuring teaspoon of Ipecac and a glass of water to the child.

3. ¿Cuántos años tiene la persona que se tragó esto?

4. ¿Cuánto pesa?

5. ¿Está respirando bien?

6. ¿Se queja de algún dolor, o de otra dificultad?

7. ¿Cuánto hace que esta persona se tragó el producto?

Aconseje al que llama que dé Jarabe dé Ipecacuana y agua según las direcciones siguientes. El agua es muy importante al principio y después de cada vómito para asegurar un lavado completo del estómago de la Ipecacuana y de la toxina.

Uno a Dos (1–2) Años

1. Déle una (1) cucharada medida de Ipecacuana y un vasito de agua.

2. Esta medicina hará que el niño/la niña vomite en veinte a treinta (20–30) minutos.

3. Vomitará tres o cuatro (3–4) veces en total.

4. Cada vez que vomite el niño/la niña, déle otro vasito de agua.

5. Si el niño/la niña se cansa de vomitar y quiere descansar, asegure que se tienda boca abajo.

Dos a Diez (2–10) Años

1. Déle una (1) cucharada medida y una (1) cucharadita medida de Ipecacuana y un vaso de agua al niño/a la niña.

2. This medicine will make the child vomit in 20–30 minutes.

3. He/she will vomit a total of three to four times.

4. Each time the child vomits, give another small glass of water.

5. If the child gets tired from vomiting and wants to rest, be sure the child lies face down.

10 Years and Older

1. Give the entire bottle of Ipecac and a large glass of water.

2. This medicine will produce vomiting in 20–30 minutes.

3. Vomiting will occur about three times.

4. Each time vomiting occurs, the person must drink another large glass of water.

Transporting to the Hospital

Administration of Ipecac at home is often advised prior to routing the patient to the hospital. This gets vomiting under way and prevents further absorption of the toxin while the patient is enroute.

If this is the case, the following instructions will be necessary:

2. Esta medicina hará que el niño/la niña vomite en veinte a treinta (20–30) minutos.

3. Vomitará tres o cuatro (3–4) veces en total.

4. Cada vez que vomite el niño/la niña, déle otro vasito de agua.

5. Si el niño/la niña se cansa de vomitar y quiere descansar, asegure que se tienda boca abajo.

Diez (10) Años y Más

1. Déle la botella entera de Ipecacuana y un vaso grande de agua.

2. Esta medicina producirá vómitos en veinte a treinta (20–30) minutos.

3. Los vómitos ocurrirán así como tres (3) veces.

4. Cada vez que vomite, la persona debe tomar otro vaso grande de agua.

Llevando al Hospital

A menudo se aconseja administrar la Ipecacuana en casa antes de llevar al paciente al hospital. Esto da principio a los vómitos y evita más absorción de la toxina mientras el paciente está en camino al hospital.

Si el caso es así, serán necesarias las siguientes instrucciones:

1. Take a pail or bucket with you in the car for the person to vomit into.

2. Bring the medicine container or product swallowed with you to the hospital.

3. Do not let the person lie down in the car.

1. Lleve consigo en el coche un balde o cubo en el cual el paciente pueda vomitar.

2. Lleve al hospital el envase de la medicina o producto que fue tragado por el paciente.

3. No permita que el paciente se acueste en el coche.

SECTION B
Medical Information

HEALTH QUESTIONNAIRE
  History of Past Illness
    Childhood
    Adult
    Operations
    Injuries
    Allergies and Sensitivities
  Family History
  Social History
  Education
  Systemic Review
    General
    Skin
    Head/Eyes/Ears/Nose
    Neck
    Respiratory
    Cardiovascular
    Gastrointestinal
    Genitourinary
    Gynecologic
    Locomotor Musculoskeletal
    Neuropsychiatric
    Hematologic
    Endocrine

ANATOMY (TERMINOLOGY)
ANESTHESIA
  Spinal Anesthesia
  Anesthesia for Obstetrics/
    Gynecology
  Outpatient Anesthesia
BACK PAIN OR PROBLEMS
BURN UNIT
  Burn Garments for Children
CARDIOLOGY
  For Adults
  Pediatric Cardiology
  Heart Attack—Useful
    Phrases
  Cardiac Surgery
COMMON MEDICAL PROB-
  LEMS (TERMINOLOGY)

DERMATOLOGY
  Psoriasis
  Skin (Terminology)
DIABETES
DRUGS
  General
  Drug Slang (Terminology)
EARS, NOSE, AND THROAT
  Ears
  Nose
  Mouth and Throat
ENDOCRINOLOGY
FAMILY PLANNING
  Contraceptives
  Terminology
GASTROINTESTINAL

GENITOURINARY
  Infection
  Obstruction
  Tumor
  Stones
  Incontinence (Leaking)
  Neurogenic
  Cystoscopy
HEADACHES/HEAD
MEDICATIONS
  Terminology
  Instructions
  Prescriptions for Those Who
    Cannot Read
  Drug Labels
  Side Effects
NEPHROLOGY
  Dialysis
  Dialysis (Terminology)
  How Dialysis Works

HEALTH QUESTIONNAIRE

Name _____

Address _____ Date _____

Telephone Number _____ Age _____

How can we contact you? _____

1. What is your name?

2. What are you here for?
   What is your problem?

3. How long have you had it?

4. Have you ever had it before?

5. Have you had a complete physical exam in the past year?

6. Are you under the care of a private physician?

7. Do you have any chronic conditions such as diabetes, heart disease or high blood pressure?

8. Are you now taking or have you taken in the past any medications on a regular basis?

9. Have you been ill or required intensive care for any amount of time in the past?

10. Are you sick or do you have any symptoms at the moment?

CUESTIONARIO DE SALUD

Nombre _____

Dirección _____ Fecha _____

Teléfono _____ Edad _____

¿Cómo podemos comunicarnos con usted? _____

1. ¿Cómo se llama usted?
   ¿Cuál es su nombre?

2. ¿De qué se queja usted?
   ¿Cuál es su problema?
   ¿Qué le molesta?

3. ¿Cuánto hace que tiene Ud. este problema?

4. ¿Lo ha tenido antes?

5. ¿Le han hecho un examen médico completo durante el último año?

6. ¿Está usted bajo la atención de un médico particular?

7. ¿Padece usted de algunas condiciones crónicas como diabetes, enfermedades del corazón, o presión alta?

8. ¿Está tomando algunas medicinas—o las ha tomado en el pasado con regularidad?

9. Por algún tiempo en el pasado, ¿ha estado enfermo(a) o ha requerido cuidado intensivo?

10. En el presente, está usted enfermo(a) o tiene algunos síntomas?

History of Past Illness

Childhood

Have you had
  measles?
  mumps?
  chickenpox?
  diabetes?
  cancer?
  rheumatic fever or heart disease?
  tuberculosis?
  congenital abnormalities?
  other serious illnesses?

Adult

Have you had any serious illness?

Have you ever been hospitalized or been under medical care for very long?

If yes, for what reason?

Operations

Have you ever had surgery?

What kind?

Injuries

Have you ever had any broken bones?

Have you had a concussion or other head injury?

Have you ever been knocked unconscious?

Historia de Enfermedades Pasadas

Niñez

¿Ha tenido usted
  sarampión?
  paperas?
  viruelas locas, varicela?
  diabetes?
  cáncer?
  fiebre reumática o enfermedades del corazón?
  tuberculosis?
  anormalidades congénitas?
  otras enfermedades serias?

Edad adulta

¿Ha tenido alguna enfermedad seria?

¿Ha sido hospitalizado o ha estado bajo atención médica alguna vez por mucho tiempo?

Si la respuesta es sí, ¿Por qué motivo?

Operaciones

¿Ha tenido alguna vez operaciones?

¿Qué clase de operaciones?

Heridas o Fracturas

¿Se le ha quebrado alguna vez un hueso?

¿Ha tenido alguna vez un daño o concusiones cerebrales?

¿Alguna vez ha perdido Ud. el conocimiento?

Allergies and Sensitivities

Do you have or have you ever had allergies?

Do you have a history of skin reaction or other untoward reaction or sickness after taking any drug or medication?

Family History

	If living		If deceased
	Age	Health	Age at death and cause
Father			
Mother			
Brother/Sister			
Husband/Wife			
Son/Daughter			

Has any blood relative ever had
  cancer?
  tuberculosis?
  diabetes?
  heart trouble?
  high blood pressure?
  stroke?
  convulsions?
  suicide?
  insanity?
  bleeding tendency?
  arthritis, gout?

Alergias y Sensibilidades

¿Tiene o ha tenido alergias alguna vez?

En el pasado ¿ha tenido reacción de la piel u otra reacción o enfermedad después de tomar alguna droga o medicina?

Historia Familiar

	Si viven		Si fallecidos
	Edad	Salud	Edad cuando murió y causa
Padre			
Madre			
Hermano/Hermana			
Esposo/Esposa			
Hijo/Hija			

¿Alguno de su familia estuvo o ha estado enfermo de
  cáncer?
  tuberculosis?
  diabetes?
  problemas cardíacos?
  presión alta?
  derrame?
  convulsiones?
  suicidio?
  locura?
  tendencia a sangrar?
  artritis, gota?

Social History

Are you single, married, separated, divorced, widowed?

Are you living with your husband/wife?

Is your sex life satisfactory?

Do you have dependents at home?

Do you consume alcoholic beverages? Never, rarely, moderately, daily, ever.

Do you use tobacco? Cigarettes? If you smoke, how many packs a day?

Are you employed? Full-time? Part-time?

What is your job?

Are you exposed to fumes, dusts, or solvents?

How much time have you lost from work because of your health during the past six months? The past year? The past five years?

Education

Years

Grade school
High school
College
Postgraduate

Historia Social

¿Es usted soltero(a), casado(a), separado(a), divorciado(a), viudo(a)?

¿Vive usted con su esposo/esposa?

¿Es satisfactoria su vida sexual?

¿Tiene familiares que dependen de usted económicamente?

¿Toma usted bebidas alcohólicas? Nunca, rara vez, moderadamente, diario, jamás.

¿Fuma tabaco? ¿cigarrillos? Si usted fuma, ¿cuántos paquetes al día?

¿Está trabajando? ¿Tiempo completo? ¿Parte del tiempo?

¿Cuál es su oficio (trabajo)?

¿Está expuesto(a) a gases, polvo o residuos químicos?

¿Cuánto tiempo ha perdido de trabajo a causa de la salud durante los últimos seis meses? ¿durante un año o cinco años pasados?

Educación

Años

Escuela elemental
Escuela secundaria
Universidad
Pos graduado

Systemic Review

General

Have you been in good general health most of your life?

Has your weight changed recently?

Skin

Do you have or have you ever had
  skin disease?
  jaundice?
  hives, eczema, or rash?
  frequent infections or boils?
  abnormal pigmentation?

Head/Eyes/Ears/Nose

Do you wear glasses?

Do you have or have you ever had
  eye disease or injury?
  double vision?
  headaches?
  glaucoma?
  itching eyes or nose?
  sneezing or runny nose?
  nosebleeds?
  chronic sinus trouble?
  ear disease?
  impaired hearing?
  dizziness or episodes of unconsciousness?

Repaso de los Sistemas

General

¿Ha estado en buena salud la mayoría de su vida?

¿Ha cambiado de peso recientemente?

La Piel

¿Tiene o ha tenido
  enfermedades de la piel?
  ictericia o piel amarilla?
  urticaria, eczema o comezón (picazón o ronchas)?
  infecciones o forúnculos (chichones) frecuentes?
  pigmentación anormal? Piel amarilla?

Cabeza/Ojos/Oídos/Nariz

¿Usa usted lentes (gafas)?

¿Tiene o ha tenido
  enfermedades de los ojos o heridas?
  visión doble?
  dolores de cabeza (jaquecas)?
  glaucoma?
  comezón de los ojos o nariz?
  estornudos o le corren las narices?
  sangramiento por la nariz?
  problemas crónicos con los senos nasales (sinusitis)?
  enfermedades de los oídos?
  empeoramiento de la audición (¿sordera?)
  mareos o pérdidas del conocimiento? ¿desmayos?

Neck

Do you have or have you ever had
  stiffness?
  thyroid trouble?
  enlarged glands?

Respiratory

Do you have URI (a cold) now?

Do you ever spit up blood?

Do you have or have you ever had
  chronic or frequent cough?
  asthma or wheezing?
  difficulty breathing?
  any trouble with lungs?
  pleurisy or pneumonia?

Cardiovascular

Do you have or have you ever had
  chest pain or angina pectoris?
  shortness of breath while walking or lying down?
  difficulty walking two blocks?
  heart trouble or heart attacks?
  high blood pressure?
  swelling of hands, feet or ankles?
  awakening in the night?
  smothering?
  heart murmur?

Cuello

¿Tiene o ha tenido
  torcimiento (tortícolis)? ¿el cuello tieso?
  problemas con la glándula tiroides?
  glándulas inflamadas o crecidas?

Respiratorio

¿Está resfriado, o tiene un catarro ahora?

¿Escupe o arroja sangre por la boca?

¿Tiene o ha tenido
  tos crónica o frecuente?
  asma o respiración silbante?
  dificultad al respirar?
  problemas con los pulmones?
  pleuresía o pulmonía?

Cardiovascular

¿Tiene o ha tenido
  dolor de pecho o angina de pecho?
  falta de respiración al caminar o al estar acost
  dificultad al caminar dos cuadras?
  problemas o ataques del corazón?
  presión alta?
  hinchazón de las manos, pies o tobillos?
  despertar durante la noche?
  ahogo o sofocación?
  soplos del corazón?

Gastrointestinal

Do you have or have you ever had
   peptic ulcer (stomach or duodenal)?
   vomiting blood or food?
   gallbladder disease?
   liver trouble?
   hepatitis?
   painful bowel movements?
   black stools?
   hemorrhoids or piles?
   recent changes in bowel movements?
   frequent diarrhea?
   heartburn or indigestion?
   cramping or pain in abdomen?
   food stuck in throat?

Genitourinary

Do you have or have you ever had
   loss of urine?
   frequent urination?
   nighttime urinating?
   burning or painful urination?
   blood in urine?
   kidney trouble?
   kidney stones?
   Bright's disease?

Gastrointestinal

¿Tiene o ha tenido alguna vez
   úlcera péptica (del estómago o del duodeno)?
   vómitos de sangre o de alimentos?
   enfermedad de la vesícula biliar (de la bilis)?
   problemas del hígado?
   hepatitis?
   defecaciones con dolor?
   defecación de color negro?
   hemorroides o almorranas?
   cambios recientes en defecar?
   diarrea frecuente?
   ardor en el pecho o indigestión?
   calambres o dolor en el abdomen?
   alimento atorado en la garganta?

Genitourinario

¿Tiene o ha tenido alguna vez
   pérdida de orina?
   que orinar con frecuencia?
   que orinar de noche?
   ardor o dolor al orinar?
   sangre en la orina?
   problemas de los riñones?
   cálculos renales?
   nefritis crónica?

Gynecologic

At what age did your periods start?

How frequent are your periods? Every _____ days.

How many days does your period usually last?

Do you have any pain with your periods?

How many times have you been pregnant?

How many miscarriages (spontaneous abortions) have you had?

How many children do you have?

When did you have your last Pap (cancer) smear? What were the results?

What was the date of the first day of your last period?

Was your last period normal?

Locomotor Musculoskeletal

Do you have or have you ever had
  varicose veins?
  weakness of muscles or joints?
  any difficulty in walking?
  any pain in calves or buttocks from walking?
  pain in the joints? Does it get better or worse with exercise?

Ginecológica

¿A qué edad empezó su menstruación (su regla)?

¿Cuál es la frecuencia de su regla? Cada _____ días.

¿Cuántos días dura su regla regularmente?

¿Tiene dolor durante la menstruación?

¿Cuántas veces ha estado embarazada?

¿Cuántas pérdidas (abortos espontáneos) ha tenido?

¿Cuántos hijos tiene?

¿Cuándo tuvo su última prueba Pap (para cáncer)? ¿Cuáles fueron los resultados?

¿Cuál fue la fecha del primer día de su última regla?

¿Fue normal su última regla?

Locomotor Músculo Esqueletal

¿Tiene o ha tenido alguna vez
  venas varicosas?
  debilidad en los músculos o coyunturas (articulaciones)?
  dificultad al caminar?
  dolor en las pantorrillas o en las nalgas al caminar?
  dolor en las coyunturas (articulaciones)? ¿Se alivia o se empeora con ejercicio?

Neuropsychiatric

Do you have or have you ever had
  psychiatric care?
  fainting spells?
  convulsions?
  paralysis?
Have you ever been advised to see a psychiatrist?

Hematologic

Do you have or have you ever had
  cuts that were slow to heal?
  blood disease?
  anemia?
  phlebitis?
  excessive bleeding after tooth extraction or surgery?

  abnormal bleeding or bruising?

Endocrine

Do you have or have you ever had
  thyroid disease?
  hormone therapy?
  any change in hat or glove size?
  any change in hair growth?
  have you become colder than before?
  has your skin become dryer?

Neuro-Psiquiátrico

¿Tiene o ha tenido alguna vez
  tratamiento psiquiátrico?
  desmayos?
  convulsiones?
  parálisis?
Alguna vez ¿le han recomendado ver a un psiquíatra?

Hematológico

¿Tiene o ha tenido alguna vez
  cortaduras que le demoran en curarse?
  enfermedad de la sangre?
  anemia?
  flebitis?
  sangramiento excesivo después de haberle extraído una
    muela o después de cirugía?
  sangramiento anormal (hemorragia) o moretones?

Endocrina

¿Tiene o ha tenido alguna vez
  enfermedad de la tiroides?
  terapia hormonal?
  cambios en medida de sombreros o guantes?
  cambio alguno en el crecimiento del pelo?
  más frío que antes?
  la piel más seca?

ANATOMY (TERMINOLOGY)

ANATOMIA (TERMINOLOGÍA)

1. abdomen
2. adrenal gland(s)
3. ankle
4. anus
5. aorta
6. appendix
7. arm
8. armpit
9. artery
10. back
    (lower) back
11. backbone

12. belly
13. birthmark
14. bladder
15. blood
16. body
17. bone
18. bowels

19. brain
    brains
20. breasts
21. buttocks

1. el abdomen
2. la glándula suprarrenal
3. el tobillo
4. el ano
5. la aorta
6. el apéndice
7. el brazo
8. la axila
9. la arteria
10. la espalda
    la cintura
11. el espinazo, la columna vertebral

12. la barriga
13. el lunar
14. la vejiga
15. la sangre
16. el cuerpo
17. el hueso
18. los intestinos, las entrañas

19. el cerebro
    los sesos
20. el pecho, los senos
21. las nalgas, las posaderas, las sentaderas

22. calf
23. cartilage
24. cervix
25. cheek (of the face)
26. chest
27. chin
28. coccyx
29. collarbone
30. diaphragm
31. duodenum
32. ear (inner)
33. ear (outer)
34. ear drum
35. ears
36. elbow
37. esophagus
38. eye
39. eyebrow
40. eyelash
41. eyelid
42. face
    facial skin
43. fallopian tube
44. finger
45. finger nail
46. fist

22. la pantorrilla, el chamorro
23. el cartílago
24. la cérviz de la matriz
25. el cachete, la mejilla
26. el pecho
27. la barbilla, el mentón
28. la cóccix
29. la clavícula
30. el diafragma
31. el duodeno
32. el oído
33. la oreja
34. el tímpano
35. las orejas
36. el codo
37. el esófago
38. el ojo
39. la ceja
40. la pestaña
41. el párpado
42. la cara
    el cutis
43. el tubo falopio
44. el dedo
45. la uña
46. el puño

47. foot	47. el pie	67. kneecap	67. la rótula, el hueso de la rodilla
sole of the foot	la planta del pie		
heel	el talón	68. larynx	68. la laringe
48. forehead	48. la frente	69. leg	69. la pierna
49. forearm	49. el antebrazo	70. ligament	70. el ligamento
50. gallbladder	50. la vesícula biliar	71. limb	71. el miembro
51. genitals	51. los genitales	72. lip	72. el labio
52. gland	52. la glándula	73. liver	73. el hígado
53. groin	53. la ingle	74. lung	74. el pulmón
54. hair (of the head)	54. el pelo, el cabello	75. mandible	75. la mandíbula
hair (of the body)	los vellos	76. molar	76. la muela
55. hand	55. la mano	77. mouth	77. la boca
palm of the hand	la palma	78. muscle	78. el músculo
56. head	56. la cabeza	79. nail	79. la uña
57. heart	57. el corazón	80. navel	80. el ombligo
58. heart valve	58. la válvula del corazón	81. neck	81. el cuello, el pescuezo (sl.)
59. heel	59. el talón	nape (of neck)	la nuca
60. hip	60. la cadera	82. nerve	82. el nervio
61. hormone	61. la hormona	83. nipples (female)	83. las tetas
62. intestines	62. los intestinos	84. nipple(s) (male)	84. el pezón, los pezones
small	el intestino delgado	85. nose	85. la nariz
large	el intestino grueso	86. nostrils	86. las narices
63. jaw	63. la quijada, la mandíbula	87. organ	87. el órgano
64. joint	64. la coyuntura, la articulación	88. ovary	88. el ovario
		89. palm	89. la palma
65. kidney	65. el riñón	90. pancreas	90. el páncreas
66. knee	66. la rodilla	91. patella	91. el hueso de la rodilla, la rótula
back of the knee	la corva		

92. pelvis	92. la cadera, la pelvis	116. stomach	116. el estómago, la panza, la barriga
93. pelvic area	93. el área pélvica		la barriga
94. penis	94. el pene, el miembro	pit of the stomach	la boca del estómago
95. pituitary gland	95. la glándula pituitaria	117. temple	117. la sien
96. prostate gland	96. la próstata, la glándula de la próstata	118. tendon	118. el tendón
		119. testicle	119. el testículo
97. pulse	97. el pulso	120. thigh	120. el muslo
98. pupil	98. la niña del ojo, la pupila	121. thorax	121. el tórax
99. rectum	99. el recto, el ano	122. thumb	122. el pulgar, el dedo gordo
100. rib	100. la costilla	123. thyroid	123. la tiroides
101. saliva	101. la saliva	124. tissue	124. el tejido
102. scalp	102. el cuero cabelludo	125. toe	125. el dedo del pie
103. scapula	103. la escápula	126. tongue	126. la lengua
104. scrotum	104. el escroto	127. tonsils	127. las anginas, las amígdalas
105. shin	105. la espinilla	128. tooth, molar	128. el diente, la muela
106. shoulder	106. el hombro	129. trachea	129. la tráquea
107. shoulder blade	107. la espaldilla	130. umbilicus, navel	130. el ombligo
108. side	108. el costado, el lado	131. urethra	131. la uretra
109. sinus	109. el seno	132. urine	132. la orina
110. skin	110. la piel	133. uterus	133. el útero, la matriz
skin of the face	el cutis	134. uvula	134. la campanilla, úvula
111. skull	111. el cráneo	135. vagina	135. la vagina
112. sole (of the foot)	112. la planta del pie	136. vein	136. la vena
113. spine	113. el espinazo, la columna vertebral	137. vocal cord	137. la cuerda vocal
		138. waist	138. la cintura
114. spleen	114. el bazo	139. womb	139. la matriz
115. sternum	115. el hueso del pecho, el esternón	140. wrist	140. la muñeca

ANESTHESIA

1. I am Dr. _____. I am going to put you to sleep tomorrow so the doctors can do the operation.
2. Have you had any operations before? What and when?
3. Do you take any medicine? What?
4. Do you have trouble taking medicines?
5. Do you have allergies?
6. Has anyone in your family had problems with anesthesia or bleeding?
7. Have you taken steroids in the past—cortisone or prednisone?
8. Do you have any loose teeth, capped teeth, or chipped teeth, or trouble opening your jaw?
9. Do you smoke? How much?
10. Do you have trouble with your chest: coughing, asthma, or shortness of breath?
11. Do you have any heart trouble?
    pain in the chest when working hard?
    trouble breathing at night?
12. Do you take pills for your heart?
    for high blood pressure?
13. Do you have any liver problems?
    hepatitis?
    jaundice (when you turn yellow)?

ANESTESIA

1. Soy Dr. _____. Le voy a poner a dormir mañana para que los médicos puedan realizar la operación.
2. ¿Ha tenido algunas operaciones antes? ¿Para qué y cuándo?
3. ¿Toma usted medicina? ¿Qué?
4. ¿Tiene problemas al tomar las medicinas?
5. ¿Tiene alergias?
6. ¿Hay alguien en su familia que haya tenido problemas con anestesia o que haya tenido hemorragias?
7. ¿Ha tomado usted esteroides en el pasado—cortisona o prednisona?
8. ¿Tiene dientes flojos, coronas o dientes astillados, o problemas al abrir la quijada (mandíbula)?
9. ¿Fuma usted? ¿Cuánto?
10. ¿Tiene problemas en el pecho: tiene tos, asma o falta de aire (respiración)?
11. ¿Padece del corazón?
    ¿Tiene dolor de pecho al trabajar mucho?
    ¿Tiene problemas al respirar en la noche?
12. ¿Toma pastillas para el corazón?
    ¿para la presión alta?
13. ¿Padece del hígado?
    ¿de hepatitis?
    ¿de ictericia (cuando la piel se pone amarilla)?

14. Do you have any kidney problems?

15. When did you eat last?

16. You must not eat or drink anything after midnight tonight. This is very important.

17. When you come to the operating room, I will give you some medicine so you will go to sleep.

18. You will feel a small needle prick now. That is your IV.

19. Take a deep breath of this oxygen. It is good for you.

20. You will feel sleepy soon.

21. Open your eyes. Take a deep breath.

22. Your operation is over, and everything went fine.

23. We are going to the recovery room now, so that you can wake up.

24. This is the recovery room. Your operation is over.

14. ¿Padece del riñón?

15. ¿Cuándo fue la última vez que comió?

16. Ud. no debe comer ni beber nada después de la media-noche. Esto es muy importante.

17. Cuando venga a la sala de operaciones, le daré medicina para que Ud. se duerma.

18. Ud. sentirá un piquete ahora. Eso es su suero intravenoso.

19. Aspire profundamente de este oxígeno. Le hará bien.

20. Ud. sentirá sueño pronto.

21. Abra los ojos. Aspire profundamente.

22. Terminó su operación. Todo salió bien.

23. Vamos a la sala de recuperación, para que Ud. pueda despertarse.

24. Esta es la sala de recuperación. Se acabó la cirugía. (Terminó su operación.)

Spinal Anesthesia

1. Turn on your side and pull your knees up.

2. This will feel cold.

3. I am putting the medicine (needle) in now.

4. We will turn you on your back. Do not help us.

Anestesia Espinal

1. Póngase de lado y encoja las rodillas.

2. Esto se sentirá frío.

3. Le estoy poniendo la medicina (la inyección). (Le estoy inyectando la medicina.)

4. Le voltearemos boca arriba ahora. No nos ayude. (No haga esfuerzo.)

5. If you must cough, sneeze, or move, tell me.
6. Does this feel sharp or dull?
7. This is oxygen to breathe. It is good for you.

Anesthesia for Obstetrics/Gynecology

1. If you have a general anesthetic, some of it will get to the baby and make him sleepy for a while, so we think an epidural anesthetic would be better.

2. We will put a small plastic catheter in between the bones of your back, and inject some local anesthetic from time to time. So you may have difficulty moving your legs.

3. You may feel some pressure, but you won't feel any pain.

4. Do you have any questions? Do you understand?

5. There is always a small statistical risk when you have an anesthetic, but I don't expect any unusual problems, so please don't worry.

6. Move over to the bed/gurney slowly.

7. When you feel a tingling (like pins and needles or a little electric shock) in your thumb or fingers, keep your arm still and tell me immediately.

8. Lift up your head, open your mouth and squeeze my hand.

9. How tall are you?

10. Please breathe from this black rubber mask.

5. Si necesita toser, estornudar o moverse, avíseme, por favor.
6. ¿Siente esto como piquete agudo o sordo?
7. Este es oxígeno para respirar. Le hará bien.

Anestesia para Obstetricia/Ginecología

1. Si Ud. recibe anestesia general, parte de ella afectará al bebé y le dará sueño por un rato. Creemos que la anestesia epidural sería mejor.

2. Le pondremos una sondita de plástico entre los huesos de la espalda para inyectar un poco de anestesia local de vez en cuando. Es posible que tenga alguna dificultad al mover las piernas.

3. Sentirá un poco de presión, pero no sentirá ningún dolor.

4. ¿Tiene algunas preguntas? ¿Entiende?

5. Siempre hay un poco de riesgo cuando Ud. reciba anestesia, pero no espero ningún problema raro, así que no se preocupe.

6. Muévase a la cama/camilla despacio.

7. Cuando sienta hormigueo (como comezón o una sacudida) en el pulgar o en los dedos, mantenga el brazo inmóvil y avíseme inmediatamente.

8. Levante la cabeza, abra la boca y apriete mi mano.

9. ¿Cuánto mide de alto?

10. Favor de respirar de esta máscara negra de goma.

Outpatient Anesthesia*

BACK PAIN OR PROBLEMS[†]

1. Where do you hurt?
2. Where is the pain?
3. What was the cause of your pain?
4. Place one finger where the pain is the strongest.
5. What aggravates the pain?
6. What relieves the pain?
7. Is the pain you are having now
   the same?
   worse?
   better?
8. Is the pain worse in the morning or the evening?
9. Does the pain awaken you at night? Can you go right back to sleep, or does it take awhile?

DOLORES O PROBLEMAS DE LA ESPALDA

1. ¿Dónde le duele?
2. ¿Dónde siente el dolor?
3. ¿Qué causó el dolor?
4. Ponga un dedo donde siente más dolor.
5. ¿Qué le aumenta el dolor?
6. ¿Qué le alivia el dolor?
7. El dolor que tiene ahora, ¿es
   igual?
   peor?
   mejor?
8. ¿Es peor el dolor en la mañana o en la noche?
9. ¿Le despierta en la noche el dolor? ¿Puede dormirse en seguida, o demora en dormirse de nuevo?

*Instructions to patients for outpatient anesthesia can be found in Section C, p. 172, Patient Information. A consent form for outpatient anesthesia can be found in Section F, p. 220, Consent Forms.

†Instructions to help with back pain and a list of things that a patient with back pain should and should not do may be found in Section C, pp. 148–149, Patient Information.

10. Do you have any
    dizziness?
    blurring of vision?
    headaches?

11. Do you have any numbness ("pins and needles" feelings) at the tips of your fingers or toes? Which fingers (toes)? All the time, or sometimes?

12. Does coughing or sneezing aggravate the pain?

13. Have you had any inability to empty your bladder?

14. What medications are you taking?

15. Have you ever had cortisone injections or pills?

16. Have X-rays been taken? Where? When?

17. I would like to examine you now. Please take off your clothes except your underwear (and bra), and put on this gown.

18. First I will test certain movements in your back. Stand with your knees straight, and bend forward to touch your toes.

19. Bend forward and slide your hands along your legs as you try to touch your toes.

20. Lean backward as far as your pain will allow.

21. Lean to the left.

22. Lean to the right.

---

10. ¿Tiene usted
    mareo o vértigo?
    vista nublada?
    jaquecas?

11. ¿Tiene entumecimiento ("hormigueo") en las yemas de los dedos de la mano o los dedos del pie? ¿Cuáles dedos? ¿Todo el tiempo o a veces?

12. ¿Le agrava el dolor la tos o los estornudos?

13. ¿Ha tenido problemas al orinar?

14. ¿Qué medicamentos está tomando?

15. ¿Le han puesto alguna vez inyecciones de cortisona, o le han dado pastillas?

16. ¿Le han tomado rayos X. ¿Dónde? ¿Cuándo?

17. Quisiera examinarlo(a) ahora. Por favor, quítese la ropa menos la ropa interior (y el sostén), y póngase este camisón.

18. Primero le voy a probar ciertos movimientos en la espalda. Párese con las rodillas rectas y dóblese hacia adelante para tocar los dedos de los pies.

19. Dóblese hacia adelante y pase las manos a lo largo de las piernas tratando de tocar los dedos del pie.

20. Dóblese hacia atrás así como el dolor le permita.

21. Dóblese hacia la izquierda.

22. Dóblese hacia la derecha.

23. Turn your shoulders to the left,
    to the right.
24. Lie face down (prone).
25. Lie face up (supine).
26. Does this cause pain?
27. Place your hands on opposite shoulders, turn to the right,
    and now to the left.
28. Now I would like you to lie down on your back to test the
    strength in your legs.
29. I would like to test your sensation with a pin. Close your
    eyes and tell me if this is sharp or dull.
30. I would like to test your reflexes. Please relax. Turn onto
    your stomach.

23. Vuelva los hombros hacia la izquierda,
    hacia la derecha.
24. Acuéstese boca abajo.
25. Acuéstese boca arriba.
26. ¿Le causa dolor esto?
27. Ponga las manos en los hombros opuestos, vuélvase a la
    derecha, ahora a la izquierda.
28. Ahora quiero que se acueste de espalda (boca arriba) para
    probar la fuerza en las piernas.
29. Quiero probar su sensibilidad con un alfiler. Cierre los ojos
    y dígame si esto siente puntiagudo o sin punta.
30. Quiero probarle los reflejos. Relájese. Póngase boca abajo.

BURN UNIT

1. I am going to take your temperature now.
2. I am going to take your blood pressure now.
3. I am going to start an IV.
4. I am going to give you your medication in the IV.
5. I am going to give you an injection.
6. It is important for you to eat.
7. It is important for you to drink liquids.
8. You are not allowed water.

DEPARTAMENTO DE QUEMADURAS

1. Le voy a tomar la temperatura ahora.
2. Le voy a tomar la presión ahora.
3. Le voy a empezar un suero.
4. Le voy a poner su medicamento en el suero.
5. Le voy a poner una inyección.
6. Es importante que usted coma.
7. Es importante que usted beba o tome líquidos.
8. No debe tomar agua.

9. We are going to put in a catheter now.

10. We are going to take out your catheter now.

11. I have to put a KAO tube (feeding tube) down your throat, because you are not eating enough.

12. We have to change your dressing twice a day.

13. We will change your dressing after your tubbing.

14. We are going to take you for your tubbing now.

15. Is the water all right?

16. Is the water the right temperature?

17. I know that hurts, but I have to do it.

18. We are going to scrub you with Betadyne now.

19. If the Betadyne is irritating you, we can use Hibiclens to scrub you.

20. Physical Therapy will come to fit you with your burn garments.

21. Have you been fitted for your burn garments yet?

Burn Garments for Children

1. This is a vest for a burned child.

2. The pressure of the vest serves to decrease the scarring.

3. It is very important for the child to use this vest for 23 hours a day.

9. Le vamos a poner una sonda (un tubo) ahora.

10. Le vamos a quitar la sonda (el tubo) ahora.

11. Tengo que ponerle un tubo por la garganta para ayudarle a comer porque usted no está comiendo lo suficiente.

12. Tenemos que cambiarle el vendaje dos veces al día.

13. Le cambiaremos el vendaje después de darle un baño de tina.

14. Ahora vamos a darle su baño de tina.

15. ¿Está bien el agua?

16. ¿Está bien la temperatura del agua?

17. Yo sé que le duele, pero tengo que hacerlo.

18. Vamos a friccionarle con Betadyne ahora.

19. Si la Betadyne le irrita, podemos usar Hibiclens para friccionarle.

20. La enfermera de fisioterapia vendrá para probarle los ajustadores (soportadores) de quemaduras.

21. ¿Le han probado ya los ajustadores para quemaduras?

Ajustadores para Quemaduras para Niños

1. Este es un chaleco para un(a) niño(a) quemado(a).

2. La presión del chaleco sirve para disminuir la cicatriz.

3. Es muy importante que el niño (la niña) use este chaleco por veintitrés horas al día.

4. The only time to remove the vest is when you bathe him/her.
5. The child will have two vests. He can wear one while the other is being washed.
6. It is necessary to wash this vest with mild soap like Ivory—never with Woolite.
7. Put the vest outside in the air to dry—never in the dryer.
8. Each vest lasts 3 to 6 months, and then the therapist can order another one.

CARDIOLOGY

For Adults

1. Have you ever had chest pain? Where?
2. Is the chest pain burning or pressure?
3. What brings it on? What makes it better?
4. How long does it last?
5. Do you have chest pains when you are resting?
6. Are the pains strongers when you are working?
7. What alleviates the pains?
8. Do the pains radiate to the back or to the left arm?
9. Do you notice any irregularity of heart beat or any palpitations?

4. Sólo puede quitarle el chaleco cuando lo/la bañe.
5. El niño (la niña) tendrá dos chalecos. Puede usar uno mientras que se lava el otro.
6. Es necesario lavar este chaleco con jabón suave como Ivory—nunca con Woolite.
7. Ponga el chaleco afuera al aire libre para secarlo—nunca en la secadora.
8. Cada chaleco dura de tres a seis (3–6) meses, entonces el terapista puede ordenar otro.

CARDIOLOGÍA

Para Adultos

1. ¿Ha tenido alguna vez dolor de pecho? ¿Dónde?
2. ¿Tiene dolor de pecho que le arde o que le causa presión?
3. ¿Qué lo causa? ¿Qué lo alivia?
4. ¿Cuánto tiempo le dura?
5. ¿Tiene dolores de pecho al descansar?
6. ¿Son más fuertes los dolores cuando está trabajando?
7. ¿Qué le alivia los dolores?
8. ¿Le corren los dolores a la espalda o al brazo izquierdo?
9. ¿Nota cualquier latido o palpitación irregular?

10. Do you get short of breath? When?

11. What makes it worse or better?

12. Can you walk up a flight of stairs without stopping? How often must you stop?

13. How many blocks can you walk before you must stop due to fatigue or shortness of breath?

14. Have you noted ankle swelling? Does it go down at night?

15. Have you noted right upper abdominal (liver) fullness or pain?

16. How many pillows do you use at night? How long do you sleep?

17. Do you have to get up at night because of shortness of breath? How often? For how long?

18. Do you take medicine for your heart? How often?

19. Do you know if you have high blood pressure?

20. Is there a history of hypertension in your family?

Pediatric Cardiology

1. Was your pregnancy with this child normal?

2. Did you have any illnesses during your pregnancy?

3. How much did your baby weigh at birth?

4. Did he (she) have a heart murmur at birth?

10. ¿Siente que le falta el aire? ¿Cuándo?

11. ¿Qué lo empeora o lo mejora?

12. ¿Puede subir las escaleras de un tramo sin pararse? ¿Cuántas veces necesita pararse?

13. ¿Cuántas cuadras puede caminar antes de que tenga que parar debido a la fatiga o a la falta de aire?

14. ¿Se le han hinchado los tobillos? ¿Se le baja la hinchazón por la noche?

15. ¿Ha tenido hinchazón o dolor en la región abdominal superior derecha (el hígado)?

16. ¿Cuántas almohadas usa para dormir en la noche? ¿Cuánto tiempo duerme?

17. ¿Tiene que levantarse en la noche debido a la falta de aire? ¿Con qué frecuencia? ¿Por cuánto tiempo?

18. ¿Toma medicina para el corazón? ¿Con qué frecuencia?

19. ¿Sabe usted si tiene la presión alta?

20. ¿Hay historia de hipertensión en su familia?

Cardiología Pediátrica

1. ¿Fue normal su embarazo con este niño(a)?

2. ¿Sufrió algunas enfermedades durante su embarazo?

3. ¿Cuánto pesó su bebé al nacer?

4. ¿Tuvo soplo de corazón al nacer?

5. Did your baby have any illnesses after birth?

6. Do (did) you breast-feed or bottle-feed?

7. What formula do you give your child?

8. Does your child drink well?

9. How many times a day does your infant eat?

10. How many ounces does your infant drink at a time?

11. How many minutes does it take for the child to drink four ounces?

12. Does your child rest a lot during the meals?

13. Does he have shortness of breath during meals?

14. Does your child sweat much during feedings?

15. Has he ever had cyanosis?

16. Does he have episodes with shortness of breath and cyanosis?

5. ¿Tuvo su bebé enfermedades después de nacer?

6. ¿Da (dio) usted el pecho o da (dio) la mamadera (el biberón)?

7. ¿Qué fórmula le da a su bebé?

8. ¿Bebe bien su niño (niña)?

9. ¿Cuántas veces al día come su bebé?

10. ¿Cuántas onzas toma su bebé cada vez?

11. ¿Cuántos minutos demora el niño(a) para beber cuatro onzas?

12. ¿Descansa mucho su bebé durante la alimentación?

13. ¿Tiene falta de aire cuando lo/la alimenta?

14. ¿Suda mucho su bebé cuando lo/la alimenta?

15. ¿Alguna vez ha tenido la piel azulada?

16. ¿A veces tiene problemas de falta de aire y con la piel azulada?

Heart Attack—Useful Phrases

1. You are in the hospital.

2. Do you know why you are in the hospital?

3. You have had a heart attack.

4. Are you lonely? Are you scared?

5. Are you in pain?

6. I want you to take your medicine.

Ataque al Corazón—Frases Útiles

1. Ud. está en el hospital.

2. ¿Sabe por qué está en el hospital?

3. Ha tenido un ataque al corazón.

4. ¿Se siente solo(a)? ¿Tiene miedo?

5. ¿Tiene dolor?

6. Quiero que tome su medicina.

7. Cough.	7. Tosa.
8. We are going to turn you.	8. Vamos a voltearle.
9. Squeeze my hand.	9. Apriete mi mano.
10. Relax. Try to sleep.	10. Relájese. Trate de dormir.

Cardiac Surgery

1. Your surgery is over. You are back in the ICU.

2. The doctors took veins from your legs for your bypass grafts.
3. Does your chest hurt?
4. How are you feeling? Where does it hurt?
5. Be sure to tell us if you have chest pains or if you feel anything unusual.
6. I'm going to listen to your chest with the stethoscope.
7. Try to breathe with the respirator.
8. I'm going to suction out your breathing tube.
9. You need to take deep breaths and cough.
10. I'm going to connect you to the monitor.
11. The computer helps us to monitor you.
12. These are electrodes that we apply to your chest to connect you with a cable to the monitor.

Cirugía Cardíaca

1. Terminó su cirugía. Ud. está ahora en la unidad de cuidado intensivo.

2. Los médicos le sacaron venas de las piernas para el injerto de desviación.
3. ¿Le duele el pecho?
4. ¿Cómo se siente? ¿Dónde le duele?
5. Debe avisarnos si tiene dolores de pecho o si siente algo anormal.
6. Le voy a escuchar su pecho con el estetoscopio.
7. Trate de respirar con el respirador.
8. Le voy a sacar el tubo para respirar.
9. Ud. necesita respirar profundamente y toser.
10. Voy a conectarlo/la al monitor.
11. El computador nos ayuda a observarlo/la.
12. Estos son electrodos que le pondremos en el pecho para conectarlo/la al cable del monitor.

13. With the monitor we are able to constantly watch your heart rhythm.
14. Please turn on your side.
15. Do you have to urinate?
16. Do you have to use the bedpan?
17. Can you walk to the bathroom?
18. Do you want to sit in the chair?
19. Do you want to go for a walk in the hall?
20. Do you want to go back to bed?
21. I'll let your family in now.

13. Con el monitor podemos vigilar constantemente el ritmo del corazón.
14. Favor de ponerse de lado.
15. ¿Tiene que orinar?
16. ¿Tiene que usar el bacín?
17. ¿Puede caminar al baño?
18. ¿Quiere sentarse en la silla?
19. ¿Quiere caminar en el pasillo?
20. ¿Quiere regresar a la cama?
21. Dejaré entrar a su familia ahora.

COMMON MEDICAL PROBLEMS (TERMINOLOGY)

PROBLEMAS MÉDICÓS COMUNES (TERMINOLOGÍA)

1. abortion
2. abscess
3. addiction
4. adenoids
5. adenoma
6. anemia
7. angina
8. appendicitis
9. arthritis
10. asthma

1. el aborto
2. el absceso
3. la adicción
4. los adenoides
5. el adenoma
6. la anemia
7. la angina
8. la apendicitis
9. la artritis
10. el asma

11. atherosclerosis
12. backache
13. blindness
14. bronchitis
15. burn (1st, 2nd, or 3rd degree)
16. bursitis
17. cancer
18. chickenpox
19. chills

11. la ateromatosis
12. el dolor de espalda
13. la ceguera
14. la bronquitis
15. la quemadura (de primer, segundo o tercer grado)
16. el bursitis
17. el cáncer
18. la varicela
19. los escalofríos

20. chorea	20. la corea	47. gall stone	47. el cálculo biliar
21. cold	21. el catarro, el resfriado	48. gangrene	48. la gangrena
22. cold sores	22. las úlceras de la boca	49. gastric ulcer	49. la úlcera gástrica
23. constipation	23. la constipación	50. glaucoma	50. la glaucoma
24. convulsion	24. la convulsión	51. gonorrhea	51. la gonorrea
25. cough	25. la tos	52. hallucination	52. la alucinación
26. cramps	26. los calambres	53. handicap	53. el impedimento
27. deafness	27. la sordera	54. harelip	54. el paladar hendido
28. diabetes	28. la diabetes		(labio leporino)
29. diarrhea	29. la diarrea	55. hay fever	55. la fiebre de heno
30. diptheria	30. la difteria	56. headache	56. el dolor de cabeza
31. discharge	31. el flujo, desecho	57. heart attack	57. el ataque al corazón
32. dizziness	32. el vértigo, el mareo	58. heartbeat	58. el latido—el pálpito
33. eczema	33. la eczema	a. irregular	a. el latido irregular
34. embolism	34. el embolismo	b. rhythmical	b. el latido rítmico
35. emphysema	35. el enfisema	c. slow	c. el latido lento
36. encephalitis	36. la encefalitis	d. fast (tachycardia)	d. taquicardia
37. epilepsy	37. la epilepsia	59. heartburn	59. la acedía (ardor)
38. fainting spell	38. el desmayo	60. heart disease	60. la enfermedad del corazón
39. fatigue	39. la fatiga	61. heart failure	61. la falla del corazón
40. fever	40. la fiebre	62. heart murmur	62. el soplo del corazón
41. fistula	41. la fístula	63. hemorrhage	63. la hemorragia
42. flu	42. la influenza, la gripe	64. hemorrhoids	64. la almorranas
43. food poisoning	43. el envenenamiento por comestibles	65. hepatitis	65. la hepatitis
		66. hernia	66. la hernia
44. fracture	44. la fractura	67. herpes	67. el herpes
45. frostbite	45. la congelación	68. high blood pressure	68. la presión alta
46. gall bladder attack	46. el ataque de la vesícula biliar	69. hit (on face)	69. la bofetada

70. hives	70. la urticaria
71. hoarseness	71. la ronquera
72. ill	72. enfermo(a)
73. illness	73. la enfermedad
74. immunization	74. la inmunización
75. infantile paralysis	75. la parálisis infantil
76. infarct	76. el infarto
77. infection	77. la infección
78. inflammation	78. la inflamación
79. injury	79. la herida, el daño
80. itch	80. la picazón—la comezón
81. jaundice	81. la piel amarilla, la ictericia
82. kidney stone	82. cálculo en el riñón piedra en el riñón
83. laceration	83. la laceración
84. laryngitis	84. la laringitis
85. lesion	85. la lesión—el daño
86. leukemia	86. la leucemia
87. lice	87. los piojos
88. lump	88. el bulto
89. malaria	89. la malaria
90. malignancy	90. la malignidad
91. malignant	91. maligno(a)
92. malnutrition	92. la mala nutrición
93. manic-depressive	93. maníacodepresivo(a) (la psicosis)
94. measles	94. el sarampión
95. meningitis	95. la meningitis
96. menopause	96. la menopausia

97. metastasis	97. la metástasis
98. migraine	98. la migraña, la jaqueca
99. mite	99. el ácaro, el órolo
100. mononucleosis	100. la mononucleosis infecciosa
101. multiple sclerosis	101. la esclerosis múltiple
102. mumps	102. las paperas
103. muscular dystrophy	103. la distrofía muscular
104. mute	104. mudo(a)
105. myocardial infarct	105. el infarto miocardíaco
106. myopia	106. la miopia
107. nephritis	107. la nefritis
108. neuralgia	108. la neuralgia
109. obese	109. obeso(a)
110. obstruction	110. la obstrucción
111. opthalmia	111. la oftalmia
112. osteomyelitis	112. la osteomielitis
113. overdose	113. la sobredosis
114. overweight	114. el sobrepeso
115. pain	115. el dolor
a. growing pain	a. el dolor de crecimiento
b. labor pain	b. el dolor del parto
c. phantom limb pain	c. el dolor de miembro fantasma
d. referred pain	d. el dolor referido
e. sharp pain	e. el dolor agudo
f. shooting pain	f. el dolor punzante
g. burning pain	g. el dolor que quema
h. intense pain	h. el dolor intensivo

pain (continued)	el dolor (seguido)	138. rheumatic fever	138. la fiebre reumática
i. severe pain	i. el dolor severo	139. roseola	139. la roséola
j. intermittent pain	j. el dolor intermitente	140. rubella	140. la rubéola
k. throbbing pain	k. el dolor pulsante	141. rupture	141. la ruptura
116. palpitation	116. la palpitación	142. scab	142. la costra
117. palsy	117. la parálisis	143. scabies	143. la sarna
118. palsy, Bell's	118. la parálisis facial	144. scar	144. la cicatriz
119. palsy, cerebral	119. la parálisis cerebral	145. scarlet fever	145. la escarlatina
120. paralysis	120. la parálisis	146. scratch	146. el rasguño
121. Parkinson's disease	121. la enfermedad de Parkinson	147. senile	147. senil
		148. shock	148. el choque
122. pellagra	122. la pelagra	149. sinus congestion	149. congestión nasal
123. pernicious anemia	123. la anemia perniciosa	150. slipped disc	150. el disco desplazado
124. pertussis	124. la tos convulsiva	151. smallpox	151. la viruela
125. pimple	125. el grano de la cara, el barro	152. snakebite	152. la mordedura de culebra
		153. sore	153. la llaga
126. plague (Bubonic)	126. la plaga bubónica	154. spasm	154. el espasmo
127. pneumonia	127. la pulmonía	155. spider bite	155. la picadura de araña
128. poison ivy, oak	128. la hiedra venenosa	156. spotted fever	156. la fiebre purpúrea
129. polio	129. la poliomielitis	157. sprain	157. la torcedura
130. polyp	130. el pólipo	158. stomachache	158. el dolor de estómago
131. psoriasis	131. la psoríasis	159. stomach ulcer	159. la úlcera del estómago
132. pus	132. el pus	160. suicide	160. el suicidio
133. pyorrhea	133. la piorrea	161. sunburn	161. la quemadura del sol
134. rabies	134. la rabia	162. sunstroke	162. la insolación
135. rash	135. la roncha, el salpullido, la erupción	163. swelling	163. la hinchazón
		164. syphilis	164. la sífilis
136. relapse	136. la recaída	165. tachycardia	165. la taquicardia
137. renal	137. renal	166. tapeworm	166. la lombriz solitaria

167. tetanus
168. thrombosis
169. thrush
170. tonsillitis

171. toothache
172. toxemia
173. trauma
174. tuberculosis
175. tumor
176. typhoid fever
177. typhus
178. ulcer
179. unconsciousness
180. undulant fever
181. uremia
182. uterus, prolapsed
183. valley fever
184. varicose veins

167. el tétano(s)
168. la trombosis
169. la afta
170. la tonsilitis,
     la amigdalitis

171. el dolor de muela
172. la toxemia
173. el trauma
174. la tuberculosis
175. el tumor
176. la fiebre tifoidea
177. el tifus
178. la úlcera
179. la insensibilidad
180. la fiebre ondulante
181. la uremia
182. el prolapso de la matriz
183. la fiebre del valle
184. las venas varicosas

185. venereal disease
     a. canker sore
     b. chancre
     c. chlamidia
     d. cold sore
     e. condyloma
     f. genital wart
     g. gonorrhea
     h. herpes genitalis
     i. monoliasis
     j. syphilis
     k. trichomonas
186. virus
187. vomit
188. wart
189. weakness
190. weal
191. wheeze
192. whiplash

193. whooping cough
194. worm(s)
195. wound
196. yellow fever

185. la enfermedad venérea
     a. la postemilla
     b. el chancro
     c. la clamidia
     d. los fuegos en la boca
     e. la condiloma
     f. la verruga genital
     g. la gonorrea
     h. el herpes genital
     i. la monoliasis
     j. la sífilis
     k. la tricomonas
186. el virus
187. el vómito, los vómitos
188. la verruga
189. la debilidad
190. el verdugón—el moretón
191. jadear, silbar
192. concusión de la espina
     cervical, lastimado del
     cuello
193. la tos ferina
194. la lombriz (las lombrices)
195. la herida
196. la fiebre amarilla

DERMATOLOGY

Psoriasis

1. You have psoriasis.
2. Psoriasis is a disease in which your skin cells are growing too fast.
3. There are medicines for psoriasis. If you use them in the right way your psoriasis will go away. The psoriasis may never come back or it may come back from time to time. If you start using the medicine as soon as you notice the psoriasis, it will clear up faster.
4. These medicines stop the skin cells from growing too rapidly:
   Anthialin
   Tars
   Steroids
   You must use them in the right way.
5. Anthialin is a strong medicine for psoriasis. It is a very good medicine, but you must use it with care.*
6. You will receive ultraviolet light treatments. The ultraviolet light also stops the skin cells from growing too fast.
7. Sunlight will also help your psoriasis clear. Try to spend some time in the sun every day.

*A set of instructions for the use of Anthialin can be found in Section C, Patient Information, p. 184.

DERMATOLOGÍA

Psoríasis

1. Usted tiene psoríasis.
2. La psoríasis es una enfermedad en la cual las células de la piel crecen muy rápidamente.
3. Hay medicinas para la psoríasis. Si las usa correctamente la psoríasis desaparecerá. La psoríasis quizás no vuelva o tal vez aparecerá de vez en cuando. Si comienza a usar la medicina tan pronto como se da cuenta, la psoríasis desvanecerá rápidamente.
4. Las siguientes medicinas detienen el crecimiento rápido de las células:
   Antialina
   La brea
   Los esteroides
   Debe de usarlas en la manera correcta.
5. La Antialina es una medicina fuerte para la psoríasis. Es una buena medicina pero debe usarla con cuidado.
6. Recibirá tratamientos con rayo ultravioleta. Este tratamiento también ayuda para que las células de su piel no crezcan tan rápido.
7. La luz del sol también ayuda que la psoríasis desvanezca. Trate de pasar un rato cada día en el sol.

8. Tars are a good medicine for psoriasis. Apply the tar medicine to the psoriasis three to four times a day.

9. Tars must be applied in the direction the hair grows. If not, you may get an infection in the hair follicles.

10. Steroids must be used sparingly. If you use too much your skin will become thin. It may tear and bruise easily.

11. Your skin problems may cause itching. If you scratch your skin, it will make the skin problem worse.

12. Try not to scratch.

13. There are pills to stop the itching.

14. If you itch, ask for the pill for the itching.

15. If you itch, take the pill for the itching.

16. The pills may make you sleepy. Do not drive or operate machinery after taking the pills.

17. Do you itch?

18. Do you need the pill for the itching?

19. Does you skin burn?

20. Is your skin burning or sore anywhere?

8. La brea es una buena medicina para la psoríasis. Aplíquesela de tres a cuatro veces por día.

9. La brea debe ser aplicada en la dirección en la cual crece el pelo. Si no se hace así, una infección puede aparecer en los folículos del pelo.

10. Los esteroides deben ser usados con cuidado. Si los usa mucho, la piel se volverá fina. Podrá romperse y causar moretones fácilmente.

11. Los problemas de la piel quizás podrán causarle salpullido. Si Ud. se rasca la piel le causará que se empeore el problema de la piel.

12. Trate de no rascarse.

13. Hay pastillas para detener la picazón (comezón).

14. Si tiene comezón (picazón) entonces pida la píldora para aliviarse.

15. Si tiene picazón tome la píldora para la picazón.

16. Las pastillas le pueden producir sueño. No maneje ni opere maquinaria después de tomar las pastillas.

17. ¿Tiene picazón o comezón?

18. ¿Necesita las píldoras para la comezón?

19. ¿Le quema la piel?

20. ¿Le quema la piel o está dolorida en alguna parte?

Skin
(Terminology)

La Piel
(Terminología)

1. abrasion, scraping off	1. abrasión, raspadura
2. abscess	2. absceso, postema
3. birthmark	3. lunar
4. blister	4. ampolla, vejiga
5. boil, carbuncle	5. grano enterrado, "tacotillo," forúnculo
6. bruise	6. moretón, magulladura
7. burn	7. quemadura
8. chilblain	8. sabañones
9. cut	9. cortada
10. cyanosis	10. cianosis, piel azulada
11. dermatitis	11. dermatitis
12. dry skin	12. piel seca
13. eczema	13. eczema
14. eruption	14. erupción
15. erysipelas	15. erisipela
16. fester, sore	16. llaga
17. inflammation	17. inflamación
18. itch	18. picazón, comezón
19. pustule	19. pústula

20. rash	20. salpullido, roncha
21. ringworm	21. empeine, tiña
22. scab, crust	22. costra
23. scabies	23. sarna
24. scald	24. escaldadura
25. scar	25. cicatriz
26. scratch	26. rasguño, raspón
27. skin, crack in	27. grieta
28. skin discoloration	28. paños, decoloración de la piel
29. skin, oily	29. piel grasosa
30. stitches	30. puntadas, puntos
31. swelling	31. hinchazón
32. tumor	32. tumor
33. ulcer	33. úlcera
34. urticaria	34. urticaria
35. wart	35. verruga
36. welt	36. roncha, verdugón

DIABETES*

1. You have diabetes.
   (You have too much sugar in your blood.)
2. To correct this, you must lose weight, exercise, and take medicine (pills or injections).
3. Your doctor will regulate your dosage.
4. You should take your medicine at the same time every day or as the doctor orders it.
5. You should eat after every injection.
6. We have to rotate the site of injection to prevent soreness.
7. Drink this glass of orange juice. It will make you feel better.

DRUGS

General

1. What drugs do you use?
   heroin?
   cocaine?
   uppers?
   downers?
   barbiturates?
   speed?

DIABETES

1. Ud. tiene diabetes.
   (Ūd. tiene demasiado azúcar en la sangre.)
2. Para remediar esto usted tiene que perder peso, hacer ejercicios y tomar medicina (pastillas o inyecciones).
3. Su médico le indicará su dosis.
4. Ud. debe tomar su medicina a la misma hora todos los días o como se lo indique su médico.
5. Ud. debe comer después de cada inyección.
6. Tenemos que alternar el sitio de la inyección para evitar molestias en la misma parte.
7. Tome este vaso de jugo de naranja. Le hará sentirse mejor.

DROGAS

General

1. ¿Cuáles drogas usa usted?
   ¿heroína?
   ¿cocaína?
   ¿estimulantes?
   ¿abajos?
   ¿diablitos o barbitúricos?
   ¿blancas?

*Mexican-American diet for diabetes can be found on p. 177. Instructions for self-administration of insulin can be found on p. 184. Directions for urine testing are on p. 181. Warning signs of hypoglycemia are on p. 188. Wallet card for diabetics can be found on p. 158.

2. When was your last fix?

3. Where do you shoot the drugs?

4. Do you have any abscesses?

5. Have you ever been through a detoxification program before?

6. Have you ever taken methadone before?
    for detoxing?
    on maintenance?

7. Have you ever overdosed on drugs?

8. Have you ever had a heart infection from using drugs?

9. Have you ever had hepatitis?

10. Do you think you might have been exposed to hepatitis recently?

2. ¿Cuándo fue el último fileraso?

3. ¿Dónde se pone usted las drogas?

4. ¿Tiene algunos abscesos?

5. ¿Ha participado alguna vez en un programa de desintoccicación?

6. ¿Ha tomado metadona alguna vez?
    ¿para desintoccicarse durante el tratamiento?
    ¿para mantenimiento?

7. ¿Alguna vez se ha sobredrogado?

8. ¿Ha sufrido alguna vez una infección cardíaca a causa del uso de drogas?

9. ¿Ha sufrido alguna vez de hepatitis?

10. ¿Cree usted que ha estado expuesto a la hepatitis recientemente?

Drug Slang (Terminology)

Jerga de Drogas (Terminología)

1. heroin
2. bag or stash of drugs
3. cocaine
4. drug paraphenalia
5. busted for drugs
6. O.D.
7. heroin user or junkie

1. **heroína, chiva, carga**
2. **clavo, o talega de drogas**
3. **coca, nieve**
4. **heré**
5. **torcido**
6. **sobredosis**
7. **drogadicto, heroínomania, tecato**

8. to mainline or shoot the drug
9. PCP or angel dust
10. Jones—that is, addiction
11. stoned
12. speed or whites
13. speed freak or one who uses speed

8. **inyectarse, chutear**
9. **PCP o polvo de ángel**
10. **prendido, adicto, "jones"**
11. **embalado, empacado**
12. **blancas**
13. **blanco**

14. downers, reds, barbiturates
15. one who uses reds
16. homemade drug capsules
17. "fix"
18. to shoot up heroin
19. drug in a capsule form
20. joint
21. cold turkey or quit suddenly
22. to get high on speed

14. rojos, diablitos, pingas y abajos
15. pingo
16. encachuchas
17. fileraso
18. filerearse, picarse, inyectarse
19. gorra, cachucha
20. griga, hierba, leño
21. kickear
22. poner blancas, "estar volando"

23. to get high on drugs (in general)
24. to push or deal
25. roach
26. tracks
27. to buy a lid
28. to swallow a drug in capsules
29. heroin bought by the spoon
30. to dissolve heroin in a spoon over a flame
31. opium
32. to deal heroin

23. ponerse loco
24. puchar
25. rocha
26. trakes, traques
27. apañar un bote
28. tragarse la cachucha
29. cuchara
30. cukear, cuquear
31. opio
32. llevar carga, llevar mula

EARS, NOSE AND THROAT

Ears

1. Have you ever had an infection of the middle ear?

2. Do you have any hearing problems?

3. Do you use a hearing aid?

4. Are you hard of hearing or deaf?

5. Do you ever have discharge from your ears?
   Did you ever have discharge from your ears?

6. Do your ears feel clogged or blocked?

LOS OÍDOS, LA NARIZ, Y LA GARGANTA

Los Oídos

1. ¿Ha tenido alguna vez una infección del oído interno?

2. ¿Tiene Ud. problemas de oír?

3. ¿Usa Ud. un audífono?

4. ¿Le es difícil oír bien? ¿Padece de sordera?

5. ¿Le supuran alguna vez los oídos?
   ¿Le han supurado los oídos alguna vez?

6. ¿Siente Ud. los oídos tapados?

7. Do your ears ring?
   Do you have ringing in your ears?
8. Do you ever have dizzy spells?

Nose

1. Do you have allergies?
2. What causes your allergies?
3. Do you have a cold?

4. How many colds did you have last year?
5. Do you have a runny nose?
6. Do you have a stuffed/stopped-up nose?
7. Do you have sinus headaches?
8. Do you have nose bleeds?

Mouth and Throat

1. Do you have sore throats frequently?
2. Are you hoarse frequently?
3. Do your gums bleed frequently?
4. Do you have gum infections often?

7. ¿Siente un tintineo o silbido en los oídos?

8. ¿Sufre de mareos algunas veces?

La Nariz

1. ¿Tiene alergias?
2. ¿Qué le causa las alergias?
3. ¿Tiene usted un resfriado/resfrío?
   ¿Tiene usted un catarro?
4. ¿Cuántos resfriados tuvo durante el año pasado?
5. ¿Le corren o le moquean las narices?
6. ¿Tiene Ud. la nariz tapada/tupida?
7. ¿Tiene jaquecas del seno nasal o jaquecas nasales?
8. ¿Le sangra la nariz a veces?

Boca y Garganta

1. ¿Le duele la garganta con frecuencia?
2. ¿Tiene ronquera con frecuencia?
3. ¿Le sangran las encías con frecuencia?
4. ¿Tiene infecciones de las encías con frecuencia?

5. Have you ever had strep throat?

6. Does your throat hurt when you swallow?

7. Does your tongue feel swollen?

8. Can you taste anything?

9. I want to take a throat culture. Open your mouth. This will not hurt.

ENDOCRINOLOGY

1. Have you been unusually thirsty, hungry, or fatigued?

2. Have you had more frequent urination? Do you get up at night to urinate? How often?

3. Have you ever had problems with your thyroid? Have you ever had irradiation to your neck for any reason?

4. Have you noted any significant weight gain or loss? What is your usual weight?

5. How is your appetite?

6. (WOMEN) How old were you when your periods started? How many days between periods? Have you ever been pregnant? How many children do you have? Ages?

5. ¿Ha tenido alguna vez "strep" (infección estreptococo de la garganta)?

6. ¿Le duele la garganta al tragar?

7. ¿Siente la lengua hinchada?

8. ¿Puede saborear algo?

9. Quiero hacer un cultivo de la garganta. Abra la boca. Esto no le va a doler.

ENDOCRINOLOGÍA

1. ¿Ha tenido Ud. sed, hambre o fatiga más de lo común?

2. ¿Ha tenido que orinar más de lo usual? ¿Se levanta por la noche para orinar? ¿Con qué frecuencia?

3. ¿Ha tenido alguna vez problemas con la tiroides? ¿Ha tenido alguna vez una irradiación en el cuello por cualquier motivo?

4. ¿Ha notado pérdida o aumento de peso? ¿Cuál es su peso usual?

5. ¿Qué tal su apetito?

6. (PARA LAS MUJERES) ¿Cuántos años tenía cuando tuvo la primera regla? ¿Cuántos días entre las reglas? ¿Ha estado embarazada? ¿Cuántos hijos tiene? ¿Edad de los hijos?

FAMILY PLANNING

1. What is your name? How do you spell it?
2. What is your address?
3. What is your zip code?
4. What is the name of your nearest relative?
5. How is he/she related to you?
6. How old are you?
7. On what day, month, and year were you born?
8. Where were you born?
9. What is your marital status?
10. When was your last menstrual period?
11. How long did it last?
12. How often do you get your menstrual period?
13. How many days does it last?
14. How old were you when you first began to menstruate?
15. Do you have vaginal secretions?
16. When was your last Pap smear?
17. Have you ever been pregnant? How many times? How many live births?
18. Have you ever had an abortion or miscarriage?
19. Are you pregnant now?

PLANEACIÓN FAMILIAR

1. ¿Cómo se llama Ud.? ¿Cómo se deletrea su nombre?
2. ¿Cuál es su dirección?
3. ¿Cuál es su zona postal?
4. ¿Cómo se llama su pariente más cercano?
5. ¿Qué parentesco tiene con Ud.?
6. ¿Qué edad tiene usted?
7. ¿En qué día, mes, y año nació usted?
8. ¿Dónde nació usted?
9. ¿Cuál es su estado civil?
10. ¿Cuándo fue su última regla? (período?) (menstruación?)
11. ¿Cuánto tiempo le duró?
12. ¿Cada cuándo le viene la menstruación?
13. ¿Cuántos días le dura?
14. ¿A qué edad tuvo su primera regla?
15. ¿Tiene secreciones vaginales?
16. ¿Cuándo fue su última prueba Pap?
17. ¿Ha estado alguna vez embarazada? ¿Cuántas veces? ¿Cuántos niños tiene?
18. ¿Ha tenido alguna vez un aborto o una pérdida (un mal parto)?
19. ¿Está usted embarazada ahora?

20. Do you want to be pregnant?
21. Do you want an abortion?

Contraceptives

1. Would you like information on birth-control methods?

2. There are various methods you may use if you do not wish to get pregnant.

3. The pill is one of the most effective means of birth control when taken correctly.

4. A condom or rubber is a narrow rubber or latex sheath (bag) worn by the man on his penis during sex. This usually works well and helps prevent the spreading of venereal disease also.

5. The diaphragm is a shallow cup made of soft rubber. The woman inserts it in her vagina before intercourse, and must leave it in for at least 6 hours afterward.

6. Contraceptive foam comes in a can or tube, and the woman must insert it into her vagina prior to sexual relations.

7. The IUD (intrauterine device) is a plastic or metal object that is placed inside the uterus. It prevents implantation of a fertilized ovum in the uterus.

20. ¿Quiere estar embarazada?
21. ¿Quiere tener un aborto?

Anticonceptivos

1. ¿Quiere Ud. información sobre los métodos del control de la natalidad (los métodos anticonceptivos)?

2. Hay varios métodos que Ud. puede usar si no quiere estar embarazada.

3. La píldora es el método más seguro para evitar el embarazo, pero es preciso tomársela como es debido.

4. El condón es una bolsa elástica de goma o hule, que el hombre se pone durante relaciones sexuales. Es efectivo para evitar el embarazo, y también ayuda a evitar las enfermedades venéreas.

5. El diafragma es un tamborcito de goma que la mujer inserta en su vagina antes de tener relaciones sexuales, y que se la debe dejar por 6 (seis) horas después de tener relaciones.

6. La espuma anticonceptiva viene en un tubo y la mujer se la unta en la vagina antes de tener relaciones sexuales.

7. El dispositivo intrauterino consiste en un objeto plástico de metal que un médico coloca dentro de la matriz. Mientras esté adentro evita implantación del óvulo en la matriz.

Family Planning
(Terminology)

Planeación Familiar
(Terminología)

1. abortion
2. birth control methods

3. biopsy
4. bladder
5. breasts
6. breast lumps
7. cauterize
8. cesarean section
9. cervix
10. clitoris
11. coitus interruptus

12. conception
13. creams
14. cyst
15. diaphragm
16. dilatation and curettage
17. discharge
18. ectopic pregnancy
19. ejaculation
20. erection
21. estrogen

1. un aborto, un malparto, una pérdida
2. métodos del control de la natalidad, métodos anti-conceptivos
3. la biopsia
4. la vejiga
5. los pechos, los senos
6. las bolitas en el pecho
7. cauterizar
8. la cesárea
9. la cerviz
10. el clítoris
11. se sale, se saca, coito interrumpido
12. la concepción
13. las cremas
14. el quiste
15. el diafragma
16. dilatación y raspado
17. el flujo, las secreciones
18. un embarazo en los tubos
19. la eyaculación
20. la erección
21. el estrógeno

22. fallopian tubes

23. family planning
24. fertilization
25. foams
26. gonorrhea
27. hormones
28. hymen
29. hysterectomy
30. IUD

31. jellies
32. laparoscopy
33. masturbation
34. menopause
35. menstruation
36. miscarriage

37. orgasm
38. ovaries
39. ovulation
40. Pap smear
41. pelvic exam
42. penis

22. los tubos de falopio, las trompas de falopio
23. la planificación familiar
24. la fecundación
25. las espumas
26. la gonorrea
27. las hormonas
28. el himen, la membrana
29. la histerectomía
30. el DIU, dispositivo intrauterino
31. las jaleas
32. la laparoscopia
33. la masturbación
34. la menopausia
35. la menstruación, la regla
36. un malparto, un aborto, una pérdida
37. el orgasmo
38. los ovarios
39. la ovulación
40. la prueba Pap
41. el examen de la pelvis
42. el pene, el miembro

43. pill
44. pregnancy
45. sexual intercourse
46. side effects
47. speculum
48. sperm
49. spermicides
50. sterilization

43. la píldora, la pastilla
44. el embarazo
45. las relaciones sexuales
46. los efectos secundarios
47. el espéculo
48. la esperma, la semilla
49. las espermaticidas
50. la esterilización

51. syphilis
52. testicles
53. tubal ligation

54. uterus
55. vagina
56. vasectomy
57. venereal disease
58. vulva

51. la sífilis
52. los testículos
53. la ligación de los tubos/
    de las trompas
54. la matriz, el útero
55. la vagina
56. la vasectomía
57. las enfermedades venéreas
58. la vulva, los labios
    vaginales

GASTROINTESTINAL

1. What foods disagree with you?
2. Do you get gas pains?
3. Do you get heartburn?
4. Do you burp a lot?
5. Do you have frequent stomach aches?
6. Do you have indigestion often?
7. Do you feel pain?
8. Where is your pain? Show me where it hurts the most.

GASTROINTESTINAL

1. ¿Qué alimentos le caen mal?
2. ¿Suele Ud. tener gases?
3. ¿Suele tener ardor en el pecho?
4. ¿Eructa usted mucho?
5. ¿Tiene usted con frecuencia dolores de estómago?
6. ¿Tiene indigestión con frecuencia?
7. ¿Tiene dolor alguno?
8. ¿Dónde le duele? Enséñeme (muéstreme) dónde le duele más.

9. Can you describe the pain?
   a. dull?
   b. strong?
   c. sharp?
   d. burning?
   e. crampy?
   f. running?
   g. achy?
10. Does the pain move? Where?
11. How long does the pain last?
12. What causes it?
13. What makes it worse?
   a. to cough?
   b. to eat?
   c. to have a bowel movement?
   d. sex?
   e. moving?
14. What makes it better?
15. Are you going to vomit?
16. Did you vomit?
17. Have you vomited?
18. Do you have blood in your vomit?
19. How many times have you had a bowel movement today?
20. What color is your bowel movement?

9. ¿Puede describir el dolor?
   a. sordo?
   b. fuerte?
   c. agudo?
   d. con ardor?
   e. con calambres?
   f. que le corre?
   g. doloroso?
10. ¿Le corre el dolor? ¿Dónde?
11. ¿Por cuánto tiempo le dura el dolor?
12. ¿Qué lo causa?
13. ¿Qué lo hace peor?
   a. al toser?
   b. al comer?
   c. al evacuar?
   d. al tener relaciones sexuales?
   e. al moverse?
14. ¿Qué se lo alivia?
15. ¿Va a vomitar (arrojar)?
16. ¿Vomitó (arrojó)?
17. ¿Ha vomitado (arrojado)?
18. ¿Tiene usted vómitos con sangre?
19. ¿Cuántas veces ha tenido defecación hoy?
20. ¿De qué color son sus evacuaciones?

21. Do you need a bedpan?	21. ¿Necesita usted un bacín?
22. How are your stools?	22. ¿Cómo son las evacuaciones (deposiciones)?
23. Are your stools hard, soft, bloody, black?	23. ¿Las evacuaciones son duras, blanditas, con sangre, o negras?
24. Are you constipated?	24. ¿Está usted estreñido (constipado)?
25. Do you have diarrhea?	25. ¿Tiene usted diarrea?
26. Is it diarrhea with mucus?	26. ¿Es diarrea con moco (mocosidad)?
27. With diarrhea, does it have a foul smell?	27. Con diarrea, ¿tiene mal olor?
28. Do you have hemorrhoids?	28. ¿Tiene usted almorranas (hemorroides)?
29. Do you have bleeding hemorrhoids?	29. ¿Tiene almorranas que sangran?
30. Do you have rectal bleeding?	30. ¿Le sale sangre por el recto?
31. Have you ever had a barium enema?	31. Ha tenido alguna vez una lavativa (un lavado) de bario?
32. Have you ever had a barium X-ray?	32. ¿Le han hecho alguna vez una prueba (radiografía) con bario?
33. When was your last menstrual period?	33. ¿Cuándo fue su última regla?
34. Are you active sexually?	34. ¿Tiene usted relaciones sexuales con frecuencia?
35. Do you use a contraceptive? What?	35. ¿Usa usted anticonceptivas? ¿Cuáles?
36. Do you have discharge?	36. ¿Tiene usted flujos (secreciones)?
37. Is your appetite good?	37. ¿Tiene buen apetito?
38. What have you eaten today?	38. ¿Qué ha comido hoy?
39. What did you eat in the last 24 hours?	39. ¿Qué comió en las últimas veinticuatro (24) horas?
40. How many times has your child had a bowel movement today?	40. ¿Cuántas veces ha tenido su hijo defecación hoy?

41. What did your child eat in the last 24 hours?
42. What color is his (her) bowel movement?
43. Have you had any change in your urine?

GENITOURINARY

Infection

1. Do you have pain with urination?

2. Do you have a burning sensation when you urinate?

3. Do you have to urinate very frequently?

4. Do you have to get up at night to urinate?

5. How many times a day do you urinate?
   How much do you urinate at one time?

6. Do you have pain over the bladder?

7. Is the urine
   a. clear?
   b. normal?
   c. cloudy?
   d. bloody?
   e. with pus?
   f. with stones?
   g. with a strange odor?

8. Is it dark red, pink, brownish?

41. ¿Qué comió su hijo/a en las últimas veinticuatro (24) horas?
42. ¿De qué color son las evacuaciones de él (de ella)?
43. ¿Ha notado algunos cambios en la orina?

GENITOURINARIO

Infección

1. ¿Tiene dolor al orinar?
   ¿Le duele al orinar?

2. ¿Siente ardor al orinar?

3. ¿Tiene que orinar con mucha frecuencia?

4. ¿Tiene que levantarse por la noche para orinar?

5. ¿Cuántas veces al día orina usted?
   ¿Cuánto orina a la vez?

6. ¿Tiene algún dolor sobre la vejiga?

7. ¿La orina es
   a. clara?
   b. normal?
   c. turbia?
   d. con sangre?
   e. con pus?
   f. con cálculos?
   g. con olor extraño?

8. ¿El color es rojo oscuro, rosado, moreno?

9. Do you have backaches?
10. Have you ever had a bladder infection?
11. Have you ever had cystitis?
12. Have you ever had a kidney infection? Chills, fever?

13. Do you have pain in your testicles?
14. Do you have a discharge from your penis?
15. Have you ever had prostatitis?
16. Have you had any operations on your kidneys (ureters)? Any operations on your bladder or urethra?

Obstruction

1. Can you urinate?
2. Do you have to urinate very frequently?
3. How many times a day do you urinate? How much do you urinate at one time?
4. Do you have to get up at night to urinate? How many times?
5. Do you have to wait very long for the urine to come out or strain to get the urine out?
6. Is the flow of urine strong and continuous?

9. ¿Padece de dolores de espalda?
10. ¿Ha tenido alguna vez una infección en la vejiga?
11. ¿Ha tenido alguna vez cistitis?
12. ¿Ha tenido alguna vez una infección de los riñones? ¿Escalofríos, fiebre?

13. ¿Tiene dolor en los testículos?
14. ¿Le supura el pene (el glande)?
15. ¿Ha tenido alguna vez problemas de la próstata?
16. ¿Ha tenido operaciones en los riñones (uréteres), o en la vejiga o uretra?

Obstrucción

1. ¿Puede usted orinar?
2. ¿Tiene que orinar con mucha frecuencia?
3. ¿Cuántas veces al día orina usted? ¿Cuánto orina usted a la vez?
4. ¿Tiene que levantarse en la noche para orinar? ¿Cuántas veces?
5. ¿Tiene que esperar mucho para que le salga la orina o hace fuerza para que salga la orina?
6. ¿Es fuerte y continuo el chorro de su orina?

Tumor

1. Do you have to urinate very frequently?
2. Is the urine
   a. clear?
   b. normal?
   c. cloudy?
   d. bloody?
   e. with pus?
   f. with stones?
3. Is there a strange odor?
4. Is it dark red, pink, brownish?
5. Do you have a lump in the testes?
6. Have you had any operations on your kidneys (ureters)? Any operations on your bladder or urethra?

Stones

1. When you have pain with urination, does the pain stay in that place or does it radiate toward the groin?
2. Have you had kidney stones?
3. Have you passed any stones?
4. Have you had any operations on your kidneys (ureters)? Any operations on your bladder or urethra?

Tumor

1. ¿Tiene que orinar con mucha frecuencia?
2. ¿La orina es
   a. clara?
   b. normal?
   c. turbia?
   d. con sangre?
   e. con pus?
   f. con cálculos, piedras?
3. ¿Tiene un olor extraño?
4. ¿El color, es rojo oscuro, rosado, moreno?
5. ¿Tiene alguna bolita en los testículos?
6. ¿Ha tenido operaciones en los riñones (uréteres), o en la vejiga o uretra?

Cálculos

1. Cuando tiene dolor al orinar, ¿es fijo el dolor en un lugar, o se le corre hacia la ingle?
2. ¿Ha tenido piedras en los riñones?
3. ¿Ha pasado algunas piedras?
4. ¿Ha tenido operaciones en los riñones (uréteres), o en la vejiga o uretra?

Incontinence (Leaking)

1. Do you lose urine when you cough or sneeze or lift something?
2. Do you ever lose urine for no reason?
3. When you have to urinate do you lose urine before getting to the toilet?

Neurogenic

1. Can you urinate?
2. Do you have to urinate very frequently?
3. Do you have to get up at night to urinate?
4. How many times a day do you urinate?
   How much do you urinate at one time?
5. Do you have to wait very long for the urine to come out or strain to get the urine out?
6. Is the flow of urine strong and continuous?
7. Do you lose urine when you cough or sneeze or lift something?
8. Do you ever lose urine for no reason?
9. Have you had any injury to the spinal cord or brain?

Incontinencia (Gotear)

1. ¿Pierde orina al toser, al estornudar o al levantar algo?
2. ¿Hay veces que pierde orina sin ninguna razón?
3. Cuando tiene que orinar, ¿pierde orina antes de llegar al retrete?

Neurogénico

1. ¿Puede Ud. orinar?
2. ¿Tiene que orinar con mucha frecuencia?
3. ¿Tiene que levantarse por la noche para orinar?
4. ¿Cuántas veces al día orina usted?
   ¿Cuánto orina a la vez?
5. ¿Tiene que esperar mucho para que le salga la orina o hace fuerza para que salga la orina?
6. ¿Es fuerte y continuo el chorro de su orina?
7. ¿Pierde orina al toser, al estornudar o al levantar algo?
8. ¿Hay veces que pierde orina sin ninguna razón?
9. ¿Ha sufrido algún daño a la médula espinal o al cerebro?

10. Any medical disorders such as
    a. diabetes?
    b. stroke?
    c. Parkinson's disease?
    d. multiple sclerosis?

Cystoscopy

1. The doctor wants to look into your bladder—the procedure is called cystoscopy—in order to find the reason for bleeding, infection, pain, etc.

2. It is necessary for you to sign a permit for him (her) to do the cystoscopy.

3. Please put on this gown and lie on this table with your legs over the stirrups, and I will wash you with an antiseptic solution and cover you with some drapes.

4. I will put some topical anesthetic into the urethra (squirt it in) and put a Q-tip (cotton swab) in the opening to keep the anesthetic in. This will make it more comfortable for you.

4. (FOR THE MALE) I will put some topical anesthetic into the urethra (squirt it in) and place a clamp on the penis to keep the anesthetic in. This will make it more comfortable for you.

10. ¿Algunas enfermedades como
    a. diabetes?
    b. ataque fulminante? derrame?
    c. enfermedad de Parkinson?
    d. esclerosis múltiple?

Cistoscopia

1. El médico quiere examinarle la vejiga—este procedimiento se llama cistoscopia—para encontrar la razón por el sangrar, la infección, el dolor, etc.

2. Es necesario que Ud. firme el permiso para que él (ella) le haga la cistoscopia.

3. Favor de ponerse este camisón y acostarse en esta mesa con las piernas sobre los estribos, y yo le lavo con una solución antiséptica y le cubro con unas cobijas (sábanas).

4. Le voy a poner anestesia (local) en la uretra (se la voy a jeringar) y le voy a aplicar un palito con algodón en la abertura para que la anestesia se quede. Esto le hará sentirse más cómoda.

4. (PARA LOS VARONES) Le voy a poner anestesia superficial en la uretra (se la voy a jeringar), y le voy a colocar una grapa en el pene para que se quede la anestesia. Esto le hará sentirse más cómodo.

5. The doctor will insert the instrument into the urethra. You should feel only some pressure. He will then look into your bladder.

5. (FOR THE MALE) You will feel some pressure in the urethra and discomfort as the instrument passes through the prostate. Try to relax and take deep breaths as this is done.

6. He must fill your bladder with some water in order to look around. If you become uncomfortable, tell us so we can let some water out (through the instrument). (The bladder collapses around the instrument.) Otherwise, he cannot see.

7. If the doctor needs urine for cystology: The doctor needs to irrigate (flush) the bladder to obtain cells for examination. This may be uncomfortable.

8. The doctor wants you to take antibiotics for one day to prevent infection. (It is possible to introduce bacteria into the bladder even if we prep the patient.)

9. You may have some discomfort (burning) on urination and perhaps a small amount of bleeding. This is not serious unless it continues. If it does, please contact us.

10. If you have problems or complications, you may call us in the clinic or at night. Call the hospital number and ask for the urology resident on call or the interpreter if necessary.

5. El médico le insertará el instrumento en la uretra. Ud. sentirá sólo un poco de presión. Entonces (luego) él le va a examinar su vejiga.

5. (PARA LOS VARONES) Sentirá algo de presión en la uretra y molestia cuando pasa el instrumento por la próstata. Trate de relajarse y respire profundamente mientras que se hace esto.

6. El debe llenarle la vejiga con agua para observar. Si usted se pone incómodo/a, avísenos para que podamos vaciar un poco del agua (por el instrumento). (La vejiga se cae alrededor del instrumento.) Si no, él no puede ver.

7. Si el médico necesita orina para la cistología: El médico tiene que limpiarle la vejiga con un chorro de agua para obtener células para la prueba. Esto puede ser incómodo.

8. El médico quiere que Ud. tome antibióticos por un día para prevenir infección. (Es posible meter bacteria en la vejiga aunque preparemos al paciente.)

9. Puede sufrir un poco de molestia (ardor) al orinar y quizás un poco de sangrar. Esto no es serio a menos que siga. Si sigue, favor de avisarnos.

10. Si tiene complicaciones o problemas, puede llamarnos en la clínica o por la noche. Llame al número del hospital y pregunte por el residente de urología de turno o por el intérprete si es necesario.

HEADACHES/HEAD

1. Do you have headaches?
2. Do you have migraines?
3. Do you ever feel dizzy?
4. How long do you feel dizzy?
5. How long do your headaches usually last?

6. Do you ever feel nauseated while you have a headache?
7. What do you do for your headaches?
8. How long have you had these headaches?
9. Where is the pain exactly?
10. Is the headache in the same place each time?
11. What causes the headaches?
12. Have the headaches occurred with vomiting?
13. Have you had recent head trauma?
14. Do you have high blood pressure?
15. Are there any changes in your vision?

DOLORES DE CABEZA/LA CABEZA

1. ¿Tiene Ud. dolores de cabeza (jaquecas)?
2. ¿Tiene Ud. migrañas (jaquecas)?
3. ¿Se siente Ud. mareado(a) algunas veces?
4. ¿Cuánto tiempo le dura el mareo?
5. ¿Cuánto tiempo le duran los dolores de cabeza (jaquecas, migrañas)?
6. Mientras tiene dolor de cabeza, ¿siente náuseas alguna vez?
7. ¿Qué hace para sus dolores de cabeza (jaquecas, migrañas)?
8. ¿Cuánto hace que tiene estos dolores de cabeza?
9. ¿Dónde le duele, exactamente?
10. ¿Siempre tiene el dolor de cabeza en el mismo sitio?
11. ¿Qué le causa los dolores de cabeza?
12. ¿Ha tenido dolores de cabeza con vómitos?
13. ¿Ha tenido recientemente trauma de la cabeza?
14. ¿Tiene usted presión alta?
15. ¿Hay algunos cambios en su vista?

MEDICATIONS

Terminology

1. alcohol
2. amphetamine
3. anesthesia
4. antacid
5. antibiotic
6. antihistamine
7. application
8. ascorbic acid

9. aspirin (for children)
10. barbiturate
11. Benzedrine (amphetamine)
12. calamine
13. calcium
14. capsule
15. castor oil

16. cocaine
17. cod liver oil

18. codeine
19. contact lens
20. contraceptive pills
21. cortisone
22. cotton

MEDICAMENTOS

Terminología

1. alcohol
2. anfetamina
3. anestesia
4. antiácido
5. antibiótico
6. antihistamina
7. aplicación
8. ácido ascórbico
   (Vitamina C)
9. aspirina (para niños)
10. barbitúrico
11. bencedrina
12. calamina
13. calcio
14. cápsula
15. aceite de ricino
    (de castor)
16. cocaína
17. aceite de hígado de
    bacalao
18. codeína
19. lentes de contacto
20. pastillas anticonceptivas
21. cortisona
22. algodón

23. cough drops, lozenges
24. cough syrup
25. digitalin
26. diuretic
27. dose
28. douche

29. dressing
30. drops
31. elastic bandage
32. enema
33. Epsom salt
34. foam
35. gauze
36. glucose
37. heroin
38. ice
39. insulin
40. iodine
41. laxative
42. liniment
43. lotion
44. milk of magnesia
45. mineral oil
46. morphine

23. pastillas para la tos
24. jarabe para la tos
25. digitalina
26. diurético
27. dosis
28. ducha, lavado interno,
    lavado vaginal
29. vendaje
30. gotas
31. venda elástica
32. enema
33. sal de higuera (de Epsom)
34. espuma
35. gasa
36. glucosa
37. heroína
38. hielo
39. insulina
40. yodo
41. laxante, purgante, purga
42. linimento
43. loción
44. leche de magnesia
45. aceite mineral
46. morfina

47. narcotic	47. narcótico
48. needle	48. aguja
49. Novocaine	49. novocaína
50. ointment	50. ungüento, crema
51. oxygen	51. oxígeno
52. pacemaker	52. marcapaso
53. penicillin	53. penicilina
54. phenobarbital	54. fenobarbital
55. pill	55. píldora, pastilla
a. birth control pill	a. píldora anticonceptiva
b. sleeping pill	b. píldora para dormir
c. thyroid pill	c. medicina para tiroides
56. powder	56. polvo
57. prosthesis	57. miembro artificial (prótesis)
58. quinine	58. quinina
59. rubber (condom)	59. goma, condón
60. salve	60. pomada, ungüento

61. sanitary napkin ("Kotex")	61. servilleta sanitaria ("Kotex")
62. sedative	62. sedante, calmante
63. serum	63. suero
64. smelling salts	64. sales aromáticas
65. Sodium Pentothal (thiopental)	65. pentotal de sodio
66. spray	66. rociada
67. stimulant	67. estimulante
68. sulfa	68. sulfa
69. sulfur	69. azufre
70. suppository	70. supositorio
71. syrup of ipecac	71. jarabe de ipecacuana
72. tablet	72. tableta
73. tampon	73. tapón
74. Terramycin (oxytetracycline)	74. terramicina
75. Vaseline (petroleum jelly)	75. Vaselina (jalea petrólea)
76. vitamin	76. vitamina

MEDICATIONS

Instructions

MEDICAMENTOS

Instrucciones

1. right	1. derecho(a)
2. left	2. izquierdo(a)
3. tablespoonful	3. cucharada
4. teaspoonful	4. cucharadita

5. one-half teaspoonful	5. media cucharadita
6. BID	6. dos veces al día
7. TID	7. tres veces al día
8. QID	8. cuatro veces al día

9. every hour
10. each day, daily
11. every other day
12. till gone
13. Let it dissolve in your mouth.
14. as needed for pain
15. insert
16. when you get up in the morning
17. Use the blow bottle like this at least three times a day.
18. apply
19. one-half hour after meals
20. one hour before meals
21. for ten days
22. now (stat)
23. before bedtime

9. cada hora
10. cada día, diariamente
11. cada otro día (cada tercer día)
12. hasta terminar (acabar)
13. Que se le disuelva en la boca
14. cuando la necesite para el dolor
15. inserte
16. al levantarse
17. Use la botella soplante así por lo menos tres veces al día.
18. aplique
19. media hora después de comidas
20. una hora antes de comidas
21. durante diez días
22. ahora (ahora mismo)
23. antes de acostarse

24. before you exercise
25. only when you really need it, because it may be habit-forming
26. Apply _____ to the affected part.
27. chew
28. mix
29. applicatorful
30. vaginally
31. dissolved in
32. Cool in the refrigerator.
33. Shake well.
34. as directed
35. scalp
36. by mouth
37. under the tongue
38. rectally
39. rub
40. gargle
41. soak

24. antes de hacer ejercicios
25. solamente cuando la necesite, porque produce hábito
26. Aplique _____ en la parte afectada.
27. mastique
28. mezcle
29. un aplicador lleno
30. en la vagina
31. disuelto en
32. Enfríe en el refrigerador.
33. Agite bien.
34. de acuerdo con las instrucciones
35. cuero cabelludo
36. por la boca
37. bajo la lengua
38. por el recto
39. frote
40. haga gárgaras
41. remoje, empape

42. Here is some medication for diarrhea. Take 1-2 tablets every 4-6 hours as needed for diarrhea.

43. Mix this package of soap with one quart of water, and wash the affected area thoroughly.

44. These pills are vitamins.

45. These pills are for pain.

46. These pills are for the infection.

47. These pills are to treat your condition.

48. Take _____ of these pills each day.

49. Here is enough medicine for _____ days.

50. Take one of these pills every _____ hours.

51. Take one pill daily for _____ days.

52. But no more than _____ a day maximum.

53. Fill the medicine dropper to this line and mix with a glass of water, juice, or milk.

42. Aquí tiene la medicina para diarrea. Tome una o dos (1-2) tabletas cada cuatro a seis (4-6) horas según las necesite para diarrea.

43. Mezcle este paquete de jabón con un litro de agua y lave completamente la parte afectada.

44. Estas pastillas son vitaminas.

45. Estas pastillas son para dolor.

46. Estas pastillas son para la infección.

47. Estas pastillas son para tratar su condición.

48. Tome _____ de estas pastillas cada día.

49. Aquí tiene suficiente medicina para _____ días.

50. Tome una de estas pastillas cada _____ horas.

51. Tome una pastilla por _____ días.

52. Pero no más de _____ en total cada día.

53. Llene el gotero hasta esta línea y mezcle con un vaso de agua, jugo, o leche.

Prescriptions for Those Who Cannot Read

The form below can be xeroxed and given along with medications to those patients who cannot read. The blanks below the pictures can be used to draw the dosage; for example, if the patient is to take two tablets four times per day, two tablets could be drawn under each time/picture.

name, nombre _____

medicine, medicina _____

what it is for, symptoms, síntomas _____

_____

dosage, dosis _____

TAKE WITH MEALS
TÓMESE A LA HORA DE LAS COMIDAS

TAKE WITHOUT FOOD
TÓMESE SIN COMIDA

NO

Reprinted with permission from David B. Werner, *Where There Is No Doctor*, p. 64.

Drug Labels

1. Avoid contact with your skin or clothing.
2. Do not crush or chew these tablets.
3. Do not take aspirin without the consent of your physician.
4. Do not take with antacids.
5. Do not take with aspirin.
6. Consult your physician for advice.
7. Do not take with dairy products or antacids.
8. Do not take with fruit juices.
9. Do not take with milk.
10. Drink a full glass of orange juice or eat a banana daily while taking this medication.
11. Filled by _____.
    Pharmacist
12. Finish all this medication unless directed otherwise by your physician.
13. Increase water intake when using this medication.
14. Keep in the refrigerator. Do not freeze.
15. Keep out of reach of children.
16. May cause drowsiness. Alcohol may intensify this effect. Use care when operating machinery or an automobile.
17. Medication may cause drowsiness. Avoid other depressants, such as alcohol.

Etiquetas de Drogas

1. Evite contacto con la piel o la ropa.
2. No moler ni masticar estas tabletas.
3. No tomar aspirina sin autorización de su médico.
4. No tomar con antiácidos.
5. No tomar con aspirina.
6. Consultar con el médico para advertencia.
7. No tomar con productos lácteos o antiácidos.
8. No tomar con jugos de frutas.
9. No tomar con leche.
10. Tómese un vaso de jugo de naranja o cómase un plátano al día mientras toma esta medicina.
11. Dispensado de _____.
    Farmacista
12. Termine esta medicina a menos que su médico no indique lo contrario.
13. Aumente tomar agua mientras usa esta medicina.
14. Guárdese en refrigerador. No congele.
15. Mantenga las medicinas fuera del alcance de los niños.
16. Puede causar somnolencia. El alcohol puede aumentar este efecto. Precaución en el uso de maquinarias o vehículos de motor.
17. Esta medicina puede causar somnolencia. Evite otros depresantes, como alcohol.

18. Not to be taken by mouth.
19. Poison.
20. Shake well.
21. Shake well and keep refrigerated.
22. Special dietary considerations are necessary while taking this medication.
23. Take by mouth.
24. Take medication immediately before or with meals.
25. Take medication on an empty stomach one (1) hour before or 2–3 hours after meals.
26. Take medication ½ hour before meals.
27. Take medication with food or milk.
28. Take medication with plenty of water.
29. This medication may discolor the urine or feces.
30. This prescription (R) may be refilled:
    0 1 2 3 4 5 6 7 8 9 10 times as needed.
31. Warning—It is dangerous to stop this medication suddenly. Please contact your physician before altering dosage.

18. No es para tomarse.
19. Veneno.
20. Agítese bien.
21. Agítese bien y guárdese en el refrigerador.
22. Consideraciones especiales en la dieta son necesarias al tomar esta medicina.
23. Tómese por boca.
24. Tómese inmediatamente antes, o con las comidas.
25. Tómese con estómago vacío una (1) hora antes o dos a tres (2–3) horas después de las comidas.
26. Tómese media hora antes de comer.
27. Tómese con leche o alimentos.
28. Tómese con abundante agua.
29. Esta medicina puede teñir la orina o heces.
30. Esta receta puede repetirse:
    0 1 2 3 4 5 6 7 8 9 10 veces según la necesidad.
31. Advertencia—Es peligroso cesar esta medicina repentinamente. Consulte con su médico antes de cambiar la dosis.

Side Effects

With this medicine you may . . .

1. be irritable
2. be depressed
3. be agitated
4. have insomnia
5. be dizzy
6. be nauseated
7. be thirsty
8. be hungry
9. lose your appetite
10. have excessive salivation
11. have diarrhea
12. be constipated
13. feel weak
14. have blurred vision
15. have double vision
16. have ringing in your ears
17. note a bad taste in your mouth
18. have a dry mouth
19. have a change in the color of your urine
20. have a different-smelling urine
21. have more vaginal secretions
22. have palpitations
23. have a rash
24. have red spots
25. be sleepy and you may not drive a car

Efectos Secundarios

Con esta medicina puede tener . . .

1. irritabilidad
2. depresión
3. agitación
4. insomnia
5. mareos
6. náusea
7. sed
8. hambre
9. falta de apetito
10. salivación excesiva
11. diarrea
12. estreñimiento
13. debilidad
14. visión nublada
15. visión doble
16. zumbido de los oídos
17. un sabor desagradable en la boca
18. la boca seca
19. cambio de color en su orina
20. un olor diferente en su orina
21. más flujo vaginal
22. palpitaciones
23. una erupción
24. manchas rojas
25. sueño y no debe manejar un carro

NEPHROLOGY

Dialysis

1. Bring me your medicine please.
2. Wash your forearm with soap.
3. Tell me, please, is it necessary to begin hemodialysis?

NEFROLOGÍA

Diálisis

1. **Tráigame su medicina, por favor.**
2. **Lávese el antebrazo con jabón.**
3. **Dígame por favor ¿es necesario empezar hemodiálisis?**

4. Breathe deeply and hold it. Breathe out.

5. Are you thirsty?

6. When did the dull pain occur in your stomach?

7. Your "K" (potassium) is very high. Do you eat a lot of avocados and beans?

8. Don't drink anything after midnight.

9. Don't drink water and you will not have cramps.

10. Clean your arm and you will not have an infection.

11. Eat breakfast before coming to dialysis.

12. Don't be afraid of the machines and you will feel better.

13. Do you have pain in your cannula?

14. Give me the blood tubing.

15. Keep your arm elevated on two pillows.

16. Take your vitamins after dialysis.

17. Take off the bandage.

18. Check the bandage for drainage.

19. Have you had drainage from the cannula?

20. How much do you weigh today?

21. How much weight do you have to lose today?

22. Did you come off at your dry weight?

23. Can you breathe all right when lying flat?

24. Where do you want me to put these needles today?

25. Are your ankles swollen?

4. Aspire profundamente y sostenga la respiración. Exhale.

5. ¿Tiene sed?

6. ¿Cuándo empezó el dolor sordo en el estómago?

7. El nivel de potasio ("K") está muy alto. ¿Come muchos aguacates y frijoles?

8. No tome nada después de la medianoche.

9. No tome agua y no tendrá calambres.

10. Limpie su brazo y no tendrá ninguna infección.

11. Tome su desayuno antes de venir a diálisis.

12. No se asuste de las máquinas y se sentirá mejor.

13. ¿Tiene dolor en su cánula?

14. Déme el tubo de sangre, por favor.

15. Mantenga su brazo elevado sobre dos almohadas.

16. Tome las vitaminas después de diálisis.

17. Quítese la venda.

18. Revise la venda por si hay drenaje.

19. ¿Ha tenido drenaje por la cánula?

20. ¿Cuánto pesa usted hoy?

21. ¿Cuánto peso tiene que perder hoy?

22. ¿Después del tratamiento pesó su peso normal?

23. ¿Puede respirar normalmente al acostarse plano?

24. ¿Dónde quiere que le ponga estas agujas hoy?

25. ¿Tiene los tobillos hinchados (inflamados)?

Dialysis
(Terminology)

Diálisis
(Terminología)

1. artery
2. blood clot
3. cannula
4. chills
5. depressed
6. end-stage renal disease

7. fistula
8. graft
9. drainage

1. arteria
2. coágulo
3. cánula
4. escalofríos
5. deprimido
6. enfermedad de los riñones de etapa final

7. fístula
8. injerto
9. drenaje

10. fever
11. irritable
12. listless
13. pain
14. redness

15. shunt
16. swelling
17. symptoms
18. weak(er)

10. fiebre
11. irritable
12. indiferente
13. dolor
14. enrojecimiento o inflamación
15. desviación
16. hinchazón
17. síntomas
18. (más) débil

How Dialysis Works

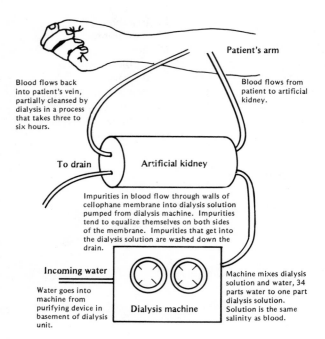

Patient's arm

Blood flows back into patient's vein, partially cleansed by dialysis in a process that takes three to six hours.

Blood flows from patient to artificial kidney.

To drain

Artificial kidney

Impurities in blood flow through walls of cellophane membrane into dialysis solution pumped from dialysis machine. Impurities tend to equalize themselves on both sides of the membrane. Impurities that get into the dialysis solution are washed down the drain.

Incoming water

Water goes into machine from purifying device in basement of dialysis unit.

Dialysis machine

Machine mixes dialysis solution and water, 34 parts water to one part dialysis solution. Solution is the same salinity as blood.

Courtesy of San Jose Mercury News.

Cómo Funciona la Diálisis

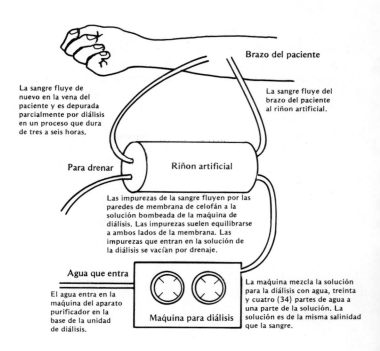

Brazo del paciente

La sangre fluye de nuevo en la vena del paciente y es depurada parcialmente por diálisis en un proceso que dura de tres a seis horas.

La sangre fluye del brazo del paciente al riñon artificial.

Para drenar

Riñon artificial

Las impurezas de la sangre fluyen por las paredes de membrana de celofán a la solución bombeada de la máquina de diálisis. Las impurezas suelen equilibrarse a ambos lados de la membrana. Las impurezas que entran en la solución de la diálisis se vacían por drenaje.

Agua que entra

El agua entra en la máquina del aparato purificador en la base de la unidad de diálisis.

Máquina para diálisis

La máquina mezcla la solución para la diálisis con agua, treinta y cuatro (34) partes de agua a una parte de la solución. La solución es de la misma salinidad que la sangre.

NEUROLOGY

1. Do you feel weak?
2. Do you feel dizzy?

3. Do you have fainting spells?
4. Do you know whether you were a normal birth or a breech birth?
5. Have you ever had a high fever?
6. Have you ever had a head injury?
7. Have you ever had a motorcycle accident?
8. Have you ever had a sports injury?
9. Do you have convulsions?
10. Do you see double?
11. Do you have blurred vision?
12. Do you have tingling sensations?
13. Do you have numbness in your hands, arms or feet?
14. Have you ever lost consciousness? For how long?
15. How frequently does this happen?
16. Have you ever had an electromyogram?
17. Do you get a ringing in your ears? Right, left, or both?

18. Relax. Repeat the words I am going to say.
19. Close your eyes.

NEUROLOGIA

1. ¿Se siente débil?
2. ¿Se siente mareado?
   (¿Tiene vértigo?)
3. ¿Tiene desmayos?
4. ¿Sabe usted si fue de parto normal o de nalgas?

5. ¿Ha tenido alguna vez una fiebre (una calentura) alta?
6. ¿Ha tenido alguna vez daño a la cabeza?
7. ¿Ha tenido alguna vez un accidente en su motocicleta?
8. ¿Ha tenido alguna vez un daño deportivo?
9. ¿Tiene convulsiones?
10. ¿Ve usted doble?
11. ¿Tiene la vista borrosa?
12. ¿Tiene hormigueos?
13. ¿Siente entumecidos las manos, los brazos o los pies?
14. ¿Perdió alguna vez el sentido? ¿Por cuánto tiempo?
15. ¿Con qué frecuencia ocurre esto?
16. ¿Ha tenido alguna vez un electromiograma?
17. ¿Siente tintineo en los oídos? ¿En el derecho, en el izquierdo o en los dos?

18. Relájese. Repita las palabras que le voy a decir.
19. Cierre los ojos.

20. Move your head to your right, to the left, back and forward like this.
21. Squeeze my fingers in your hand as hard as you can.
22. Pull your arm toward your shoulder.
23. Say yes when you feel something touching you.
24. Is this hot or cold?
25. Do you feel the vibrations?
26. Put your feet together.
27. Am I sticking you with the point or the head of the pin?

28. Am I sticking you with two points or with one?
29. Do you feel it more on one side than on the other?

Electroencephalogram (EEG)

The electroencephalogram (EEG) is a brain wave test. It is a written record of the electrical activity of the brain.

Before the test be sure to ask your doctor what drugs you should take.

Come to the laboratory on the day and the hour of your appointment. You will then be seated in a chair and asked to keep your eyes open or closed. The lights may or may not be dimmed. Discs will be placed on areas of your scalp. A special paste will be used.

20. Mueva la cabeza hacia la derecha, hacia la izquierda, hacia atrás y hacia adelante, así.
21. Apriete mis dedos en su mano lo más fuerte que pueda.
22. Suba el brazo hacia el hombro.
23. Diga "sí" cuando sienta que algo le toca.
24. ¿Está frío o caliente esto?
25. ¿Siente las vibraciones?
26. Junte los pies.
27. ¿Le estoy pinchando con la punta o con la cabeza del alfiler?

28. ¿Le estoy pinchando con dos puntas o con una?
29. ¿Lo siente más en un lado que en el otro?

Electroencefalograma

El electroencefalograma es una prueba de las ondas cerebrales. Es una grabación escrita de la actividad eléctrica del cerebro.

Antes de la prueba recuerde preguntarle a su médico qué drogas debe tomar usted.

Venga al laboratorio el día y a la hora de su cita. Luego usted se sentará en una silla y mantendrá los ojos abiertos o cerrados. Las luces serán disminuidas o no. Le pondrán electrodos de metal en áreas de su cuero cabelludo. Se usa una pasta especial.

During the test a technician is at the controls of the machine monitoring the procedure. You may feel dizzy at times and will be asked to breathe deeply.

The EEG takes about one and a half hours.

EMG Examination

The EMG (electromyographic) examination is a test of the electrical activity of nerves and muscles. The test gives your physician information about the health and functioning of the nerves and muscles in your body; this information can be of importance in making decisions regarding diagnosis and/or treatment of a number of different conditions in which the nerves and muscles may be affected.

The human body contains a large number of nerves and a correspondingly large number of individual muscles. The nature of the examination that will be carried out in your particular case depends in large part upon the nature of your problem. Generally speaking, the examination consists of two parts: nerve conduction testing and electromyography proper.

Nerve conduction tests (NCV) are usually performed by pasting small metal discs on the skin of a hand or foot and then activating a nerve leading to the hand or the foot with a small stimulus pulse. The pulse produces a movement of the hand or foot, and this movement is photographed and later measured to determine whether the nerve response is normal or not.

El Examen EMG

Durante la prueba un técnico está en los controles de la máquina encargado del procedimiento. Ud. puede tener mareo a veces y se le pedirá respirar profundo.

Esta prueba demora una hora y media (1½).

El examen EMG (electromiográfico) es una prueba de la actividad eléctrica de los nervios y músculos. La prueba da a su médico información acerca de la salud y la función de los nervios y músculos de su cuerpo. Esta información puede ser de importancia en hacer decisiones tocante a la diagnosis y/o tratamiento de diferentes condiciones en las cuales los nervios y los músculos pueden ser afectados.

El cuerpo humano contiene un gran número de nervios y un gran número correspondiente de músculos individuales. El género de la prueba que se llevará a cabo, en su caso particular, depende en mayor parte en el género de su problema. En general, la prueba consiste en dos (2) partes: un examen de la conducción de los nervios, y la electromiografía misma.

Las pruebas de la conducción de los nervios (NCV) generalmente se hacen pegando pequeños discos metálicos en la piel de la mano o del pie, y luego activando, con un leve pulso de estímulo, un nervio que se dirige a la mano o al pie. El pulso produce un movimiento de la mano o del pie, y este movimiento es fotografiado y después medido para determinar si la respuesta del nervio es normal o no.

The electromyographic (EMG) examination proper consists of testing the responsiveness of different muscles. In order to do this, it is necessary to administer a small pin-prick in each muscle as it is being tested.

The extent of your particular examination (whether both NCV and EMG tests will be done, or whether just one or the other will suffice; and which nerves and which muscles are to be examined) depends entirely on the nature of your symptoms and the kind of examination requested by your physician. In general, the examination takes between 30 and 60 minutes. If you have other questions, please feel free to ask them at the time of your examination.

Spinal Tap

You will need to have a spinal tap (lumbar puncture). The doctor will put a little medicine (like a dentist uses novocain) into your back to numb it. It will sting a little for a few seconds. Lie on your side with head bent forward and knees pulled up to your stomach. The inserting of the needle afterwards may feel like a blood test in the arm. If any tingling or pain occurs in one leg, tell the doctor. For the rest of the day lying down is recommended as much as possible. If a headache develops, lying down and taking aspirin will help.

El examen EMG (electromiográfico) propio consiste en probar el responder de los diferentes músculos. Para hacer esto, es necesario administrar un leve piquete de alfiler en cada músculo cuando se está examinando.

La extensión de su examen particular (ya sea que ambos exámenes NCV y EMG se hagan, o que sólo uno sea suficiente; y cuales nervios y músculos han de ser examinados) depende enteramente género de sus síntomas, y en la clase de examen pedida por su médico. En general, el examen dura de treinta (30) a sesenta (60) minutos. Si tiene otras preguntas, favor de hacerlas al tiempo del examen.

La Punción Lumbar

Se le deberá hacer una punción lumbar. El médico le pondrá un poco de medicina en su espalda (como usa novocaína el dentista) para entumecer el área. Le picará un poco por unos segundos. Acuéstese al lado con la cabeza doblada hacia adelante y con las rodillas alzadas hasta el estómago. El insertar de la aguja después se puede sentir como una prueba de la sangre en el brazo. Si siente algún hormigueo o dolor en una pierna avísele al médico. Durante el resto del día se recomienda que se acueste lo más posible. Si llega dolor de cabeza le ayudará acostarse y tomar aspirina.

Pediatric Outpatients—EEG Lab

General Preparation for All

1. May eat normal meals, but no carbonated soft drinks.
2. Continue medication ordered by doctor.
3. Wash hair night before test. Apply no hair dressing or hair spray.
4. Do not let child sleep on the way to test.
5. Important to be on time. If you cannot, please call _____ immediately.

Test Procedure

1. Painless, simple test.
2. Test involves applying small metal discs on scalp with sticky paste. No needles.
3. Takes 1-2 hours, depending upon how quickly child goes to sleep.

Infants Up to 2 Years of Age

1. If your child takes a bottle, bring one so that child may be fed just before test.
2. No nap before the test.

Pacientes Ambulatorios de Pediatria—Laboratorio de Electroencefalograma (EEG)

Preparación General Para Todos

1. Se puede comer comidas regulares pero no tomar gaseosas.
2. Que siga tomando la medicina recetada por el médico.
3. Lávele el pelo la noche antes de la prueba, no le aplique grasa, ni laca, ni ningún otro líquido para el pelo.
4. No deje dormir al niño en camino a la prueba.
5. Es importante llegar a tiempo, si no, favor de llamar _____ en seguida.

Procedimiento de la Prueba

1. Es una prueba sencilla sin dolor.
2. Le pondrán unos pequeños electrodos de metal o discos en ciertas áreas del cuero cabelludo con una pasta especial. No se usan agujas.
3. Dura una a dos (1-2) horas según tan pronto se duerma el niño (la niña).

Criaturas Hasta 2 Años de Edad

1. Si su niño toma el biberón, traiga uno para que el niño pueda alimentarse inmediatamente antes de la prueba.
2. Ninguna siesta antes de la prueba.

Ages 3 Years to Teens

1. The night before the test, keep child up until 12:00 midnight (if possible). Get child up at 5:00 a.m.

2. Do not let child nap before appointment time.

Adult Outpatients—EEG Lab

General Preparation for All

1. May eat normal meals—no coffee or tea the night before test.

2. Continue medication ordered by doctor.

3. Wash hair night before test, apply no hair dressing or hair spray.

4. Important to be on time. If you cannot, please call _____ immediately.

Awake EEG Only

1. Painless, simple test.

2. Takes approximately 1 hour.

3. Test involves applying small metal discs on scalp with sticky paste. No needles.

Edades 3 Años Hasta Los Años 13–19

1. La noche antes de la prueba mantenga al niño despierto hasta las doce (12:00) de la noche (la medianoche) (si es posible). Despierte al niño a las cinco (5) de la mañana.

2. No deje al niño dormir una siesta antes de la cita.

Pacientes Adultos y Ambulatorios—Laboratorio de Electroencefalograma (EEG)

Preparación General Para Todos

1. Se puede comer comidas regulares. No tome café ni té la noche antes de la prueba.

2. Siga tomando la medicina recetada por el médico.

3. Lávese el pelo la noche antes de la prueba, no se aplique grasa, ni laca, ni ningún otro líquido para el pelo.

4. Es importante llegar a tiempo. Si no, favor de llamar _____ en seguida.

Prueba de Electroencefalograma (EEG) (Despierto Sólo)

1. Es una prueba sencilla sin dolor.

2. Dura más o menos una (1) hora.

3. Le pondrán unos pequeños electrodos de metal o discos en ciertas áreas del cuero cabelludo con una pasta especial. No se usan agujas.

Sleep EEG   EEG

1. No sleep 24 hours before appointment. It helps to have someone stay up with you.

2. <u>Painless</u>, simple test.

3. Takes 1-2 hours.

4. Test involves applying small metal discs on scalp with sticky paste. <u>No needles.</u>

5. <u>DO NOT DRIVE.</u> Arrange transportation to and from the hospital. It may be necessary to give you mild medication to help you sleep.

NUCLEAR MEDICINE

General

1. Return at this time tomorrow.

2. We are going to take some pictures of your brain/liver/kidney.

3. This test takes two days.

4. Take this capsule now and come back tomorrow at this time.

5. There is no preparation for this test.

6. You may have anything to eat or drink before this test.

Prueba de Electroencefalograma (EEG) (Dormido)

1. No duerma veinticuatro (24) horas antes de la cita. Ayuda tener alguien que se quede despierto con usted.

2. Es una prueba sencilla <u>sin dolor.</u>

3. Dura una a dos (1-2) horas.

4. Le pondrán unos pequeños electrodos de metal o discos en ciertas áreas del cuero cabelludo con una pasta especial. <u>No se usan agujas.</u>

5. <u>NO MANEJE.</u> Arregle transporte al hospital y de vuelta. Es posible que usted reciba medicina ligera para ayudarle a dormir.

MEDICINA NUCLEAR

General

1. Regrese mañana a esta hora.

2. Le vamos a sacar unas radiografías de su cerebro/hígado/riñón.

3. Este examen (esta prueba) demora dos días.

4. Tome esta cápsula ahora y regrese mañana a esta hora.

5. No hay preparativos para esta prueba.

6. Puede tomar o comer lo que quiera antes de la prueba.

7. Save all your urine for 24 hours. (Schilling test)

8. The doctor wants to examine your neck.

9. Is your neck enlarged?

10. Can you feel any lumps in your neck?

11. Can you swallow and breathe without pain?

12. Have you lost or gained weight?

13. How much and in what period of time?

14. Is your hair falling out?

15. Does the hot or cold weather bother you?

16. How is your appetite?

17. Are you a nervous person?

18. Is your skin dry?

19. Do your nails break easily?

20. Do you perspire very much?

21. Have you had an X-ray in the past six months?

22. Do you take any medications?

23. Are you pregnant?

7. Guarde toda su orina durante un período de veinticuatro (24) horas para una prueba de Schilling.

8. El doctor desea examinarle su cuello.

9. ¿Está agrandado su cuello?

10. ¿Siente alguna masa (o bolita) en el cuello?

11. ¿Puede tragar y respirar sin dolor?

12. ¿Ha perdido o ha ganado peso?

13. ¿Cuánto y en cuánto tiempo?

14. ¿Se le cae el pelo?

15. ¿Le molesta cuando hace calor o cuando hace frío?

16. ¿Cómo está su apetito?

17. ¿Es usted una persona nerviosa?

18. ¿Está seca su piel?

19. ¿Se le quiebran las uñas con facilidad?

20. ¿Suda usted mucho?

21. ¿Le han sacado un rayo X durante los últimos seis meses?

22. ¿Toma usted alguna medicina?

23. ¿Está usted embarazada (preñada)?

Questions for Female Patients

If the patient is female, the following questions should be asked prior to any administration of radioactive nuclides.

1. Have you completed menopause?
2. Have you had a hysterectomy?
3. Date of the last menstrual period?
4. Are you taking birth control pills?
5. Do you have an IUD?
6. Is there any possibility of pregnancy?

Bone Scanning

If the patient is female, the following questions should be asked prior to any administration of radioactive nuclides.

1. Have you completed menopause?
2. Have you had a hysterectomy?
3. Date of the last menstrual period?
4. Are you taking birth control pills?
5. Do you have an IUD?
6. Is there any possibility of pregnancy?
7. I'm going to give you an injection into a vein.

Preguntas para Pacientes Hembras

Si el paciente es una mujer, se le deben hacer las siguientes preguntas antes de administrarle núclidos radioactivos.

1. ¿Ha terminado su menopausia?
2. ¿Ha tenido una histerectomía?
3. ¿La fecha del último período menstrual?
4. ¿Toma usted píldoras anticonceptivas?
5. ¿Usa un aparato intrauterino?
6. ¿Hay alguna posibilidad de embarazo?

Exploración de Hueso

Si el paciente es una mujer, se le deben hacer las siguientes preguntas antes de administrarle núclidos radioactivos.

1. ¿Ha terminado su menopausia?
2. ¿Ha tenido una histerectomía?
3. ¿La fecha del último período menstrual?
4. ¿Toma usted píldoras anticonceptivas?
5. ¿Usa un aparato intrauterino?
6. ¿Hay alguna posibilidad de embarazo?
7. Voy a ponerle una inyección en una vena.

8. Please return in 2½ hours so that I may take pictures of your bones. This takes 1 hour.

9. You may eat or drink anything in the interim.

10. If you have any pain, tell me so that I can take special pictures of that area.

11. The report will be sent to your doctor. Please contact your doctor for the results of this test.

Liver-Spleen Scanning

If the patient is female, the following questions should be asked prior to any administration of radioactive nuclides.

1. Have you completed menopause?

2. Have you had a hysterectomy?

3. Date of the last menstrual period?

4. Are you on birth control pills?

5. Do you have an IUD?

6. Is there any possibility of pregnancy?

7. I'm going to give you an injection in the vein.

8. I am going to take pictures of your liver and spleen. This takes 1 hour.

9. The report of this test will be sent to your doctor. Please contact your doctor for the results.

---

8. Por favor, regrese dentro de dos horas y media (2½ horas) para poder sacar fotos (radiografías) de los huesos. Esto demorará una (1) hora.

9. Entre tanto, Ud. puede tomar o comer cualquier cosa.

10. Si tiene algún dolor, dígame para poder sacar radiografías especiales de esa area.

11. El informe se mandará a su doctor. Favor de llamar a su doctor si quiere averiguar los resultados.

La Exploración del Hígado y del Bazo

Si el paciente es una mujer, se le deben hacer las siguientes preguntas antes de administrarle núclidos radioactivos.

1. ¿Ha terminado la menopausia?

2. ¿Ha tenido una histerectomía?

3. ¿La fecha del último período menstrual?

4. ¿Toma usted píldoras anticonceptivas?

5. ¿Usa un aparato intrauterino?

6. ¿Hay alguna posibilidad de embarazo?

7. Le voy a poner una inyección en la vena.

8. Voy a sacar radiografías de su hígado y del bazo. Esto demorará una (1) hora.

9. El informe de esta prueba será enviado a su doctor. Favor de llamar a su doctor para los resultados.

Thyroid Scanning

If the patient is female, the following questions should be asked prior to any administration of radioactive nuclides.

1. Have you completed menopause?
2. Have you had a hysterectomy?
3. Date of the last menstrual period?
4. Are you on birth control pills?
5. Do you have an IUD?
6. Is there any possibility of pregnancy?
7. Have you taken anything by mouth this morning?
8. Please return in 6 hours so that we may take pictures of your neck.

9. Please return tomorrow morning at _____ to complete the test.

La Exploración de la Tiroides

Si el paciente es una mujer, se le deben hacer las siguientes preguntas antes de administrarle núclidos radioactivos.

1. ¿Ha terminado la menopausia?
2. ¿Ha tenido una histerectomía?
3. ¿La fecha del último período menstrual?
4. ¿Toma usted píldoras anticonceptivas?
5. ¿Usa un aparato intrauterino?
6. ¿Hay alguna posibilidad de embarazo?
7. ¿Ha tomado o comido algo esta mañana?
8. Por favor, regrese dentro de seis (6) horas para que podamos sacar fotos (radiografías) de su cuello.

9. Por favor, regrese mañana a las _____ de la mañana para terminar el examen.

OBSTETRICS AND GYNECOLOGY

Prenatal Record

DATE _____   CHART NUMBER _____

Please fill in all of the following information and bring this form to the doctor.

Name _____ Birthdate _____ Race _____ Religion _____

Address _____ City _____

Phone or number where messages may be given _____

Head of household _____ Birthdate _____ Occupation _____

PRESENT PREGNANCY HISTORY:
Date of last normal period _____
Date of prior menstrual period _____
When did you first feel the baby move? _____
Expected date of delivery _____

Please circle the medications you are taking now:

Vitamins	Sleeping pills	Pills for special illness or disease
Iron pills	Pain pills	Liquid medicine
Tranquilizers	Pep pills	Shots or injections
Antibiotics	Diet pills	Other

OBSTETRICIA Y GINECOLOGÍA

Registro Prenatal

FECHA _____   NUMERO DE EXPEDIENTE _____

Favor de llenar toda la información siguiente y traer esta forma al médico.

Nombre _____ Fecha de nacimiento _____ Raza _____ Religión _____

Dirección _____ Ciudad _____

Teléfono o número donde se pueden dejar mensajes _____

Dueño de la familia _____ Fecha de nacimiento _____ Ocupación _____

HISTORIA DEL EMBARAZO ACTUAL:
Fecha de la última regla normal _____
Fecha de la regla anterior _____
¿Cuándo fue la primera vez que Ud. notó que el bebé se estaba moviendo? _____
Fecha aproximada del parto _____

Favor de circundar las medicinas que Ud. está tomando ahora:

Vitaminas	Píldoras para dormir	Píldoras para enfermedades especiales
Píldoras de hierro	Píldoras para dolor	Medicina líquida
Tranquilizantes	Píldoras para animar	Inyecciones
Antibióticos	Píldoras de dieta	Otra

Please check (**X**) A the symptoms you have had since this pregnancy began.
Please check (**X**) B the symptoms you still have this week.

	A	B		A	B
Spots before eyes	____	____	Chills and fever	____	____
Nausea and vomiting	____	____	Heartburn	____	____
Swelling of hands and feet	____	____	Painful rectum	____	____
Burning on urination	____	____	Hemorrhoids (piles)	____	____
Constipation	____	____	Vaginal discharge	____	____
Cramping	____	____	Water from vagina	____	____
Lumps in breasts	____	____	Backache	____	____
Headache	____	____	Dizziness	____	____
Bleeding	____	____	Varicose veins	____	____
Frequent tiredness	____	____	Emotional upsets	____	____
Frequent colds or illness	____	____	Dental problems	____	____
Loss of appetite	____	____	Loss of balance	____	____

PREVIOUS OBSTETRICAL HISTORY: Full term _____ Premature _____ Abortions _____ Living children _____

Date	Weeks pregnant	Type of delivery (spontaneous, forceps, breech, cesarean section)	Hours of labor	Child Weight	Sex	Where delivered	Complications

Favor de marcar (X) A los síntomas que Ud. ha tenido desde que este embarazo empezó.
Favor de marcar (X) B los síntomas que Ud. todavía tiene esta semana.

	A	B		A	B
Manchas frente a los ojos	___	___	Escalofríos y fiebre	___	___
Náuseas y ganas de vomitar	___	___	Acedía (Ardor)	___	___
Hinchazón de las manos y de los pies	___	___	Recto doloroso	___	___
Ardor al orinar	___	___	Hemorroides (almorranas)	___	___
Estreñimiento	___	___	Desecho vaginal	___	___
Calambres	___	___	Agua de la vagina	___	___
Bultos en los senos	___	___	Dolor de espalda	___	___
Dolor de cabeza	___	___	Mareos	___	___
Hemorragia	___	___	Venas varicosas	___	___
Cansancio frecuente	___	___	Problemas emocionales	___	___
Resfriados frecuentes o enfermedad frecuente	___	___	Problemas dentales	___	___
Pérdida de apetito	___	___	Pérdida de equilibrio	___	___

HISTORIA OBSTETRICIA PREVIA: Embarazo a término _____ Prematuro _____ Abortos _____ Hijos viviendos _____

Fecha	Semanas del embarazo	Tipo de parto (espontáneo, fórceps, nalgas, cesárea)	Horas de dolores de parto	Hijo(a) Peso	Sexo	Lugar del parto	Complicaciones

PATIENT'S PAST HISTORY: (Please circle diseases you have had and indicate your age when disease discovered)

Mumps	Measles	Chicken pox
Whooping cough	Scarlet fever	Rheumatic fever
Allergies	Tuberculosis	Diabetes
Cancer	Syphilis	Heart trouble
High blood pressure	Blood disease	Lung trouble
Digestion or bowel trouble	Dental disease	Arthritis
Kidney trouble	Other handicaps	Mental or emotional illness
Problems with muscles or bones	Serious injuries	

What years have you been hospitalized for illness? _____ Why? _____

What years have you had operations? _____ Why? _____

Have you ever had unusual complications from taking drugs? _____

Anesthesia? _____ Medical treatments? _____

Have you ever needed blood transfusions? _____ Spinal fluid tests? _____

Radiation therapy? _____

MENSTRUAL HISTORY: Age it began _____ Number of days period lasts? _____

Number of days from first day of one period to first day of next period? _____

If periods are irregular please explain _____

Have periods ever caused you to seek medical treatment or take medication? Explain: _____

_____

FAMILY HISTORY:

MOTHER:	Age _____	General health _____	Date and cause of death _____
FATHER:	Age _____	General health _____	Date and cause of death _____
BROTHERS:	How many _____	General health _____	Date and cause of death _____
SISTERS:	How many _____	General health _____	Date and cause of death _____

HISTORIA MÉDICA DE LA PACIENTE: (Favor de circundar las enfermedades que Ud. ha tenido y de indicar su edad cuando la enfermedad fue descubierta)

Paperas	Sarampión	Varicela
Tos ferina	Escarlatina	Fiebre reumática
Alergias	Tuberculosis	Diabetes
Cáncer	Sífilis	Enfermedad del corazón
Presión alta	Enfermedad de la sangre	Problemas de los pulmones
Problemas con la digestión o las entrañas	Enfermedad dental	Artritis
Problemas de los riñones	Otras inhabilidades	Enfermedades mentales o emocionales
Problemas con músculos o huesos	Heridas serias	

Fechas de hospitalizaciones _____   Razones _____

Fechas de operaciones _____   Razones _____

¿Jamás ha tenido Ud. complicaciones extraordinarias de tomar drogas? _____

¿Anestesia? _____   ¿Tratamientos médicos? _____

¿Jamás ha tenido Ud. una transfusión de sangre? _____   ¿Pruebas del flúido de la espina? _____

¿Terapia de radiación? _____

HISTORIA MENSTRUAL: Edad de empezar _____   ¿Cuántos días le duran las reglas? _____

Número de días desde el primer día de la regla hasta el primer día de la regla siguiente _____

Si las reglas no son regulares favor de explicar _____

¿Ha buscado Ud. tratamiento médico o ha tomado medicinas a causa de sus reglas? Explique: _____

_____

HISTORIA DE LA FAMILIA:

MADRE:	Edad _____	Salud _____	Fecha y causa de muerte _____
PADRE:	Edad _____	Salud _____	Fecha y causa de muerte _____
HERMANOS:	¿Cuántos? _____	Salud _____	Fecha y causa de muerte _____
HERMANAS:	¿Cuántas? _____	Salud _____	Fecha y causa de muerte _____

PLEASE CIRCLE CONDITIONS THAT ARE OR HAVE BEEN IN YOUR FAMILY—INCLUDING YOUR OWN GRANDPARENTS:

Tuberculosis	Problems with blood pressure or disease	Convulsions or fits
Cancer	Physical birth defects	Allergies
Diabetes	Mental retardation	Twins or multiple births
Heart trouble	Nervous disorders	Varicose veins

DO NOT WRITE BELOW THIS LINE

TO BE COMPLETED BY MD   EDC _____

Weight and blood pressure today _____

Suspicious urine or other test results _____

_____

Findings or high risk factors _____

_____

Follow-up plans in clinic _____

Follow-up plans for PHN _____

PPD given left forearm _____

Other comments (referrals and services suggested) _____

_____

FAVOR DE CIRCUNDAR LAS CONDICIONES QUE ESTÁN O HAN ESTADO EN SU FAMILIA-INCLUYENDO SUS PROPIOS ABUELOS:

Tuberculosis	Problemas con presión o enfermedad de sangre	Convulsiones
Cáncer	Defectos de nacimiento	Alergias
Diabetes	Retardación mental	Gemelos o partos múltiples
Enfermedades del corazón	Enfermedades de los nervios	Venas varicosas

---

NO ESCRIBA BAJO ESTA LINEA
DO NOT WRITE BELOW THIS LINE

TO BE COMPLETED BY MD   EDC _____

Weight and blood pressure today _____

Suspicious urine or other test results _____

_____

Findings or high risk factors _____

_____

Follow-up plans in clinic _____

Follow-up plans for PHN _____

PPD given left forearm _____

Other comments (referrals and services suggested) _____

_____

Early Pregnancy

1. When was your last menstrual period?
2. Do you have any vaginal discharge?
   How much?
3. Have you ever been pregnant?
   How many times?
4. Are you pregnant now?
5. I need a urine specimen from you.
6. You are pregnant.
   You are not pregnant.
7. Do you want an abortion?
8. Your baby is due on _____.
9. What was your normal weight before pregnancy?
10. While you are pregnant it is important not to smoke, drink alcohol, or drink too much coffee.
11. Have you taken any medicines while you were pregnant?

Danger Signs during Pregnancy

1. Nausea and continuous vomiting.
2. Persistent headache.
3. Blurred vision.
4. Dizziness.

Early Pregnancy

1. ¿Cuándo tuvo su última regla?
2. ¿Tiene secreciones vaginales?
   ¿Qué tanto?
3. ¿Ha estado embarazada alguna vez?
   ¿Cuántas veces?
4. ¿Está embarazada ahora?
5. Necesito una muestra de su orina.
6. Ud. está embarazada.
   Ud. no está embarazada.
7. ¿Quiere tener un aborto?
8. Su bebé nacerá el _____.
9. ¿Cuál fue su peso normal antes del embarazo?
10. Mientras que Ud. esta embarazada no debe fumar, ni tomar alcohol, ni tomar demasiado café.
11. Tomó algunas medicinas mientras estaba embarazada?

Síntomas de Peligro durante el Embarazo

1. Náusea y vómitos continuos.
2. Dolor de cabeza constante.
3. Vista nublada (borrosa).
4. Mareos.

5. Swelling of feet, hands, ankles and face.

6. Small amount of urine passed during the day.

7. Spotting or hemorrhage.

8. Water coming from the vagina.

9. Any other symptom that worries you.

Labor and Delivery

1. Has your bag of waters broken? When?

2. When did your pains begin?

3. How many minutes apart are they now?

4. Do you have a lot of pain?

5. Open your mouth and breathe. Do not push.

6. Everytime the pain comes, push.

7. I need to examine you internally.

8. I have to examine you vaginally.

9. Put your feet in these stirrups.

10. Spread your knees and legs apart.

11. It is not possible for your baby to be born vaginally; we are going to do a cesarean section. Do you understand?

12. Your baby is in a difficult breech position, and it is safer to have your baby with a cesarean section.

5. **Hinchazón de los pies, de los tobillos, de las manos, y de la cara.**

6. **Poca orina pasó durante el día.**

7. **Manchas de sangre o hemorragias.**

8. **Agua que sale de la vagina.**

9. **Cualquier otro síntoma que le preocupe.**

Parto

1. **¿Se le rompió la bolsa de agua(s)? ¿Cuándo?**

2. **¿Cuándo le comenzaron los dolores?**

3. **¿Cuántos minutos pasan entre uno y otro dolor?**

4. **¿Tiene usted mucho dolor?**

5. **Abra la boca y respire por la boca. No empuje.**

6. **Cuando le venga el dolor, empuje.**

7. **Necesito hacerle un examen interno.**

8. **Tengo que examinarle por la vagina.**

9. **Ponga los pies en estos estribos.**

10. **Abra las rodillas y las piernas.**

11. **No es posible que su bebé nazca por la vagina; por eso vamos a hacerle una cesárea. ¿Entiende?**

12. **Su bebé está en posición de nalgas y es mejor que hagamos una cesárea.**

13. A cesarean section is an operation in which your baby is born via an incision made abdominally. There are two possible types of anesthesia. With epidural, you will be awake and can see your baby right away, but you won't be able to feel the incision. With full anesthesia you will be able to see your baby when you come out of the recovery room.

14. I'm going to listen to the baby's heartbeat.

15. This is a fetal monitor which enables us to check the baby's heartbeat continually.

16. We have to catheterize you. It will be a little uncomfortable.

17. We have to start an IV in your arm. It will help keep fluids in you.

18. I'm going to give you some medication to make your pains stronger—Pitocin (oxytocin).

19. I am going to give you some medication for the pain through your IV.

20. Roll over on your side.

21. Grab your knees and push.

22. Congratulations, you have a healthy baby boy/girl.

23. Your baby has some medical problems. We will call an interpreter.

13. Una operación cesárea (un nacimiento cesáreo) es una operación en la que nace su bebé cuando hacemos una incisión (cortada) en el abdomen. Hay dos tipos de anestesia que se pueden usar: con la epidural usted está despierta y puede ver al bebé inmediatamente pero no podrá sentir la incisión (cortada); con la anestesia general podrá ver al bebé cuando usted salga de la sala de recuperación.

14. Voy a escuchar los latidos del corazón del bebé.

15. Este es un monitor del feto que nos ayuda a examinar (revisar) el latido del corazón del bebé.

16. Tenemos que ponerle un catéter. Le será un poco incómodo.

17. Tenemos que ponerle un suero en su brazo. Ayudará a mantenerle los flúidos.

18. Le voy a dar una medicina para hacerle los dolores más fuertes.

19. Le voy a dar una medicina para el dolor por medio del suero.

20. Póngase al lado. (Voltéese.)

21. Agarre las rodillas y empuje.

22. Felicidades, Ud. tiene un niño/una niña sano/sana.

23. Su bebé tiene unos problemas médicos. Llamaremos a un intérprete para que se los explique.

Postpartum*

1. Are you planning to breast-feed or bottle-feed?
2. Do you want "rooming-in," or do you want the nurses to watch your baby in the nursery?
3. Your baby weighs _____ lb. (kilograms) _____ oz. (grams).
4. It is important that both you and your baby rest so that you are both strong when you go home.
5. Do you have any questions about caring for your baby? If so, I can call an interpreter to explain things to you.
6. You should not have sexual relations for six weeks.
7. If your flow becomes very heavy or painful, call your doctor immediately.
8. Do you fully understand what circumcision is and what it requires?
9. Would you like more information?
10. Circumcision involves surgically removing the foreskin from the penis. It is done very quickly.
11. Do you want your baby circumcised?
12. Generally the plastic ring will fall off about 5 to 8 days after the circumcision. The baby can be bathed and his diapers can be changed as if he had not been circumcised.

Después del Parto

1. ¿Piensa darle pecho al nene o darle el biberón?
2. ¿Quiere "rooming-in" (quiere decir tener al bebé en el cuarto con usted siempre) o prefiere que las enfermeras le cuiden a su bebé en la sala de los recién nacidos?
3. Su bebé pesa _____ libras (kilos) _____ onzas (gramos).
4. Es importante que Ud. y su bebé descansen para que los dos estén fuertes cuando se vayan a casa.
5. ¿Tiene preguntas sobre el cuidado de su bebé? Si es así, puedo llamar a un intérprete para que le explique.
6. No debe tener relaciones sexuales por seis semanas.
7. Si le sale mucho flujo o si siente dolores, llame a su médico inmediatamente.
8. ¿Entiende bien lo que significa la circuncisión y lo que requiere?
9. ¿Quiere más información?
10. La circuncisión envuelve el remover quirúrgicamente el prepusio del pene. Se hace rápidamente.
11. ¿Quiere que su niño sea circuncidado?
12. Generalmente el anillo plástico cae de los cinco (5) a ocho (8) días después de la circuncisión. El bebé puede ser bañado y sus pañales pueden ser cambiados como si no hubiera sido circuncidado.

*A list of clothing and other equipment for newborns can be found on p. 107, in the Pediatrics section.

Gynecology

1. At what age did you begin to menstruate?

2. How often do you get your periods?

3. How far apart are your periods?
4. How long do they last?
5. When was your last menstrual period?
6. Describe your menstrual flow.
   Very heavy? With pain?
7. Do you bleed heavily?
8. How many sanitary pads or tampons do you use during a period?
9. Have your periods always been regular until now?
10. Have you ever had menstrual problems?
11. How is your mood during your menstrual flow?
12. Do you spot between periods?
13. Do you have vaginal discharge?
14. Describe the discharge.
15. When was your last Pap smear?

Ginecología

1. ¿A qué edad tuvo el primer período?
   ¿A qué edad tuvo la primera regla?
2. ¿Cada cuándo le viene la regla?
   ¿Cada cuándo menstrúa Ud.?
3. ¿Con qué frecuencia tiene los períodos?
4. ¿Cuánto le duran?
5. ¿Cuándo fue su última regla?
6. Describa su hemorragia (flujo) menstrual.
   ¿Muy abundante? ¿Con dolor?
7. ¿Sangra mucho?
8. ¿Cuántas toallas higiénicas o tampones usa durante la regla?
9. ¿Han sido regulares sus reglas hasta ahora?
10. ¿Ha tenido alguna vez problemas menstruales?
11. ¿Cómo es su humor durante su regla?
12. ¿Tiene manchas de sangre entre los períodos?
13. ¿Tiene flujos vaginales?
14. Describa los flujos, de qué color.
15. ¿Cuándo fue su última prueba Pap?

Pelvic Exam	Examen Pélvico
1. I am going to do a pelvic exam.	1. Le voy a hacer un examen pélvico.
2. Have you ever had a pelvic exam before?	2. ¿Ha tenido alguna vez un examen pélvico?
3. I am going to insert my fingers into your vagina in order to examine you internally.	3. Voy a insertarle mis dedos en la vagina para examinarle por dentro.
4. This will not hurt.	4. Esto no le va a doler.
5. Slide down the table and bend your legs, putting your feet in the stirrups. Then let your legs relax and open.	5. Muévase hasta el borde de la mesa y doble las piernas, ponga los pies en los estribos. Relaje las piernas y ábralas.
6. I am going to insert this speculum in your vagina in order to see your vagina and cervix. It might be a little cold.	6. Le voy a insertar este espéculo en su vagina para vérsela y también la cervix. Lo sentirá un poco frío.
7. Now I am going to put my finger in your rectum. Relax. This will not hurt.	7. Ahora le voy a poner mi dedo en su recto. Relájese. No le va a doler.
8. You can slide back now and sit up. I am finished.	8. Ahora puede moverse y sentarse. He terminado.
9. You can get dressed now.	9. Puede vestirse ahora.

OPHTHALMOLOGY

1. Have you had pain in your eyes?
2. Do you have eyeaches?
3. Do you wear glasses?
4. Were you exposed to anything that could have injured your eye?
5. Do you see things double sometimes?

OFTALMOLOGÍA

1. ¿Ha tenido dolor en los ojos?
2. ¿Sufre de dolores en los ojos?
3. ¿Usa usted anteojos/gafas/lentes/espejuelos?
4. ¿Fue expuesto a cualquier cosa que pudiera haberle dañado el ojo?
5. ¿Ve las cosas dobles algunas veces?

6. Do you ever have blurred vision?

7. Do your eyes burn?
8. Do you have a discharge from your eyes?
9. Do your eyes water much?
10. Do your eyes tire when reading?
11. I am going to put drops in your eyes in order to examine them. This medicine may burn at first.
12. I am putting in these drops to dilate your eyes.
13. This medicine may burn for a few seconds.
14. I am going to patch your right/left eye.
15. Please return in _____ days for reevaluation.
16. I'm shining this light in your eye as part of the exam.

17. Please look into this apparatus.

6. ¿Ve nublado a veces?
   ¿Tiene la vista borrosa a veces?

7. ¿Le arden los ojos?
8. ¿Le supuran los ojos?
9. ¿Le lagrimean mucho los ojos?
10. ¿Se le cansan los ojos cuando lee?
11. Le voy a poner gotas en los ojos para examinarlos. Esta medicina puede arderle al principio.
12. Le estoy poniendo estas gotas para dilatarle los ojos.
13. Esta medicina puede arderle por unos segundos.
14. Le voy a cubrir su ojo derecho/izquierdo.
15. Favor de regresar en _____ días para más evaluación.
16. Estoy alumbrando su ojo con esta luz como parte del examen.

17. Favor de mirar dentro de este aparato.

ORTHOPEDICS

1. Have you been in an accident?
2. How long ago?
3. Where is the pain?
4. Do you feel pain when you stand?
5. Do you feel pain when you bend?

ORTOPEDIA

1. ¿Ha tenido algún accidente?
2. ¿Cuánto hace?
3. ¿Dónde le duele?
4. ¿Siente dolor al pararse?
5. ¿Siente dolor al doblarse?

6. Do the pains shoot down toward the legs?
7. You have a pulled muscle.

8. You have a broken bone.
9. You have a sprain.
10. You have sprained your _____.
11. We need to take some x-rays.
12. You must wear a sling whenever you are out of bed.
13. I'm going to put a pillow under your leg.
14. Can I help you into the chair? I will hold your leg for you.

15. Place the walker in front of you.
16. Put most of your weight on your hands and take a step into the walker.
17. You must keep your knee straight for the surgery to be successful.
18. Wiggle toes to aid circulation.
19. Do you want something for the pain?
20. Is this traction helping you?
21. Do you want a shot or pain pills?
22. Leave your dressing or hip alone.

6. Le corren los dolores hacia las piernas?
7. Ud. tiene un músculo distendido.
   Ud. tiene un músculo jalado.
   Ud. tiene un músculo rasgado.
8. Ud. tiene un hueso quebrado (roto).
9. Ud. tiene una torcedura.
10. Ud. se ha torcido su _____.
11. Necesitamos tomarle unos rayos X.
12. Ud. debe llevar un cabestrillo cuando no esté en la cama.
13. Le voy a poner una almohada debajo de la pierna.
14. ¿Puedo ayudarle a sentarse en la silla? Le agarraré la pierna.
15. Ponga el andador en frente de Ud.
16. Ponga su peso en las manos y dé un paso con el andador.
17. Ud. debe mantener la rodilla recta para que tenga éxito la cirugía.
18. Mueva los dedos del pie para ayudar la circulación.
19. ¿Quiere algo para el dolor?
20. ¿Le ayuda esta tracción?
21. ¿Quiere una inyección o pastillas para el dolor?
22. No se toque el vendaje ni la cadera.

Hand Splint

1. This is a splint to protect your hand.
2. To care for it wash it in warm (lukewarm) water.
3. If you wash it in hot water it will melt.
4. Do not leave it in the sun or in any very hot place (dashboard of a car or on the radiator).
5. You can wash the padding also.
6. It is very dense and does not absorb water.
7. Just brush it briskly and it will dry immediately.
8. Be careful to check the fit.
9. Your wrist should rest snugly in the curve.
10. Watch it, and adjust it if the edge slips down on your arm.
11. This edge should stay between your knuckles and the second joint on your finger.
12. Because of the surgery, the tendon that used to bend your ring finger now bends your thumb.
13. Practice touching the tip of your thumb to the tips of your fingers.
14. Squeeze this gauge. It measures the strength in your hand. Grip and pinch.

Tablilla de Mano

1. Esta es una tablilla para proteger su mano.
2. Para cuidarla lávela en agua tibia.
3. Si la lava en agua caliente se ablanda.
4. No la deje en el sol o en un lugar demasiado caliente (en el guardabarros de un carro o en el radiador).
5. También el relleno se puede lavar.
6. Es muy denso y no absorbe agua.
7. Nomás cepíllela ligeramente y se secará en seguida.
8. Cuidado de revisar el ajuste.
9. Su muñeca debe reposar bien en la curva.
10. Revísela, y ajústela si el borde se zafa por el brazo.
11. Este borde debe estar entre los nudillos y la segunda coyuntura del dedo.
12. Por razón de la cirugía el tendón que antes doblaba su dedo de anillo ahora dobla su dedo pulgar.
13. Practique tocar la punta del pulgar a las puntas de los dedos.
14. Apriete este calibrador. Mide la fuerza de su mano. Apriételo y pellizque.

PEDIATRICS

Pediatric Equipment List

1. A and D ointment

2. alcohol
3. bassinette
4. bath towel

5. bathtub

6. blankets
7. bottles
8. cotton
   a. cotton balls
   b. cotton swabs, Q-Tips
9. cream (lotion)
10. crib
11. Desitin
12. diapers
    a. disposable diapers
    b. diaper pins
    c. diaper pail

13. drops
14. gauze (sterile)
15. high chair
16. kimono
17. lotion
18. nightgown

19. nipples
20. oil
21. pail (diaper)
22. petroleum jelly, Vaseline

23. powder
24. Q-Tips, cotton swabs
25. shampoo
26. shirts
27. sheets
28. sweater
29. towels
30. Vaseline

PEDIATRÍA

Lista de Equipo Pediátrico

1. ungüento de A y D, crema de A y D

2. alcohol
3. moisés
4. manta de baño, toalla de baño

5. bacín para el niño, bañera

6. cobijitas
7. biberones
8. algodón
   a. bolas de algodón
   b. palitos de algodón
9. crema (loción)
10. cuna
11. crema de Desitin
12. pañales
    a. pañales desechables
    b. alfileres de seguridad
    c. balde para pañales

13. gotas
14. gasa (estéril)
15. silla alta
16. quimono
17. loción
18. camiseta de dormir, batita de dormir

19. teteros
20. aceite
21. balde para pañales
22. jalea de petróleo, Vaselina

23. talco, polvos
24. palitos de algodón
25. champú
26. camisetas interiores
27. sábanas
28. suéter
29. toallitas
30. Vaselina

History Form (for new patients,
to be filled out by parent prior to visit)

Name of child _____

Birthdate _____

Is this child being seen for a routine visit ( ), for a school exam ( ), etc., or for a particular problem ( )? If so, please specify. _____

Pregnancy and Birth

1. Is the child yours by birth _____, adopted _____, stepchild _____, other _____?

2. Did you have an illness or bleeding during your pregnancy?   No   Yes

3. Did you take any medications or have any x-rays during the pregnancy? (Circle which one.)   No   Yes

4. Was it a premature delivery?   No   Yes
   Full-term?   Yes   No

5. Was the delivery normal?   Yes   No
   If not, was it breech, by cesarean section, induced, by forceps? Full term?

6. Was the baby born strong and healthy?   Yes   No

7. Where was the child born? _____

8. What was the birth weight?_____
   Length? _____

Historia (para pacientes que vienen por primera vez, y a ser llenado por los padres antes de la visita)

Nombre del niño _____

Fecha de nacimiento _____

¿Es ésta una visita de rutina o chequeo ( ), un examen para la escuela ( ), etc., o viene Ud. por un problema particular ( )? De ser así por favor especifique el problema. _____

Embarazo y Nacimiento

1. ¿Es su hijo por nacimiento _____, adoptado _____, hijastro _____, otro _____?

2. ¿Tuvo Ud. enfermedades, sangramiento o hemorragias durante su embarazo?   No   Sí

3. ¿Tomó Ud. alguna medicina, o le hicieron alguna radiografía durante su embarazo? (Indique cual con un círculo)   No   Sí

4. ¿Fue el parto prematuro?   No   Sí
   ¿Nació a término?   Sí   No

5. ¿Fue el parto normal?   Sí   No
   Si no, fue un parto de nalgas, cesárea, inducido, fórceps? ¿Nació a término?

6. ¿Nació el bebé fuerte y de buena sulud?   Sí   No

7. ¿Dónde nació el niño? (Ciudad y País) _____

8. ¿Cúanto pesó al nacer? _____
   ¿Cuánto midió? _____

9. Did your baby have any trouble starting to breathe?	No	Yes
10. Did the baby have any trouble while in the hospital? (Jaundice, difficulty breathing, blueness, vomiting)	No	Yes
11. Did the baby leave the hospital when you (mother) left?	Yes	No

Feeding and Digestion

1. Was there severe colic or any unusual feeding problem the first 3 months?	No	Yes
2. Is your child's appetite usually good?	Yes	No
3. Is it good now?	Yes	No
4. Has there been any change in your child's appetite recently?	No	Yes
5. Are there any foods he cannot eat?	No	Yes
6. Does your child often have diarrhea?	No	Yes
7. Has constipation ever been much of a problem?	No	Yes
8. Does he take vitamins? _____ iron? _____ fluoride? _____ other medicine? _____		

Comida y Digestión

9. ¿Tuvo su bebé algún problema para empezar a respirar?	No	Sí
10. ¿Tuvo el niño alguna enfermedad o trastorno mientras que estaba en el hospital? (Ictericia, problemas o trastornos respiratorios, piel azulada, vómitos?)	No	Sí
11. ¿Se pudo ir el niño a casa al mismo tiempo que la madre?	Sí	No
1. ¿Tuvo el niño severos cólicos o algún trastorno inusual para alimentarse en los primeros tres meses?	No	Sí
2. ¿Es el apetito de su niño generalmente bueno?	Sí	No
3. ¿Cómo está su apetito actualmente?	Bueno	Malo
4. ¿Ha tenido su niño cambios de apetito recientemente?	No	Sí
5. ¿Hay algunas comidas que no pueda comer?	No	Sí
6. ¿Tiene su niño diarrea frecuentemente?	No	Sí
7. ¿Está su niño estreñido, o lo ha sido, causándole problemas?	No	Sí
8. ¿Toma él: vitaminas _____, Hierro _____, Fluoruro _____, Otra medicina _____?		

Family History

1. Circle any of the following diseases that this child's grand-parents, parents, aunts, uncles, brothers, or sisters have had:

   diabetes   cancer
   tuberculosis   seizures
   congenital defects   high blood pressure
   heart attack   stroke
   nervous breakdown   bleeding disorder or anemia
   kidney disease   rheumatic fever
   asthma or hay fever   any inherited or family
                                          diseases

2. Are the child's parents both in good health?   Yes   No
   Mother's age _____ Ht _____ Wt _____
   Father's age _____ Ht _____ Wt _____

3. List name, birthdate, and general health of brothers and sisters and their general state of health (good, regular, etc.)

   _____

   _____

   _____

4. Are the parents separated (date)? _____
   Divorced (date)? _____

5. Does the mother work outside of the home?   No   Yes

Historia de la Familia

1. Ponga un círculo alrededor de alguna de estas enfermedades si alguno de los padres, abuelos, tíos o hermanos de su niño los ha tenido:

   diabetes   cáncer
   tuberculosis   ataques o convulsiones
   defectos congénitos   tensión o presión alta
   ataque al corazón   infarto o embolia, derrame
   problemas nerviosos   problemas de la sangre o
                                    anemia
   enfermedades del riñón   fiebre reumática
   asma o rinitis, fiebre   algunas enfermedades
       del heno   familiares o hereditarias

2. ¿Están los padres del niño en buena salud?   Sí   No
   Edad de la madre _____ Estatura _____ Peso _____
   Edad del padre   _____ Estatura _____ Peso _____

3. Ponga aquí el nombre de los hermanos del niño, su fecha de nacimiento, y su estado general de salud (bueno, regular, etc.)

   _____

   _____

   _____

4. ¿Están los padres del paciente separados (desde cuándo)? _____
   ¿Divorciados (desde cuándo)? _____

5. ¿Trabaja la madre fuera de la casa?   No   Sí

6. Have any of your children died?	No	Yes
7. Have you had any abortions or miscarriages?	No	Yes
8. Does the family include any stepchildren, or half-brothers, half-sisters, foster children, or grandparents?	No	Yes

Infections, Illnesses, Miscellaneous Problems, and Development

1. Has your child:
   a. Had as many as three attacks of ear trouble? No Yes
   b. Had more than three colds or throat infections with fever per year? No Yes
   c. Had any trouble with urination? No Yes
   d. Had any trouble hearing? No Yes
   e. Had any trouble with vision? No Yes
   f. Ever been unconscious or had convulsions at any time? No Yes

2. At what age did your child:
   Sit alone? _____
   Walk alone? _____
   Say words? _____

3. At what age was he toilet trained:
   daytime? _____ (years)
   night time? _____ (years)

4. Does your child have any trouble sleeping? No Yes

5. Does your child have dental problems? No Yes

6. ¿Se le ha muerto algún hijo?	No	Sí
7. ¿Ha tenido Ud. abortos o pérdidas?	No	Sí
8. ¿Está la familia integrada con algún hijastro, medio hermano, niño adoptado o abuelos?	No	Sí

Infecciones, Enfermedades, Problemas Misceláneos, Desarrollo

1. Ha tenido su niño
   a. ¿a lo menos tres inflamaciones o infecciones del oído? No Sí
   b. ¿más de tres resfriados, gripes o infecciones de la garganta con fiebre en un año? No Sí
   c. ¿problemas al orinar? No Sí
   d. ¿problemas auditivos? No Sí
   e. ¿problemas de visión? No Sí
   f. ¿Ha estado inconsciente o ha sufrido convulsiones alguna vez? No Sí

2. ¿A qué edad
   Se sentó solo _____ su niño.
   Caminó solo _____ su niño.
   Dijo palabras _____ su niño.

3. ¿A qué edad dejó de orinarse
   de día? _____ (años)
   de noche? _____ (años)

4. ¿Tiene su niño algún problema para dormir? No Sí

5. ¿Tiene su niño problemas con los dientes? No Sí

6. In this list of illnesses, circle any that your child has had:

"red" measles	mumps
chickenpox	scarlet fever
	German or "3-day" measles
whooping cough	serious accidents
pneumonia	removal of tonsils and
broken bones	adenoids

other operations (specify) _____

other diseases (what?) _____

hospitalizations (for what and for how long?) _____
_____

7. (For teenage girls): At what age was onset of menstruation? _____

Allergies

1. Has your child ever had:
   a. Eczema or hives?   No   Yes
   b. Wheezing, asthma, hay fever?   No   Yes

   c. Allergies or reactions to any medicines   No   Yes
      or injections?

2. Does your child tend to have a stuffy   No   Yes
   nose or "constant cold" (sinus trouble)?

6. En esta lista de enfermedades, haga un círculo alrededor de la(s) que su niño haya tenido:

sarampión	parotiditis o paperas
varicelas (lechina o viruelas	fiebre escarlatina
locas)	rubéola
tos ferina	accidentes serios
pulmonía	operación de las amígdalas o
huesos quebrados	adenoides

otras operaciones (especifique)_____

otras enfermedades (especifique) _____

hospitalizaciones (especifique el motivo y duración) _____
_____

7. (Para niñas): ¿A qué edad empezó a menstruar? _____

Alergias

1. ¿Ha tenido su hijo:
   a. Eczema o urticaria?   No   Sí
   b. Disnea (silbido o problemas al respirar),   No   Sí
      asma, fiebre del heno?

   c. Reacción o alergia a alguna medicina o   No   Sí
      ampolleta (vacuna o inyección)?

2. ¿Suele su niño tener la nariz tapada o   No   Sí
   refriados "constantes" (enfermedad del seno
   nasal)?

Behavior

1. Does your child get along well in school?   Yes   No
2. Does your child get along well with other   Yes   No
   children, adults, teachers?
3. Does your child have any behavior   No   Yes
   problems that cause you concern?

Tests and Immunizations

1. Has your child been vaccinated against:
   a. Smallpox (successfully)? Date _____   Yes   No
   b. DPT: or diphtheria, tetanus and   Yes   No
      whooping cough?
      Date of last booster _____
   c. Polio (all three doses by mouth)?   Yes   No
   d. Polio (by injection)   Yes   No
      Any booster polio immunizations given?   Yes   No
   e. Measles? Date _____   Yes   No
   f. Mumps? Date _____   Yes   No
   g. German measles? Date _____   Yes   No
2. Has your child had a skin test for   Yes   No
   tuberculosis? Give date of last test _____
   Negative or positive? _____

Conducta

1. ¿Se lleva bien su niño en la escuela?   Sí   No
2. ¿Tiene su niño buenas relaciones con otros   Sí   No
   niños, adultos, maestros?
3. ¿Tiene su niño algún problema de conducta   No   Sí
   que le preocupa a Ud?

Pruebas e Inmunizaciones

1. ¿Ha sido su niño inmunizado (vacunado) contra:
   a. La viruela (con éxito)? Fecha _____   Sí   No
   b. D.P.T. (tétanos, difteria, tos ferina)?   Sí   No
      Fecha de última vacuna _____
   c. El polio (todas las tres dosis por   Sí   No
      la boca)?
   d. Polio (en forma de inyección)   Sí   No
                                                   Sí   No
   e. Sarampión (inyección)? Fecha_____   Sí   No
   f. Parotiditis o paperas (inyección)?   Sí   No
      Fecha _____
   g. Rubéola (inyección)? Fecha _____   Sí   No
2. ¿Ha tenido su niño pruebas de tuberculina   Sí   No
   (tuberculosis)?
   Fecha de última prueba _____
   ¿Positiva o negativa? (indique) _____

3. Has your child's hearing been tested?   Yes   No

4. Has your child's vision been tested?   Yes   No

5. When did your child last see a dentist? _____

6. Name and address of child's last pediatrician or general physician _____

_____

Postpartum Breast-feeding Questions and Instructions

1. Did the baby nurse well?

2. Nurse your baby only 5 minutes on each breast.

3. Be sure to burp the baby when changing to the other breast.

4. I know you don't have any milk yet. The baby's nursing will stimulate your milk to come in sooner.

5. Before your milk comes in the baby gets something called colostrum when he nurses. It is very nutritious and good for the baby.

6. Are you having cramps or pain with your stitches?

7. Everytime you go to the bathroom fill this bottle with warm water and spray yourself off. Use the whole bottle.

8. Pat yourself dry, do not rub. Try not to go over the same area twice.

3. ¿Ha sido examinada la audición de su niño?   Sí   No

4. ¿Ha sido examinada la vista de su niño?   Sí   No

5. ¿Cuándo vio su niño por ultima vez al dentista? _____

6. Nombre y dirección del último pediatra o médico del niño

_____

_____

Amamantando al Bebé Después del Parto Preguntas e Instrucciones

1. ¿Mamó bien el/la bebé?

2. Dé de mamar a su bebé sólo cinco (5) minutos de cada pecho.

3. Haga eructar al (a la) bebé al cambiar al otro pecho.

4. Sé que todavía no tiene leche. El mamar del bebé la estimulará para que venga la leche más pronto.

5. Antes de que venga la leche el bebé obtiene algo llamado colostro cuando mama. Es muy alimenticio y bueno para el bebé.

6. ¿Tiene calambres o dolor en sus puntados?

7. Cada vez que vaya al baño llene esta botalla con agua tibia y dúchese. Use toda la botella.

8. Séquese a palmaditas, no se frote. Trate de no pasar sobre la misma área dos (2) veces.

Illness in Infants*

1. What kind of food has the baby been eating at home?
2. Is there any food/medicine that makes the baby sick?

3. Feed the baby the same as you were before.

4. The baby is getting a little bit better.
5. Bring the baby to the clinic on _____.
6. Call the clinic on _____ morning so we can tell you the time of your next appointment.

Conversational Phrases with Children

1. Hello, my name is _____. I am your nurse/doctor.
2. This is a hospital.
3. You are going to have an operation.
4. You won't feel anything.
5. It's the same as being asleep.
6. When you wake up you will be here in your bed, and you may feel a little pain.

Enfermedades de los Niños

1. ¿Qué clase de comida ha estado comiendo el bebé en casa?
2. ¿Hay algunos alimentos/algunas medicinas que le hacen mal a su bebé?
3. Siga dándole al bebé la misma clase de comida que le daba antes.
4. El bebé se está mejorando.
5. Traiga al bebé a la clínica el _____.
6. Llame a la clínica el _____ por la mañana para que le digamos la fecha de su próxima visita.

Frases Conversacionales con los Niños

1. Hola, me llamo _____. Soy la enfermera, soy la doctora/el doctor.
2. Este es un hospital.
3. Tú vas a tener una operación.
4. No sentirás nada.
5. Es lo mismo que dormir.
6. Cuando te despiertes, estarás aquí en la cama y tendrás un poco de dolor.

*Instructions for fever reduction in children can be found in Section C, Patient Information, p. 176.
Directions for treating diarrhea in children can be found in Section C, Patient Information, p. 186.

7. Your Mommy and Daddy will be able to visit you.
8. Do you want some juice, milk, or anything?
9. We have a play room where you may play
   —when you feel better
   —when the doctor says it's all right.
10. When you have to go to the bathroom, press the button and I will help you.
11. You have to stay in bed. Please don't move.
12. Are you
    a. sleepy?
    b. hungry?
    c. scared?
    d. angry?
    e. sad?
13. I'm going to put an IV in your arm.
14. The food will go into your veins through this needle.

15. Please don't move. It won't hurt once it's in place.

16. Thank you.
17. Sit down/lie down (go to bed)/get up.

7. Tu mamá y papá pueden visitarte.
8. ¿Quieres jugo, leche, otra cosa?
9. Tenemos un cuarto de recreo donde puedes jugar
   —cuando estés mejor
   —cuando el doctor diga que esté bien.
10. Cuando necesites ir al baño, aprieta el botón y te ayudaré.
11. Necesitas guardar cama. Por favor, no te muevas.
12. ¿Tienes
    a. sueño?
    b. hambre?
    c. miedo?
    d. ¿Estás enojado(a)?
    e. ¿Estás triste?
13. Te voy a poner un suero en el brazo.
14. El alimento intravenoso pasará por tus venas a través de esta aguja.
15. Por favor, no te muevas. No te va a doler cuando esté en su sitio.
16. Gracias.
17. Siéntate/acuéstate/levántate.

Vocabulary*	Vocabulario
1. juice	1. **jugo**
2. milk	2. **leche**
3. toys	3. **juguetes**
4. doll	4. **muñeca**
5. animal	5. **animal**
6. bottle	6. **botella**
7. diaper	7. **pañal**
8. pee	8. **(hacer) pipi**
9. poo	9. **(hacer) caca (popó)**

10. play	10. **jugar**
11. read	11. **leer**
12. sing	12. **cantar**
13. dance	13. **bailar**
14. baby	14. **bebé, nene**
15. Mickey Mouse	15. **Ratón Mickey**
16. Donald Duck	16. **Pato Donaldo**
17. Come here.	17. **Ven acá.**
18. Give me your hand.	18. **Dame la mano (manita).**

Developmental Milestones

Naturally most children will have reached these developmental milestones months before the time limit given. Should a child lag behind, then the parents might welcome the opportunity to have their child examined. When I describe a behavior, please tell me whether you have noticed your child doing it. I may ask the child to perform some simple tasks.

1. 3 months
   a. Lifts head up while on stomach
   b. Responds to bell or similar sound
   c. Vocalizes, not crying (coos, chuckles)
   d. Smiles responsively to mother or familiar person or object

Etapas de Desarrollo

La mayoría de los niños llegarán naturalmente a estas etapas de desarrollo meses antes del plazo indicado. Si el niño se demora, se supone que sus padres puedan apreciar la oportunidad de hacer que el niño sea examinado. Cuando yo describa un comportamiento, por favor dígame si ha notado que su niño(a) lo hace. Es posible que yo le diga al niño (a la niña) que haga algunas cosas sencillas.

1. tres (3) meses
   a. Levanta la cabeza mientras que está boca abajo
   b. Responde a una campana o a otro sonido semejante
   c. Vocaliza sin llorar (intenta hablar, se ríe)
   d. Responde con sonrisas a la mamá o a una persona u objeto familiar

*With toddlers and small children the term "mi hijo/mi hija" is used by many members of the family besides the parents and may well be used by the medical worker when soothing or calming a toddler.

2. 6 months
   a. Supports upper body with arms while on stomach

   b. Sits with support, head steady
   c. Rolls over
   d. Grasps rattle
   e. Reaches for object
   f. Follows object moving across his line of vision (4 mo.)

   g. Laughs and squeals (5 mo.)
   h. Smiles spontaneously
3. 9 months
   a. Bears some weight on legs
   b. Sits without support
   c. Transfers object from one hand to another
   d. Turns to voice or loud noise
   e. Feeds self cracker
   f. Works for toy out of reach
4. 12 months
   a. Stands holding on
   b. Pulls self to sitting position
   c. Grasps small object with thumb and index finger
   d. Hands toy on request
   e. Imitates speech sounds (dada, baba, mama)
   f. Plays peek-a-boo
   g. Holds onto toy if someone tries to pull it away
   h. Responds to name

2. seis (6) meses
   a. Soporta el tronco del cuerpo con los brazos mientras que está boca abajo
   b. Se sienta con soporte, con la cabeza firme
   c. Roda el cuerpo de un lado a otro
   d. Agarra la sonaja
   e. Alcanza con las manos hacia algún objeto
   f. Con los ojos sigue un objeto que cruza su línea de vista (cuatro meses)
   g. Se ríe y hace chillidos de gusto (cinco meses)
   h. Sonríe espontáneamente
3. nueve (9) meses
   a. Soporta algo de su peso con las piernas
   b. Se sienta sin soporte.
   c. Cambia un objeto de una mano a otra
   d. Se voltea al oír alguna voz o ruído fuerte
   e. Come una galleta por sí mismo(a)
   f. Hace el esfuerzo de sujetar un juguete fuera de su alcance
4. doce (12) meses
   a. Se mantiene de pie soportándose
   b. Levanta el cuerpo para sentarse
   c. Agarra un objeto con el pulgar y el dedo índice
   d. Entrega un juguete cuando se le pide
   e. Imita sonidos de la voz ("papá," "bebé," "mamá")
   f. Juega a las escondidas con la cabeza
   g. No suelta un juguete si alguien trata de quitárselo
   h. Responde a su nombre

5. 18 months
    a. Likes pull toys and being read to
    b. Stoops and recovers object
    c. Walks alone
    d. Plays ball
    e. Indicates wants, not crying
    f. Drinks holding cup
6. 2 years
    a. Throws and kicks ball
    b. Walks backward
    c. Walks up steps, climbing
    d. Identifies one body part (for example, Where is your hair?)
    e. Correctly uses several words (other than mama, dada)
    f. Uses spoon, spilling little
    g. Removes garments
7. 3 years
    a. Throws ball overhand
    b. Follows two or three simple directions
    c. Alternates feet on stairs
    d. Stands momentarily on one foot
    e. Feeds self
    f. Jumps in place
    g. Pedals trike
    h. Uses sentences of two or more words
    i. Can copy the letter "O" (only 50% of the children tested)

5. dieciocho (18) meses
    a. Le gustan los juguetes que se jalan; le gusta que le lean
    b. Se agacha y levanta un objeto
    c. Camina sin ayuda
    d. Juega a la pelota
    e. Indica lo que quiere, sin llorar
    f. Bebe agarrando la taza
6. dos (2) años
    a. Tira y patea la pelota
    b. Camina hacia atrás
    c. Sube escalones, trepando
    d. Identifica partes del cuerpo (por ejemplo, ¿Dónde está tu pelo?)
    e. Usa varias palabras correctamente (más que "mamá," "dadá")
    f. Usa la cuchara, derramando poco
    g. Se quita la ropa
7. tres (3) años
    a. Lanza la pelota
    b. Lleva a cabo dos o tres mandatos sencillos
    c. Alterna los pies en las escaleras
    d. Momentáneamente se para en un pie
    e. Se alimenta a sí mismo(a)
    f. Salta en su lugar
    g. Pedalea el triciclo
    h. Habla en oraciones de dos o más palabras
    i. Puede copiar la letra "O" (sólo cincuenta por ciento—50%—de los niños examinados pasaron esta prueba)

8. 4 years
   a. Gives first and last name
   b. Washes and dries hands
   c. Understands "cold," "tired," and "hungry" (at least two of the three words alone)
   d. Puts on shoes
   e. Dresses with supervision
   f. Uses plural words
   g. Plays games like tag with other children
   h. Can copy plus sign (+) (only 50% of children tested)

8. cuatro (4) años
   a. Da su nombre y apellido
   b. Se lava y se seca las manos
   c. Entiende "frío," "cansado," y "tener hambre" (a lo menos dos de las tres palabras solas)
   d. Se pone los zapatos
   e. Se viste, con dirección
   f. Usa palabras plurales
   g. Juega juegos como "tócame tú" con otros niños
   h. Puede copiar la señal de más (+); (sólo cincuenta por ciento)—50%—de los niños examinados pasaron esta prueba)

Denver Developmental Test

Pre-test forms for the Denver Developmental Screening Test are available in Spanish as well as in English.

The pre-test forms cover development of children from 3 months to 6 years of age. They are to be filled out by a parent before the health practitioner administers the test.

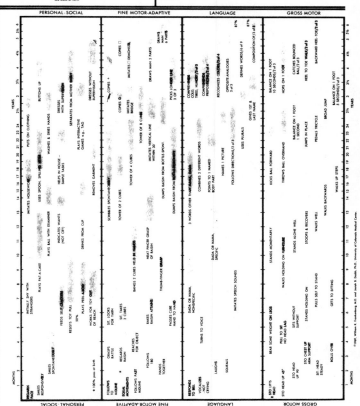

PULMONARY-RESPIRATORY

1. Do you have difficulty breathing?
2. Can you breathe well now?
3. How long can you hold your breath?
4. Are you short of breath?
5. Do you smoke? How many packs a day?
6. Do you cough a lot?
7. How long have you been coughing?
8. Does it hurt when you cough?
9. Do you cough up phlegm?
10. What is the color of the phlegm?
    a. clear?
    b. gray?
    c. white
    d. yellow?
    e. green?
    f. red?
    g. brown?
    h. black?
11. Do you cough up blood?
12. Do you spit up blood?
13. Do you wheeze?
14. Have you ever had asthma?

PULMONAR-RESPIRATORIA

1. ¿Tiene alguna dificultad para respirar?
2. ¿Puede Ud. respirar bien ahora?
3. ¿Por cuánto tiempo puede retener la respiración?
4. ¿Le falta aire para respirar? Tiene falta de aire?
5. ¿Fuma usted? ¿Cuántos paquetes al día?
6. ¿Tose usted mucho?
7. ¿Desde cuándo tiene tos?
8. ¿Le duele cuando tose?
9. ¿Al toser, escupe usted flema(s)?
10. ¿De qué color es la flema?
    a. clara?
    b. gris?
    c. blanca?
    d. amarilla?
    e. verde?
    f. roja?
    g. marrón?
    h. negra?
11. Al toser, ¿arroja usted sangre?
12. ¿Escupe usted sangre?
13. ¿Le silba a usted el pecho?
14. ¿Ha tenido asma alguna vez?

15. Have you ever had:
    a. tuberculosis?
    b. pneumonia?
    c. emphysema?
    d. bronchitis?
16. When was the last time you had your chest X-rayed? What were the results?
17. I am going to listen to your lungs.
18. Breathe deeply.
19. Exhale. Exhale with force (very strongly).
20. Again, please.
21. Relax. Relax your arm/leg.
22. Don't pull out the tube.
23. You need the tube to be able to breathe.

PSYCHIATRY

Current Mental Status

1. Why are you seeking hospital treatment now?
2. Can you cope at home, work?
3. Do you have a psychiatrist (therapist) now?
4. How are you feeling?
5. Do you want to hurt yourself or someone else?

15. ¿Ha tenido alguna vez:
    a. tuberculosis?
    b. pulmonía?
    c. enfisema?
    d. bronquitis?
16. ¿Cuándo fue su última radiografía (rayos-X) del pecho? ¿Cuáles fueron los resultados?
17. Le voy a escuchar los pulmones.
18. Aspire profundamente. (Respire profundo.)
19. Exhale. Exhale con fuerza (muy fuerte).
20. Otra vez, por favor.
21. Relájese. Afloje el brazo/la pierna.
22. No jale el tubo.
23. Ud. necesita el tubo para poder respirar.

PSIQUIATRÍA

Actual Estado Mental

1. ¿Por qué busca tratamiento del hospital ahora?
2. ¿Puede manejar en casa, en el trabajo?
3. ¿Tiene un psiquíatra (terapista) ahora?
4. ¿Cómo se siente?
5. ¿Le dan ganas a Ud. de dañarse o de dañar a otra persona?

6. Do you want to die?

7. Do you hear voices?

8. Do you get messages from the television or radio?

9. Do you get messages from other places?

10. Can/do people control your thoughts?

11. Do voices or thoughts inside your head ever tell you or command you to do things? To yourself or to others?

12. How long have you had this problem?

13. We will help you maintain control.

Behavior Changes

1. When did the patient's behavior begin to change?

2. What were the changes?
   a. Did the patient stop eating? When?
   b. Did the patient stop sleeping? When?
   c. Did the patient become withdrawn/stop talking?

3. What is the patient usually like behaviorally?

Substance Use

1. Does the patient use alcohol?
   a. What kind?
   b. How much per day and for how long?

6. ¿Desea Ud. morir?

7. ¿Oye Ud. voces?

8. ¿Recibe Ud. mensajes por televisión o por radio?

9. ¿Recibe Ud. mensajes por otros modos (lugares)?

10. ¿Controlan otros sus pensamientos?

11. ¿Algunas veces le mandan a Ud. hacer algo las voces, a los pensamientos que lleva? ¿A sí mismo(a) o a otras personas?

12. ¿Desde cuándo tiene este problema?

13. Le ayudaremos a mantener control.

Cambios de Comportamiento

1. ¿Cuándo empezó a cambiar el comportamiento del paciente?

2. ¿Cuáles fueron los cambios?
   a. ¿Dejó de comer el paciente? ¿Cuándo?
   b. ¿Dejó de dormir? ¿Cuándo?
   c. ¿Se puso retirado el paciente? ¿Dejó de hablar?

3. ¿Cómo es el comportamiento del paciente regularmente?

Uso de Substancias

1. ¿Usa alcohol el paciente?
   a. ¿De qué tipo?
   b. ¿Cuánto por día y por cuánto tiempo?

2. Does the patient use street drugs (pot, pills, coke)?

   a. What kind?
   b. How much per day and for how long?

3. Does the patient use any drugs prescribed by the doctor or bought from the drug store?
   a. What kind?
   b. How much and for how long?

Family Psychiatric History

1. Has anyone in the patient's family ever had a mental illness?
2. Has anyone in the family had a drug or alcohol problem?

3. Who was the relative? (relationship to the patient)
4. What kind of a problem did he/she have?
5. Was he/she treated by a doctor or hospitalized for the problem?

Medical Problems

1. Is the patient currently being seen by a doctor for any medical problem?
2. Who is the doctor? Name, phone number?

2. ¿Usa el paciente drogas corrientes de calle (marijuana, forma de píldoras, cocaína)?
   a. ¿De qué tipo?
   b. ¿Cuánto por día y por cuánto tiempo?

3. ¿Usa el paciente drogas recetadas por médico o compradas en la farmacia?
   a. ¿De qué tipo?
   b. ¿Cuánto y por cuánto tiempo?

Historia Familiar Psiquiátrica

1. ¿Alguna vez ha tenido enfermedad mental algún miembro de la familia del paciente?
2. ¿Ha tenido alguno de la familia algún problema con drogas o con alcohol?
3. ¿Quién era el pariente? (parentesco del paciente)
4. ¿Qué tipo de problema tenía él/ella?
5. ¿Fue atendido(a) por un médico o internado(a) en el hospital por el problema?

Problemas Médicos

1. ¿Está el paciente bajo el cargo de un médico a causa de algún problema médico?
2. ¿Quién es el médico? ¿Su nombre, número de teléfono?

3. What are you (the patient) being seen for?

4. Is the patient allergic to any medications or foods?

4b. Are you allergic to any medications or foods?
5. Do you have a psychiatrist presently?
6. Who is the psychiatrist, phone number?
7. When did you last see a psychiatrist or medical doctor?

Finance and Insurance

1. Do you have medical insurance?
2. Do you have a Medi-Cal Card?
3. Does your insurance cover psychiatric treatment and hospitalization?
4. Do you have a job? Where do you work?
5. What type of income do you have?
6. Are you receiving Social Security? Disability, unemployment?
7. How do you support yourself?

3. ¿Para qué lo/la está atendiendo el médico a Ud. (el paciente)?

4. ¿Tiene el paciente alergias a algunos medicamentos o alimentos?

4b. ¿Es usted alérgico(a) algunos medicamentos o alimentos?
5. ¿Tiene Ud. un psiquíatra ahora?
6. ¿Quién es el psiquíatra? ¿Su número de teléfono?
7. ¿Cuándo fue la última vez que Ud. vio a un psiquíatra o médico?

Finanzas y seguro

1. ¿Tiene usted seguro médico?
2. ¿Tiene Ud. una tarjeta de Medi-Cal?
3. ¿Su seguro paga tratamiento psiquiátrico y hospitalización?
4. ¿Tiene usted empleo (tratajo)? ¿Dónde trabaja?
5. ¿Qué tipo de ingresos tiene Ud.?
6. ¿Recibe Ud. Seguro Social? ¿Ayuda por incapacidad o por falta de empleo?
7. ¿Cómo se mantiene Ud.?

Living Situation

1. Where have you been living?
2. Who was taking care of you or were you taking care of yourself?
3. Where will you live when you leave the hospital?
4. Can you return to the place where you were living?

Significant Others

1. Names and phone numbers for family members, friends and neighbors, and the hours when they can be reached.
2. Any doctor, counselor, or therapist who has treated patient in the past.

Patient Intake

1. Read these unit rules and rights of patients.
2. Do you have any questions?
3. You are restricted to this unit (area).
4. Please sign the conditions of admission.
5. You are on a 72-hour hold.
6. Routine medications are given at 9 a.m., 1 p.m., 5 p.m., and 9 p.m.

Situación de Vivienda

1. ¿Dónde ha estado viviendo?
2. ¿Quién lo/la ha cuidado, o se cuidaba a sí mismo/a?
3. ¿Dónde vivirá Ud. cuando salga del hospital?
4. ¿Puede regresar Ud. a donde vivía?

Otros Significantes

1. Nombres y números de teléfono de miembros de la familia, de amigos y vecinos, y las horas cuando se puedan llamar.
2. Cualquier médico, consejero o terapista que haya atendido al paciente en el pasado.

Ingreso del Paciente

1. Lea estas reglas de la unidad y los derechos de los pacientes.
2. ¿Tiene alguna pregunta?
3. No se permite salir de esta unidad (área).
4. Favor de firmar esta forma de condiciones de ingreso.
5. Ud tiene que quedarse por 3 días (72 horas).
6. Se dan medicinas de rutina a las nueve, a la una, a las cinco y a las nueve de la noche.

RADIOLOGY

1. Good morning (good day). Good afternoon.
2. Are you able to stand up?
3. Do you have any pain?
4. Where does it hurt?
5. I am going to take a picture/X-ray of your gallbladder.
6. I am going to take a picture/X-ray of your colon.
7. I am going to take an intravenous pyelogram.

8. Please change your clothes. Put on a hospital gown. One ties in the front and one ties in the back.
9. Please lie on the table, face up/face down.
10. The table may be a little cold.
11. Turn on your left/right side.
12. Turn over.
13. Let me put you in the right position.
14. Swallow this mixture.
15. Stand here and place your chest against this plate.
16. Rest your chin here.
17. Put your hands on your hips with the palms facing out.
18. Don't move.
19. Take a deep breath. Hold it. Now breathe normally.

RADIOLOGÍA

1. Buenos días. Buenas tardes.
2. ¿Puede Ud. estar de pie?
3. ¿Tiene Ud. algún dolor?
4. ¿Dónde le duele?
5. Le voy a hacer una radiografía (rayos-X) de la vesícula biliar.
6. Le voy a hacer una radiografía (rayos-X) del colon.
7. Le voy a hacer una radiografía (rayos-X) de los riñones (pielograma intravenoso).

8. Favor de cambiarse la ropa. Póngase el camisón. Haga un lazo en frente y el otro detrás.
9. Por favor, acuéstese sobre la mesa, boca arriba/boca abajo.
10. La mesa puede estar un poco fría.
11. Voltéese al lado izquierdo/al lado derecho.
12. Voltéese al otro lado.
13. Déjeme ponerle en la postura correcta.
14. Trague esta mezcla.
15. Párese aquí y apoye el pecho contra esta placa.
16. Apoye el mentón aquí.
17. Ponga las manos en las caderas con las palmas hacia afuera.
18. No se mueva.
19. Aspire profundamente. Manténgalo. Ahora respire normalmente.

20. We have to take another picture.
21. You are almost finished.
22. When you are finished, you can go back to your room/go home.
23. You are finished.
24. You may put your clothes on and go home.
25. Sit down on the wheelchair and wait for the orderly.
26. The orderly will take you back to your room.

Ultrasound

1. Your bladder is too full. You may go to the bathroom and urinate ½ or 1 cup only.
2. Did you drink your water?
3. You were supposed to drink 4 large glasses of water or liquids.
4. Does your bladder feel full?
5. Your bladder has to be full. The sound passes through and outlines your uterus and ovaries. When your bladder is full, it pushes your bowel or intestines out of the way. The sound will not go through air. So if there is air in your intestines, we will not see anything. It blocks the sound.
6. You'll have to wait until your bladder fills up.
7. When was the last time you ate or drank anything?

20. Tenemos que tomar otra foto.
21. Ud. va a terminar muy pronto.
22. Cuando termine, puede regresar a su cuarto/regresar a casa.
23. Ud. ha terminado.
24. Ud. puede ponerse la ropa ahora e ir a casa.
25. Siéntese en la silla de ruedas y espere al ayudante.
26. El ayudante le llevará a su cuarto.

Ultrasonido

1. Su vejiga está demasiado llena. Puede ir al baño y orinar solamente media taza o una taza.
2. ¿Tomó Ud. su agua?
3. Ud. debería haber tomado cuatro vasos grandes de agua o líquidos.
4. ¿Siente llena su vejiga?
5. Su vejiga tiene que estar llena. El sonido pasa por y delinea el útero y los ovarios. Cuando la vejiga está llena empuja su intestino a un lado. El sonido no puede pasar por el aire. Así que si hay aire en sus intestinos, no podemos ver nada. Obstruye el sonido.
6. Ud. tiene que esperar hasta que se llene su vejiga.
7. ¿Cuándo fue la última vez que Ud. comió o tomó algo?

8. Do you have any pain? Where? Point to it (show me where).

9. Have you had any bleeding? Was it spotting? Did you pass any clots?

10. Have you had any pelvic infections? What kind? Yeast? Gonorrhea? Syphilis?

11. Have you had any operations on your uterus or ovaries? Did they take out the ovary or tube?

12. Have you had a hysterectomy?

13. When the doctor examined you, did he feel a mass or lump on either side? Which side? Did he say how large it was or what he thought it might be?

14. Have you ever been pregnant before? How many children do you have?

15. How many months along are you?

16. When are you due?

17. Have you ever had an ultrasound test before? What did you have it done for?

18. This test will not hurt you or the baby.

19. We use sound waves and not X-rays. We rub mineral oil on your skin. The sound passes through the oil better. The sound goes into your body. Then it bounces off the organs inside and returns into this apparatus. It then gives us an image, or outline, of what is inside, on our screen. Then we take pictures of what we see.

8. ¿Tiene Ud. dolor? ¿Dónde? Enséñeme.

9. ¿Ha tenido sangramiento? ¿Había manchas de sangre? ¿Había coágulos?

10. ¿Ha sufrido de infecciones vaginales? ¿De qué clase? ¿Sacaromiceto? ¿Gonorrea? ¿Sífilis?

11. ¿Ha tenido operaciones en el útero o en los ovarios? ¿Le sacaron el ovario o tubo falopio?

12. ¿Ha tenido una histerectomía?

13. Cuando el médico le examinó, ¿sintió él un bulto en cualquier lado? ¿En qué lado? ¿Dijo él qué grande era? ¿Dijo qué creía que podía ser?

14. ¿Ha estado embarazada antes? ¿Cuántos hijos (niños) tiene?

15. ¿Cuántos meses ha estado embarazada?

16. ¿Cuándo espere al bebé? ¿Cuál es la fecha del parto?

17. ¿Ha tenido alguna vez una prueba de ultrasonido? ¿Para qué?

18. Esta prueba no le va a doler a Ud. ni al bebé.

19. Usamos ondas de sonido y no rayos-X. Frotamos aceite mineral en su piel. El sonido pasa mejor por el aceite mineral. El sonido entra en su cuerpo. Luego rebota de los órganos adentro y regresa en este aparato. Entonces nos da una imagen o bosquejo de lo que está dentro, por la pantalla. Luego sacamos fotos de lo que vemos.

Body CT*

This X-ray examination, a form of computed tomography, uses a CT scanner to produce a series of cross-sectional images of a selected part of your body. The examination will be conducted by a technologist, an expert in the use of this specialized equipment.

The results will be evaluated by a radiologist, who is a physician specializing in medical diagnosis by X-ray. Each separate CT image can be likened to a slice of an orange. By studying several images in sequence, the radiologist can build up a three-dimensional picture of the part of the body being examined.

Be sure to follow your doctor's instructions carefully. If you don't, the examination may have to be repeated at a later date.

How the Body CT Works

The ring encircling your body contains an X-ray tube and a receptor which are mounted opposite each other. These rotate around your body, which is positioned in the exact center of the ring.

With each rotation, or scan, thousands of X-ray beams pass through your body. Some of the energy in each beam is absorbed by the structures inside your body. The rest passes through and strikes the receptor. The receptor measures this amount and feeds the information into a computer.

*Courtesy of PAS Publishing Co.

CT (Tomografía Computarizada) del Cuerpo

Este examen por rayos X, una forma de tomografía computada, usa un contador CT para producir una serie de imágenes de sección transversal de una parte seleccionada del cuerpo. El examen será conducido por un tecnólogo, un experto en el uso de estos instrumentos especializados.

Los resultados se evaluarán por un radiólogo quien es un médico que especializa en la diagnosis médica por rayos X. Cada una de las imágenes de CT se puede semejar a una tajada de naranja. Estudiando varias imágenes en secuencia, el radiólogo puede componer un retrato en tres dimensiones de la parte del cuerpo examinada.

Asegúrese seguir con mucho cuidado las instrucciones de su médico. Si no, puede ser necesario repetir el examen más tarde.

Cómo Funciona la CT para el Cuerpo

El círculo rodeando su cuerpo contiene un tubo de rayos X y un receptor que están soportados en posiciones opuestas. Estos giran alrededor del cuerpo que está puesto en el centro exacto del círculo.

Con cada vuelta, o exploración, miles de emisiones de rayos X pasan por su cuerpo. Algo de la energía en cada emisión es absorbido por las estructuras dentro de su cuerpo. Lo demás pasa y da con el receptor. El receptor mide esta cantidad y entrega la información a un computador.

The computer calculates the density of each area within the body, based on the energy absorbed as the scanner rotates. This density is a number that is assigned either a particular color or a shade of grey which is then displayed on a viewing screen.

Because thousands of X-ray beams are emitted during each scan, it is possible to recreate on the screen an accurate and highly detailed picture of the structures inside your body. The calculations that are required by each scan take the computer only a few seconds to make, but would take a human being years of effort.

What Happens during a Body CT

- For the examination, you may be asked to remove part or all of your clothing, and to wear a gown.

- After you enter the examination room, the technologist will position you on a special table.

- Once you are securely in place, you will be moved into the ring of the scanner. The technologist will control the scanner and monitor the progress of the examination from an adjacent room.

- As you are moved through the scanner, relax and remain as still as possible. You will be asked to hold your breath for a few seconds as each scan is made.

- You will hear the sounds of gears and motors in the ring as the X-ray equipment scans your body. After each image, or scan, is made, the table will move you into position for the next scan.

El computador calcula la densidad de cada área dentro del cuerpo, basada en la energía absorbida, así como el aparato exploratorio da la vuelta. Esta densidad es un número al que se le asigna un color particular, o un matiz de gris, que luego se exhibe en una pantalla.

Porque miles de emisiones de rayos X se lanzan durante cada exploración es posible recrear en la pantalla un retrato preciso y sumamente detallado de las estructuras dentro de su cuerpo. Los cálculos que son requeridos por cada exploración son hechos en pocos segundos por el computador, lo que le costaría a un ser humano años de esfuerzo para llegar al mismo resultado.

Lo que Ocurre Durante una CT del Cuerpo

- Para el examen se le puede pedir que se quite toda o parte de la ropa y que se ponga un camisón.

- Después de entrar en la sala de exámenes, el tecnólogo lo/la arreglará en una mesa especial.

- Ya que esté bien asegurado/a en su lugar, se le moverá dentro del círculo del contador. El tecnólogo controlará el instrumento y vigilará el progreso del examen desde un cuarto contiguo.

- Mientras que se pase por el instrumento, relájese y permanezca lo más inmóvil posible. Se le pedirá no respirar por unos segundos mientras se haga cada escudriña.

- Oirá el sonido del engranaje y de motores en el círculo mientras el aparato de rayos X explore su cuerpo. Después de que se haga cada imagen o retrato, la mesa lo/la moverá en posición para la imagen que sigue.

- Frequently, it may be necessary to use a medication called a contrast medium to highlight certain internal structures. The way the contrast medium is introduced depends on the part of the body examined. Usually it is given orally or injected into a vein. The radiologist can give you specific information about the contrast medium before the examination begins.

- After all the required scans have been obtained, you'll wait while the radiologist examines them to make sure they contain all the necessary information. Occasionally, more scans may be needed.

- ALLOWING TIME   The examination itself usually takes less than an hour. It's wise, though, to allow more time for your entire visit. Your doctor's office can advise you on just how long you should plan to spend.

- FINDING OUT THE RESULTS   The radiologist will study your examination and give his impression to your physician. Your doctor will discuss these results with you and explain what they mean in relation to your health.

- AFTERWARDS   The contrast medium will be eliminated through your urine, and should not discolor the urine or stool. You can resume your regular diet immediately after the examination, unless told otherwise by your doctor.

- SPECIAL NOTE   If you've ever had an examination involving a contrast medium before, and experienced any discomfort, tell the radiologist or technologist. Any woman who is or thinks she may be pregnant should tell her doctor prior to the test.

- Frecuentemente será necesario usar medicación llamada medio de contraste, para hacer destacar ciertas estructuras internas. El modo en que el medio de contraste se introduce depende de la parte del cuerpo examinada. Generalmente se da por boca o se inyecta en una vena. El radiólogo le puede dar información específica acerca del medio de contraste antes de que comience el examen.

- Después de que se obtengan todas las imágenes requeridas, Ud. se esperará mientras que el radiólogo las examine para asegurar que contienen toda la información necesaria. De vez en cuando, más exploraciones se pueden necesitar.

- APARTANDO TIEMPO   El examen propio dura generalmente menos de una hora. Sin embargo, sería bueno conceder más tiempo para la visita entera. La oficina de su médico le puede aconsejar aproximadamente cuanto tiempo debe apartar para el examen.

- DESCUBRIENDO LOS RESULTADOS   El radiólogo estudiará el examen y dará su impresión a su médico. Su doctor discutirá estos resultados con Ud., y le explicará lo que significan en relación con su salud.

- DESPUÉS   El medio de contraste se eliminará por la orina y no debe descolorear la orina o las heces. Puede volver a su dieta regular inmediatamente después del examen, a menos que su médico le diga diferente.

- NOTA ESPECIAL   Si alguna vez ha tenido un examen en el cual se usó un medio de contraste y sintió malestar, dígaselo al examinador. Cualquiera mujer que está preñada, o que cree que lo sea debe decirle a su médico antes del comienzo del examen.

Head CT*

This X-ray examination, a form of computed tomography, uses a CT scanner to produce a series of cross-sectional images of your head. The examination will be conducted by a technologist, who is an expert in the use of this specialized equipment.

The results will be evaluated by a radiologist, who is a physician specializing in medical diagnosis by X-ray. Each separate CT image can be likened to a slice of an orange. By studying several images in sequence, the radiologist can build up a three-dimensional picture of the structures inside your head.

- You'll want to wear loose-fitting, comfortable clothes for the examination.

- Avoid wearing any metal objects on your head, such as hairpins or earrings, and keep your hairdo simple.

How the Head CT Works

The ring encircling your head contains an X-ray tube and a receptor which are mounted opposite each other. These rotate around your head, which is positioned in the exact center of the ring.

*Courtesy of PAS Publishing Co.

CT (Tomografía Computarizada) de la Cabeza

Este examen por rayos X, una forma de tomografía computada, usa un contador CT para producir una serie de imágenes de sección transversal de la cabeza. El examen será conducido por un tecnólogo, un experto en el uso de estos instrumentos especializados.

Los resultados se evaluarán por un radiólogo quien es un médico que especializa en la diagnosis médica por rayos X. Cada una de las imágenes de CT se puede semejar a una tajada de naranja. Estudiando varias imágenes en secuencia, el radiólogo puede componer un retrato en tres dimensiones de la estructura dentro de la cabeza.

- Ud. querrá llevar ropa suelta y confortable para el examen.

- Evite llevar objetos de metal en la cabeza, como horquillas o aretes, y arregle su pelo sencillamente.

Cómo Funciona la CT para la Cabeza

El círculo rodeando su cabeza contiene un tubo de rayos X y un receptor que están soportados en posiciones opuestas. Estos giran alrededor de la cabeza que está puesta en el centro exacto del círculo.

With each rotation, or scan, thousands of X-ray beams pass through your head. Some of the energy in each beam is absorbed by the structures inside your head. The rest passes through and strikes the receptor. The receptor measures this amount and feeds the information into a computer.

The computer calculates the density of each area within the head, based on the energy absorbed as the scanner rotates. This density is a number that is assigned either a particular color or a shade of grey which is then displayed on a viewing screen.

Because thousands of X-ray beams are emitted during each scan, it is possible to recreate on the screen an accurate and highly detailed picture of the structures inside your head. The calculations that are required by each scan take the computer only a few seconds to make, but would take a human being years of effort.

What Happens during a Head CT

- After you enter the examination room, the technologist will position you on a special table. If you're wearing glasses, you will probably be asked to remove them.

- Your head will be positioned in a cradle and secured with a restraining device, such as a strap, which should not cause discomfort.

- You will then be moved into the ring of the scanner. The technologist will control the scanner and monitor the progress of the examination from an adjacent room.

Con cada vuelta o exploración, miles de emisiones de rayos X pasan por la cabeza. Algo de la energía en cada emisión es absorbido por las estructuras dentro de la cabeza. Lo demás pasa y da con el receptor. El receptor mide esta cantidad y entrega la información a un computador.

El computador calcula la densidad de cada área dentro de la cabeza, basada en la energía absorbida, así como el aparato exploratorio da la vuelta. Esta densidad es un número al que se le asigna un color particular, o un matiz de gris, que luego se exhibe en una pantalla.

Porque miles de emisiones de rayos X se lanzan durante cada exploración, es posible recrear en la pantalla un retrato preciso y sumamente detallado de las estructuras dentro de la cabeza. Los cálculos que son requeridos por cada exploración son hechos en pocos segundos por el computador, lo que le costaría a un ser humano años de esfuerzo para llegar al mismo resultado.

Lo que Ocurre durante una CT de la Cabeza

- Después de entrar en la sala de exámenes el tecnólogo le arreglará en una mesa especial. Si lleva lentes, se le pedirá quitárselos.

- La cabeza se le pondrá en una cuna, y será asegurada con un aparato refrenador, como una venda, que no debe causar malestar.

- Luego se le moverá dentro del círculo del contador. El tecnólogo controlará el contador, y vigilará el progreso del examen desde un cuarto contiguo.

- As you are moved through the scanner, relax and do not move your head.

- You will hear the sounds of gears and motors in the ring as the X-ray equipment scans your head. After each image, or scan, is made, the table will move you into position for the next scan.

- Frequently, it may be necessary to use a medication called a contrast medium to highlight certain internal structures. If so, the contrast medium will be injected into a vein, probably in your arm. The vein may be made to stand out by a tourniquet. This medication may be injected from a syringe, or it may flow gradually from an intravenous bottle.

- During the injection, you may feel warm and flushed, and have a metallic taste in your mouth. This is a normal reaction to the contrast medium. It will last only a minute or so and is not cause for concern. But do let the examiner know if you begin to itch, feel short of breath, or are otherwise uncomfortable.

- After all the required scans have been obtained, you'll wait while the radiologist examines them to make sure they contain all the necessary information. Occasionally, more scans may be needed.

- ALLOWING TIME   The examination itself usually takes less than an hour. It's wise, though, to allow more time for your entire visit. Your doctor's office can advise you on just how long you should plan to spend.

- Mientras que pasa por el contador, relájese y no mueva la cabeza.

- Oirá el sonido del engranaje y de motores en el círculo, mientras el aparato de rayos X explore su cabeza. Después de que se haga cada imagen o retrato, la mesa lo/la moverá en posición para la imagen que sigue.

- Frecuentemente será necesario usar medicación llamada medio de contraste, para hacer destacar ciertas estructuras internas. En ese caso, el medio de contraste se le inyectará en una vena, probablemente en el brazo. La vena se hará resaltar con un torniquete. La medicación se le puede inyectar de una jeringa o gradualmente fluirá de un frasco intravenoso.

- Durante la inyección se sentirá con calor y ruborizado, y tendrá un sabor metálico en la boca. Esta es una reacción normal al medio de contraste. Durará sólo como un minuto y no debe causar inquietud. No obstante, deje saber al examinador si empieza a sentir comezón, falta de respiración, o si de otro modo se siente incómodo(a).

- Después de que se obtengan todas las imágenes requeridas, Ud. se esperará mientras que el radiólogo las examine para asegurar que contienen toda la información necesaria. De vez en cuando, más exploraciones se pueden necesitar.

- APARTANDO TIEMPO   El examen propio dura generalmente menos de una hora. Sin embargo, sería bueno conceder más tiempo para la visita entera. La oficina de su médico le puede aconsejar aproximadamente cuanto tiempo debe apartar para el examen.

- FINDING OUT THE RESULTS   The radiologist will study your examination and give his impression to your physician. Your doctor will discuss these results with you and explain what they mean in relation to your health.

- AFTERWARDS   The contrast medium will be eliminated through your urine, and should not discolor the urine or stool. You can resume your regular diet immediately after the examination, unless told otherwise by your doctor.

- SPECIAL NOTE   If you've ever had an examination involving a contrast medium before, and experienced any discomfort, tell the radiologist or technologist.

- **DESCUBRIENDO LOS RESULTADOS**   El radiólogo estudiará el examen y le dará su impresión a su médico. Su doctor discutirá estos resultados con Ud., y le explicará lo que significan en relación con su salud.

- **DESPUÉS**   El medio de contraste se eliminará por la orina y no debe descolorear la orina o las heces. Puede volver a su dieta regular inmediatamente después del examen, a menos que su médico le diga diferente.

- **NOTA ESPECIAL**   Si alguna vez ha tenido un examen en el cual se usó un medio de contraste y sintió malestar, dígaselo al radiólogo o al tecnólogo.

Anatomy
Especially for
Radiology

**Anatomía
Especialmente
para la
Radiología**

1. aorta	1. **aorta**	9. ovarian cyst	9. **quiste ovario**
2. artery	2. **arteria**	10. ovaries	10. **ovarios**
3. bile ducts	3. **conductos biliares**	11. spine	11. **espina**
4. bladder	4. **vejiga**	12. umbilical cord	12. **cordón umbilical**
5. brain	5. **cerebro**	13. umbilical vein	13. **vena umbilical**
6. gallbladder	6. **vesícula biliar**	14. uterus	14. **útero**
7. kidneys	7. **riñones**	15. vein, inferior vena cava	15. **vena, vena cava inferior**
8. liver	8. **hígado**		

Intravenous Pyelogram*

1. I am going to inject an iodine dye in your arm.
2. Then we'll take some X-rays of your kidneys.
3. This is called an intravenous pyelogram.
4. We want to determine whether there are cysts or kidney stones.

REHABILITATION ASSESSMENT

Ambulation History

1. Can you walk without assistance?
2. Do you use equipment (canes, crutches, braces)?
3. Do you use a wheelchair?
4. Is there a limit to how far you can walk (or use your wheelchair) outside the home?
5. Can and do you go out visiting friends, or to restaurants, theaters, or stores?
6. Do you have falls?
7. Do you drive a car?
8. Can you climb stairs?

Pielograma Intravenoso

1. Le voy a inyectar una tinta de yodo en el brazo.
2. Entonces, vamos a hacer unas radiografías (rayos-X) los riñones
3. Esto se llama un pielograma intravenoso.
4. Queremos determinar si hay quistes o piedras (cálculos) en los riñones.

APRECIO DE REHABILITACIÓN

Historia Ambulatoria

1. ¿Puede caminar sin ayuda?
2. ¿Usa equipo (bastones, muletas, abrazaderas)?
3. ¿Usa usted una silla de ruedas?
4. ¿Hay límite para la distancia en que puede caminar (o usar su silla de ruedas) fuera de casa?
5. ¿Puede salir o actualmente visitar a sus amigos o ir a los restaurantes, a los teatros, o a las tiendas?
6. ¿Hay ocasiones en que se cae?
7. ¿Maneja usted un carro?
8. ¿Puede usted subir las escaleras?

*A diet to be used the day before an intravenous pyelogram is done can be found in Section I, Other Medical Personnel, p. 245.

Transfer History

1. Can you get in and out of bed unaided?

2. Can you get on and off a toilet unaided?

3. Can you get in and out of the tub unaided?

Dressing History

1. Do you dress in street clothes daily?
2. Can you put on without assistance your shirt, pants, dress, undergarments, etc?
3. Do you need help with shoes and socks?

Eating History

1. Can you feed yourself unassisted?
2. Can you cut meat?
3. Do you have trouble holding glasses and cups?

Historia del Trasladarse

1. ¿Puede Ud. subirse a la cama y bajarse de la cama sin ayuda?
2. ¿Puede sentarse y levantarse del retrete (excusado) sin ayuda?
3. ¿Puede meterse en la tina y salir de la tina sin ayuda?

Historia del Vestirse

1. ¿Se viste en ropa para afuera todos los días?
2. ¿Puede ponerse sin ayuda su camisa, sus pantalones, su vestido, su ropa interior, y demás ropa?
3. ¿Necesita usted ayuda con sus zapatos y calcetines?

Historia de Comer

1. ¿Puede alimentarse sin ayuda?
2. ¿Puede cortar la carne?
3. ¿Tiene problemas en agarrar vasos y tazas?

Personal Hygiene History

1. Can you shave (use makeup) and comb your hair unaided?
2. Can you shower or bathe without assistance?
3. Can you use a toilet unaided?
4. Do you need help in cleaning up after a bowel movement?
5. Are bladder and bowel accidents a problem for you?

Historia de la Higiene Personal

1. ¿Puede afeitarse (ponerse maquillaje) y peinarse sin ayuda?
2. ¿Puede ducharse y bañarse sin ayuda?
3. ¿Puede usar el excusado sin ayuda?
4. ¿Necesita ayuda en limpiarse después de defecar o después de intestinos?
5. ¿Son accidentes de la vejiga y de los intestinos problemas para usted?

SURGERY

General Medical Surgical Nursing

1. How do you feel?
2. Do you have pain?
3. Do you feel short of breath?

4. Do you need the bedpan?
5. Do you need anything now?
6. When did you have your last bowel movement?

7. Do you need a pill for pain?
   One or two?
8. Do you urinate frequently?

CIRUGÍA

Cuidado Médico Quirúrgico General

1. ¿Cómo se siente?
2. ¿Tiene dolor?
3. ¿Tiene dificultad en respirar?
   ¿Tiene falta de aire al respirar?

4. ¿Necesita la chata (el bacín)?
5. ¿Necesita algo ahora?
6. ¿Cuándo obró últimamente?

7. ¿Necesita una pastilla para dolor?
   ¿Una o dos?
8. ¿Orina con frecuencia?

9. Do you have pain with urination?

10. Do you have allergies?

11. Have you had a bad reaction from any medicine?

12. Have you had sickness from any medicine?

13. Have you had anything to eat or drink since midnight?

14. You must have nothing to eat or drink after midnight.

Preoperative

1. My name is _____. I will make sure that everything will go fine today.

2. What is your name?

3. Where are you from?

4. How many children do you have?

5. Did you receive an injection before coming to the Operating Room?

6. How are you feeling?

7. Are you cold?

8. Did someone take a sample of your blood?

9. Are you allergic to anything? Medicines, drugs, foods, insect bites?

10. Do you use contact lenses, dentures? Do you have loose teeth, removable bridges, or any prosthesis?

9. ¿Tiene dolor al orinar?

10. ¿Tiene alergias?

11. ¿Ha tenido una reacción mala de alguna medicina?

12. ¿Le ha caído mal alguna medicina?

13. ¿Ha comido o tomado algo desde la medianoche?

14. No debe comer ni tomar nada después de la medianoche.

Antes de la Cirugía

1. Me llamo _____. Aseguraré que todo salga bien hoy.

2. ¿Cómo se llama usted?

3. ¿De dónde es usted?

4. ¿Cuántos hijos (niños) tiene usted?

5. ¿Le pusieron una inyección antes de venir a la Sala de Operaciones?

6. ¿Cómo se siente?

7. ¿Tiene frío?

8. ¿Le han tomado una muestra de sangre?

9. ¿Es usted alérgico(a) a algo?—¿Medicinas, drogas, alimentos, picaduras de insectos?

10. ¿Usa usted lentes de contacto, dentadura postiza? ¿Tiene dientes flojos, dientes postizos, o cualquier prostesis?

11. Don't be afraid.
12. You will feel fine during the procedure.
13. The operation will take only _____ hours.
14. It is important to bring your knees to your abdomen and your chin down toward your chest and push your back out toward the doctor.
15. I'm going to place this ground plate under your hip. It's going to be cold and sticky but it will warm up soon and you will forget it is there.

Preparation for Surgery

1. You will know the results tomorrow.
2. I'm going to shave you.
3. The pill will make you sleep.
4. We need to move you onto this gurney to take you to the Operating Room.

Postoperative

1. I must check for bleeding.
2. I must check your IV.
3. Your IV is not running. I must try to fix it.
4. You must lie flat.

11. No tenga miedo.
12. Ud. se sentirá bien durante el procedimiento.
13. La operación durará _____ horas.
14. Es importante levantar las rodillas hasta el abdomen y bajar la mentón hacia el pecho y empujar la espalda hacia el doctor.
15. Le voy a poner esta placa antieléctrica bajo la cadera. Estará fría y pegajosa pero se calentará pronto y Ud. olvidará de que está allí.

Preparación para Cirugía

1. Ud. sabrá los resultados mañana.
2. Le voy a rasurar.
3. La pastilla le hará dormir.
4. Necesitamos moverle a esta camilla para llevarle a la Sala de Operaciones.

Postoperatorio

1. Debo revisar para ver si está sangrando.
2. Debo revisar su suero.
3. Su suero no funciona. Debo tratar de arreglarlo.
4. Debe extenderse completamente.

5. Has the anesthesia worn off yet?

6. Do you still have numbness?

7. You may not eat or drink anything yet, because you may vomit; and the doctor wants you to rest your stomach.

8. This shot will make you sleep.

9. The doctor wants you to stay in bed.

10. I want to take your temperature.

11. Please take deep breaths and cough strongly to help prevent pneumonia.

12. Hold your incision with a pillow and cough.

13. I'm going to suction the tube.

14. This will make you cough.

15. You have fluid in your lungs.

16. Practice on this machine. Try to get all the balls to the top as you take a deep breath.

17. You may take a small amount of ice chips only.

18. What did you drink today?

19. We must measure how much you drink.

20. The doctor wants you to drink more fluids.

21. Please save your urine for us to check.

22. We need a specimen, so please save it.

5. ¿Se le ha pasado ya la anestesia?

6. ¿Todavía siente adormecimiento?

7. No puede comer ni beber nada todavía, porque puede vomitar; el doctor quiere que Ud. descanse el estómago.

8. Esta inyección le hará dormir.

9. El médico quiere que se quede en cama (que guarde cama).

10. Quiero tomarle la temperatura.

11. Por favor, respire profundamente y tosa fuertemente para ayudar a prevenir la pulmonía.

12. Ponga presión sobre la herida con una almohada y tosa.

13. Voy a aspirar el tubo.

14. Esto le va a hacer toser.

15. Ud. tiene líquido en los pulmones.

16. Practique con esta máquina. Trate de poner todas las bolas en la parte de arriba al respirar profundamente.

17. Puede tomar solamente un poco de hielo triturado.

18. ¿Qué bebió hoy?

19. Debemos medir cuánto bebe.

20. El doctor quiere que beba más líquidos.

21. Por favor, guarde su orina para que la analicemos.

22. Necesitamos una muestra, de manera que guárdela, por favor.

23. Please let us know when you have a bowel movement.

24. Have you noticed any bleeding from the rectum, vagina, mouth?

VENEREAL DISEASES

1. Do you have a urethral discharge?

2. Do you have burning with urination?
3. Do you have a vaginal discharge?
4. Do you have abdominal pain?
5. Have you noticed fever or chills?
6. Do you have an IUD in place?
7. How long have you had the symptoms you describe?
8. When did you last have intercourse?
9. With whom?
10. Oral? Rectal?
11. Have you ever had Gonorrhea or Syphilis?
12. Was it treated? With what?
13. Are you allergic to Penicillin or Tetracycline?

23. Por favor, díganos cuándo haya obrado.

24. ¿Ha notado flujo de sangre del recto, de la vagina, de la boca?

ENFERMEDADES VENEREAS

1. ¿Tiene descarga (flujo) de la uretra?
   (¿Le supura de la uretra?)
2. ¿Tiene ardor al orinar?
3. ¿Tiene descargas vaginales?
4. ¿Tiene dolor en el abdomen?
5. ¿Ha notado fiebre (calentura) o escalofríos?
6. ¿Le han puesto un aparato intrauterino?
7. ¿Desde cuándo tiene los síntomas que usted describe?
8. ¿Cuándo fue la última vez que tuvo relaciones sexuales?
9. ¿Con quién?
10. ¿Por boca? ¿Por recto?
11. ¿Ha tenido Gonorrea o Sífilis alguna vez?
12. ¿Le dieron tratamientos? ¿Con qué?
13. ¿Es usted alérgico a la Penicilina o a la Tetraciclina?

VITAL SIGNS

1. Please step on the scale.
2. I am going to take your temperature.
   Open your mouth.
3. You have a high fever.
4. You have a slight fever.
5. I'm going to take your blood pressure.
6. Roll up your sleeve. Relax.
7. Your blood pressure is normal.
8. Your blood pressure is low.
9. Your blood pressure is too high.
10. Let me feel your pulse.
11. Your pulse is too rapid.
12. I'm going to listen to your chest.
13. Take a deep breath.
14. Breathe slowly.
15. Breathe rapidly.
16. Cough please. Again.
17. Hold your breath.
18. Bend your elbow.
19. Make a fist.
20. Here is a prescription to reduce your blood pressure.

SIGNOS VITALES

1. Súbase a la báscula, por favor.
2. Le voy a tomar la temperatura.
   Abra la boca.
3. Ud. tiene una temperatura (calentura) muy alta.
4. Ud. tiene un poco de fiebre.
5. Le voy a tomar su presión de sangre.
6. Súbase la manga. Relájese.
7. Su presión es normal.
8. Su presión es baja.
9. Su presión es demasiado alta.
10. Déjeme tomarle el pulso.
11. Su pulso es demasiado rápido.
12. Le voy a escuchar su pecho.
13. Respire profundo.
14. Respire despacio.
15. Respire rápido.
16. Tosa, por favor. Otra vez.
17. Mantenga la respiración.
18. Doble el codo.
19. Haga un puño. (Cierre la mano.)
20. Aquí tiene una receta para bajar la presión de sangre.

SECTION C

Patient Information

TO HELP YOU WITH BACK PAIN

Bed

Bed rest is recommended. If it is necessary to work, try to take periods of rest during the working day. In any case, try to rest as much as possible in bed, going to bed earlier and resting during the weekend. Use a firm mattress.

Board

A board (¾ inch or 1 inch thick) should be put between the mattress and the boxspring. This will help to alleviate the back pain. If you can't get such a board in the stores, you can get one in a lumberyard.

Temperature

Moist heat will help. Rest in a hot bath for 20 minutes in the morning and at night. At other times put hot towels on your back. Repeat this two to three times a day.

SPECIAL INSTRUCTIONS _____
_____
_____
_____
_____

PARA AYUDARLE CON LOS DOLORES DE ESPALDA

Cama

Se recomienda descanso en cama. Si es necesario trabajar, trate de tener ratos de descanso durante el día de trabajo. En cualquier caso, haga lo posible para pasar más tiempo en cama, acostándose más temprano y descansando durante el fin de semana. Use un colchón firme.

Tabla

Una tabla de tres cuartos a una pulgada de gruesa debe ponerse entre el colchón y el resorte de la cama. Esto hará menos el dolor de la espalda. Si no puede conseguir tal tabla en las tiendas puede conseguirla en una maderería.

Temperatura

El calor húmedo es preferible. Descanse en un baño caliente por veinte minutos por la mañana y por la noche. Otras veces póngase toallas calientes en la espalda. Repita esto dos a tres veces por día.

INSTRUCCIONES ESPECIALES _____
_____
_____
_____
_____

What You Must or Must Not Do

<u>Bending down or lifting something heavy</u>: You should not lift anything with your knees stiff. Always bend your knees and your hips. Don't lift things from cars. Don't open windows that are over furniture, and so on.

<u>Sitting</u>: Try to sit with your knees higher than your hips. A little stool would help with this.

<u>Sleep</u>: Sleep on your side with your knees raised enough to curve your back a little.

<u>Driving</u>: Push the seat so that you can put your knees higher than your hips, curving your back a bit.

<u>Walking</u>: Don't walk a lot. Wear shoes with low-heels. Don't curve your back. Keep the points of your feet straight. Any movement can injure your back.

CANCER—THE SEVEN SIGNS OF DANGER

1. Abnormal bleeding.
2. A lump or hardening in the breast or other area.
3. A sore that does not heal.
4. Changes in the usual pattern of bowel movement.
5. Hoarseness or cough.

Lo Que Debe Hacer Y Lo Que No Debe Hacer

<u>Agacharse o levantar algo pesado</u>: No debe levantar nada con las piernas tiesas. Siempre doble las rodillas y la cadera. Sobre todo no levante cosas de los coches. No abra ventanas que estén sobre muebles, ni haga esfuerzos de ese tipo.

<u>Sentarse</u>: Trate de sentarse con las rodillas más altas que la cadera. Un banquito ayudaría para esto.

<u>Dormir</u>: Duerma de lado con las rodillas levantadas bastante para curvar su espalda un poco.

<u>Manejar</u>: Empuje el asiento para que pueda poner las rodillas más altas que la cadera, curvando un poco la espalda.

<u>Caminar</u>: No camine mucho. Use zapatos de tacón bajo. No curve la espalda; mantenga rectas las puntas de los pies. Cualquier movimiento puede lastimar la espalda.

CÁNCER—LOS SIETE AVISOS DE PELIGRO

1. Pérdida anormal de sangre o flujo.
2. Un bulto o dureza en el pecho u otra parte.
3. Una úlcera que no cicatriza.
4. Cambios en el ritmo habitual de las eliminaciones intestinales o urinarias.
5. Ronquera o tos.

6. Indigestion or difficulty in swallowing.

7. Changes in a mole or birthmark.

If any of these symptoms last more than 14 days, see your doctor.

CARE OF SUTURES (STITCHES)

1. Keep clean and dry.
   a. Cover with light dressing if possible or necessary during the day. Leave open at night.
   b. Tape plastic over wound when bathing so sutures do not get wet.
2. Check daily for:
   a. redness
   b. swelling
   c. drainage from wound or around stitches

3. Call physician if any of the above is noted.
4. Sutures out in _____ days.

6. Indigestión o dificultad al tragar.

7. Cambios en una verruga o en un lunar.

Si alguno de estos síntomas dura más de 14 días, vea a su doctor.

CUIDADO DE SUTURAS (PUNTADAS)

1. Manténgalas limpias y secas.
   a. Cúbralas con vendajes ligeros si es posible o es necesario durante el día. De noche déjelas destapadas.
   b. Protéjalas con plástico asegurado con cinta adhesiva al bañarse, para que no se le mojen las puntadas.
2. Revíselas cada día para:
   a. enrojecimiento o irritación
   b. hinchazón o inflamación
   c. líquido que sale de la herida o alrededor de las puntadas

3. Llame a su médico si se nota alguno de estos síntomas.
4. Se le quitarán las puntadas dentro de _____ días.

CARE OF YOUR BURN AT HOME

Bacteria can cause infection and prevent healing of the burn. Following the instructions below can keep bacteria from growing and help your wound heal better.

If you notice any special problems such as a strong sour smell, greenish or puslike fluid around the burn area, or fever greater than 101°F or 39°C call the hospital or your doctor.

Bathing

Bathing the burn will help keep it clean. The burn should be cleansed every day in a bathtub, sink, or a dishpan until healing becomes apparent. Be sure the washing basin is clean. Use soap powder or liquid to wash the tub. If the burn is on a small child be sure the room is warm and check the water to be sure it is not too hot.

1. Add a gentle detergent powder or liquid to the warm water.
2. Gently splash the water over the burned area.
3. Do not use a washcloth on the burn.
4. Ten to twenty minutes in the bath is enough.

EL CUIDADO DE UNA QUEMADURA EN CASA

Bacteria puede causar una infección y evitar que sane la quemadura. Siga las instrucciones que siguen para prevenir infección por bacteria y así ayudar a que sane la herida.

Si usted nota algo como lo siguiente, llame al hospital o a su médico: un olor fuerte y apestoso, flúido verde o como pus alrededor del área de la quemadura, o fiebre más de 101.0°F (ciento uno grados F) o 39°C (treinta y nueve grados C).

Baños

Para mantener limpia la quemadura debe bañarla. Se debe bañar cada día en una tina, fregadero o vacija hasta que se empiece a formar una cicatriz. Asegúrese de que la tina o fuente esté limpia. Use jabón en polvo o líquido para lavar el baño antes de usarlo. Si el quemado es un niño asegure que el agua que usa para lavarlo no esté muy caliente.

1. Añada un polvo detergente suave o líquido detergente suave al agua tibia que va a usar.
2. Con cuidado eche agua al área quemada.
3. No use toallita o trapo para lavar la quemadura.
4. 10–20 (diez a veinte) minutos de baño son suficientes para lavar la quemadura.

5. Pat the good skin dry with a clean towel. DO NOT dry the burn with a towel.

6. A little lotion can be put on the unburned skin if it is irritated.

Medication

After each bath, the burn dressing should be applied. Clean hands will help keep the burn from becoming infected. Gently spread on the dressing to a layer about this thick _____. Wrap with a gauze bandage, and secure this with adhesive tape. If the burn is on a sensitive area, you should add a layer of loosely wadded gauze before applying the tape. This will serve as a cushion.

Clothing

Loose clothing can be worn over the burn if necessary. Button-type clothes are the easiest to wear over the burn. However, it is best to leave the burn uncovered except for the medication and the dressing. Any clothing worn should be clean.

5. Con cuidado seque la piel que está normal con una toalla limpia. NO SEQUE LA QUEMADURA con una toalla.

6. Si la piel normal está irritada puede usar una loción para la piel.

Medicinas

Después de cada lavada la herida debe cubrirse con medicina y vendajes. Las manos deben estar absolutamente limpias para evitar una infección en la quemadura. Con cuidado cubra la herida con una capa de medicina más o menos así de gruesa _____. Envuelva la herida con un vendaje de gasa y asegure todo con cinta adhesiva. Si la llaga está en un lugar sensible, añada gasa suelta antes de poner la cinta adhesiva. Esto le servirá de protección.

Ropa

Sobre la quemadura se puede usar ropa suelta si es necesario. La ropa con botones es más fácil para usar sobre la quemadura. Sin embargo, es mejor no cubrir la herida con ropa, sólo con medicina y vendajes. Cualquier ropa que se use debe estar bien limpia.

General Considerations

It is important to exercise the area of the burn to keep from getting stiff. This is especially important if arms or legs have been burned. You SHOULD use the arm or leg which is burned.

Some swelling is normal and should decrease by the third day. Swelling can be minimized by keeping the injured part elevated above the heart. If your lower arm or hand has been burned remove any jewelry.

CARE OF SPRAINS

Follow these instructions to help healing and prevent further injury.

1. Keep off the injured part and avoid using it until the pain decreases.
2. Elevate your injured arm or leg above the level of your heart to reduce the amount of swelling.
3. Apply an ice bag during the first 24 hours to reduce pain and swelling.
4. Wiggle your toes or fingers often to prevent swelling.

5. Limit your activity for _____ days as directed by your physician. If pain persists or swelling persists for more than one week, seek followup care with your own doctor or call the Orthopedic Clinic at _____.

Consideraciones Generales

Es importante ejercitar el área de la quemadura para evitar la rigidez. Esto es especialmente importante si las áreas que se quemaron están en los brazos, o las piernas. SE DEBE usar el brazo o la pierna que está quemada.

Hinchazón ocurre normalmente con una quemadura, y por lo general se reduce al tercer día. Se puede reducir la hinchazón si el área que está quemada se mantiene levantada sobre el nivel del corazón. Si el brazo o la mano se ha quemado debe quitarse sus alhajas.

CUIDADO DE TORCEDURAS

Siga estas instrucciones para acelerar la curación y para prevenir más daño.

1. No ponga peso en la parte dañada y no la use hasta que disminuya el dolor.
2. Mantenga el brazo o pierna dañada sobre el nivel del corazón para reducir la hinchazón.
3. Durante las primeras veinticuatro (24) horas aplique una bolsa de hielo para disminuir la hinchazón y el dolor.
4. Mueva los dedos de los pies o de la mano muchas veces para prevenir la hinchazón.

5. Limite su actividad durante _____ días de acuerdo con las instrucciones de su médico. Si el dolor o la hinchazón persiste más de una semana, llame a su médico particular o llame a la Clínica Ortopédica a _____.

CAST CARE INSTRUCTIONS

You have just had a cast applied as part of the treatment of your injury. Because of the nature of your injury and of the Plaster of Paris used to make your cast, there are certain precautions you should take to prevent serious problems.

1. Keep the injured limb elevated (propped up) continuously for the next 48 hours. This is to prevent swelling of the limb, and to be effective, your arm or leg must be arranged so that your fingers or toes are at least 12 inches above your heart.

2. Rarely, there is sufficient swelling within the cast to interfere with the circulation or nerve supply. Signs you should look out for are excessive blueness, paleness, numbness (loss of feeling), or coldness of your fingers or toes. This is a serious condition and it is absolutely necessary that you return to the hospital at once.

3. The pain of your injury should subside rapidly. You may have some mild aching, but this should respond to aspirin. If your doctor feels you need stronger medication he will prescribe it. If the pain medication does not work within 30 to 45 minutes, you should call your doctor for advice.

INSTRUCCIONES PARA EL CUIDADO DE UN YESO

Como parte del tratamiento de su daño se le ha puesto un yeso. A causa del carácter de su herida y del yeso, hay ciertas precauciones que se deben tomar para prevenir problemas serios.

1. Mantenga el miembro dañado constantemente elevado (soportado hacia arriba) durante las próximas cuarenta y ocho (48) horas. Esto previene la hinchazón del miembro, y para que sea efectivo, arregle el brazo o la pierna de tal manera que los dedos de la mano o los dedos del pie estén por lo menos doce (12) pulgadas más altos que el corazón.

2. Rara vez hay inflamación dentro del yeso que pueda interferir con la circulación de la sangre o con los nervios. Las señales que se deben notar son: piel demasiada morada o azulada, palidez, entumecimiento (pérdida de sensación), o frío de los dedos de la mano o los dedos del pie. Si usted tiene alguna de estas señales, puede ser muy serio. Es absolutamente necesario que regrese al hospital inmediatamente.

3. El dolor de su herida debe pasar pronto. Puede sufrir un poco de dolor al principio, pero se puede aliviar con aspirina. Si su doctor cree que usted necesita medicina más fuerte, le dará una receta. Si la medicina no le alivia el dolor en treinta a cuarenta y cinco (30–45) minutos, llama al doctor para que le diga lo que usted tiene que hacer.

4. Do not get your cast wet. If you do, it will only fall apart and no longer perform its proper function.

5. Never put anything under your cast. No matter how good it would feel to scratch that itch, you are asking for trouble from infected pressure sores or scratches if you put anything under your cast. If you have trouble with itching, call your doctor. He can prescribe medicine to deal with the problem.

6. Your cast will be set in a few minutes, but it requires 48 hours to harden completely. If it has a walking heel, do not walk on it for 48 hours.

7. For proper treatment of your injury, you should come to all your appointments on time.

8. If for any reason you are concerned about your cast or your injury, do not hesitate to call your doctor.

CATHETERIZATION

1. What is the Intermittent Catheterization Program?

   A hollow tube called a catheter is passed into your bladder every 8 hours to allow the urine to drain out. On this program, you must not drink more than ½ liter of fluids per 8 hours.

4. No deje que se moje el yeso. Si se moja, se hará trozos, y será ineficaz.

5. Nunca ponga nada debajo del yeso. No rasque el área cubierta por el yeso, de ningún modo. Esto puede causar una infección. Si la comezón persiste, llame al doctor para que le dé alguna medicina.

6. El yeso se seca en unos minutos, pero requiere cuarenta y ocho (48) horas para endurecerse completamente. Si usted tiene un yeso con tacón, no camine por cuarenta y ocho (48) horas.

7. Mantenga todas sus citas con el doctor para asegurarse tratamiento adecuado.

8. Si, por cualquier razón, usted está preocupado por su yeso, o por su herida, llame a su médico.

EL PROGRAMA DE CATETERIZACIÓN

1. ¿Qué es El Programa de Cateterización Intermitente?

   Un tubo hueco que se llama un catéter es pasado hasta entrar la vejiga cada ocho (8) horas para permitir que la orina se desagüe. Durante este programa Ud. no debe tomar más de medio (½) litro de flúidos cada ocho (8) horas.

2. Why must I limit my intake of fluids to ½ liter per 8 hour shift?

   Because a large percentage of the fluids you drink is processed by your kidneys to produce urine which is stored in the bladder until you urinate. Since your spinal cord injury, your bladder cannot empty itself.

3. Why not leave the catheter in the bladder rather than reinsert it every 8 hours? Then I could drink as much as I wanted.

   A catheter could be placed in your bladder and left there, but the risk of infection is very high. There is much less risk of infection being catheterized every 8 hours.

4. I can't feel my bladder anymore. So what's the harm if it gets too full?

   There is a possibility that in 3–6 months, even though you will still be unable to feel your bladder, it might start emptying by itself when it gets full. If you stretch the bladder by filling it too full now, the muscles which surround your bladder will tear and these spontaneous emptyings will never occur after that.

5. How can I prevent this tearing of the bladder muscles?

   By being careful to drink only ½ liter of liquids every 8 hours. Also you should limit coffee or tea to one cup per day, and no alcoholic drinks of any kind. Coffee, tea or alcohol make your kidneys produce urine at a very fast speed, even if you have only had ½ liter to drink in the last 8 hours.

2. ¿Por qué debo limitar mi ingestión de flúidos a medio litro cada ocho (8) horas?

   A causa de un porcentaje grande de los flúidos que Ud. toma es sometido por sus riñones para producir orina que es acumulada en la vejiga hasta que Ud. orine. Por el daño a su espina dorsal, su vejiga no puede vaciarse por sí misma.

3. ¿Por qué no dejar puesto el catéter en la vejiga en vez de volverlo a meter cada ocho (8) horas? En esta manera yo podría beber cuanto quisiera.

   Podríamos meter un catéter en su vejiga y dejarlo allí, pero el riesgo de infección es muy alto. Hay menos riesgo de infección si usamos el catéter cada ocho (8) horas.

4. Ya no puedo sentir mi vejiga. Así, ¿qué importa si se pone demasiado llena?

   Hay posibilidad que, dentro de tres a seis (3–6) meses, aunque Ud. no pueda sentir la vejiga, podrá empezar a vaciarse cuando se llene. Si Ud. estira la vejiga por llenarla demasiado ahora, los músculos alrededor de la vejiga se romperán y estos desagües espontáneos nunca ocurrirán otra vez.

5. ¿Cómo puedo prevenir este rompimiento de los músculos de la vejiga?

   Tenga cuidado en tomar sólo medio (½) litro de líquidos cada ocho (8) horas. También, Ud. debe limitar café o té a una taza al día, y no tome bebidas alcohólicas de ninguna clase. Café, té o alcohol hacen a sus riñones producir orina a gran velocidad, aunque Ud. haya tomado solo medio (½) litro en las últimas ocho (8) horas.

CHRONIC CONSTIPATION

Milk of Magnesia or Mineral Oil: 30 cc before going to bed for three days.

If there is no bowel movement by 10 or 11 a.m. use one glycerine suppository for three days.

Begin this diet to prevent the constipation.

Every day include:
1. One serving of bran cereal or a slice of wheat bread.

2. A serving of fresh vegetables.

3. Eight ounces of prune, pear or pineapple juice.

4. Increase liquids.

If constipation returns (stools are hard or painful) you may use Milk of Magnesia or glycerine suppositories as prescribed before. Call the clinic first to make sure there is no other problem.

CONSTIPACIÓN CRÓNICA

Leche de Magnesia o Aceite Mineral: 30 (treinta) cc antes de acostarse por 3 (tres) días.

Si no usa el baño en la mañana, espere hasta las 10 (diez) o las 11 (once) a.m. (de la mañana) use un supositorio de glicerina por tres días.

Empiece esta dieta para prevenir la constipación.

Todos los días incluya:
1. Una porción de cereal de salvado o una rebanada de pan de trigo.

2. Una porción de vegetales frescos.

3. 8 (ocho) onzas de jugo de ciruela, de pera o de piña.

4. Aumente los líquidos.

Si la constipación le vuelve, por ejemplo si el excremento es duro o doloroso al usar el baño, puede usar leche de magnesia y los supositorios de glicerina como se le han recetado. Primero llame a la clínica para asegurarse que no existe otro problema.

DIABETIC I.D. CARD

I AM DIABETIC

(I am not intoxicated)

If you find me unconscious or acting in an abnormal way, my condition is due to an overdose of insulin.

SEE REVERSE

SOY DIABÉTICO

(No estoy embriagado)

Si me hallan inconsciente o actuando en forma anormal, mi estado se debe a una dosis excesiva de insulina.

VEA EL REVERSO

I am a diabetic. Please give me a little sugar or something sweet. But if this does not revive me within 15 minutes, call my doctor or send me immediately to a hospital.

Name _____

Address _____

Name of my doctor _____

Address _____ Telephone _____

Name of relative _____ Telephone _____

Soy diabético. Tenga la bondad de darme un poco de azúcar o algo dulce, pero si esto no me reanima dentro de unos quince minutos, llame a mi médico o mándeme inmediatamente a un hospital.

Nombre _____

Dirección _____

Nombre de mi médico _____

Dirección _____ Teléfono _____

Nombre del pariente _____ Teléfono _____

DIABETES URINE TESTING*

Directions

1. Collect urine in clean receptacle. With dropper in upright position, place 5 drops of urine in test tube. Rinse dropper and add 10 drops of water in test tube.

2. Drop 1 tablet into test tube. Watch while complete reaction takes place. (See Interpretation of Test.) Do not shake test tube during reaction nor for 15 seconds after boiling inside test tube has stopped.

3. At end of 15-second waiting period, shake test tube gently, compare with color chart.

Interpretation of Test

NEGATIVE: No sugar (glucose)—the liquid will be blue at the end of a waiting period of 15 seconds. The whitish sediment that may form has no bearing on the test.

POSITIVE: Sugar present—the liquid will change color. The more sugar, the greater the change and the more rapidly it occurs.

*Courtesy of Ames Division of Miles Laboratories, Inc.

PRUEBA DIABÉTICA PARA LA ORINA

Instrucciones

1. Colecte la orina en un recipiente limpio. Con el gotero en posición vertical agregue 5 gotas de orina en el tubo, enjuague el gotero y añada 10 gotas de agua.

2. Deposite una tableta en el tubo. Asegúrese que la reacción se lleve a cabo completamente. (Véase Interpretación de los Resultados.) No se agite el tubo durante la reacción ni durante los primeros 15 segundos después de terminada la ebullición.

3. Después de 15 segundos agítese suavemente y compárese con la carta de color.

Interpretación de los Resultados

NEGATIVO: Sin azúcar (glucosa)—el líquido será azul a los 15 segundos de terminada la ebullición. La formación de un sedimento blanco no afecta el resultado.

POSITIVO: Azúcar presente—el líquido cambiará de color. A mayor cantidad de azúcar corresponde un desarrollo de color más rápido y más intenso.

The amount of sugar is determined by comparing the color of the solution in the test tube with the color chart at the end of the 15-second waiting period. Color changes developing after the 15-second waiting period should be disregarded.

IMPORTANT: Careful observance of the solution in the test tube while reaction takes place and during the 15-second waiting period is necessary to detect rapid "pass-through" color changes caused by amounts of sugar over 2%. Should the color rapidly "pass-through" bright orange to a dark brown or greenish-brown, record as over 2% sugar without comparing final color development with the Color Chart.

EMERGENCY TELEPHONE NUMBERS

A doctor should be called immediately in all cases of serious injury or poisoning.

_____
Doctor's Telephone Number

In case of emergency, if a doctor cannot be located, call the Poison Control Center of your area, or take the child to the emergency unit of the nearest hospital.

_____
Telephone Number of Poison Control Center _____

La cantidad de azúcar se determina comparando el color de la solución en el tubo con la carta de color después de 15 segundos de terminada la ebullición. Los cambios posteriores a los 15 segundos no deben considerarse.

IMPORTANTE: Es necesario observar la solución en el tubo durante la reacción y durante los 15 segundos posteriores a la misma para detectar cambios rápidos de color causados por cantidades superiores a 2% de azúcar. Si hubiera un cambio rápido, de anaranjado brillante a café obscuro o a café verdoso, considérese como superior a 2% de azúcar sin comparar el color final con el de la carta de color.

TELÉFONOS DE EMERGENCIA

Se debe de llamar a un médico en seguida en todos los casos de lesiones serias o cuando se sospeche que ha habido envenenamiento.

_____
Número del Teléfono del Doctor

En caso de una emergencia, si usted no puede localizar a su médico, llame al Centro de Control de Venenos de su localidad o lleve a su hijo a la sala de emergencia del hospital más cercano.

_____
Centro de Control de Venenos. Teléfono: _____

HEAD INJURY OBSERVATION SHEET

A person who has had a blow to the head needs to be watched closely following the accident. Awaken the injured person every hour during the first 18 hours. IF ANY OF THESE SYMPTOMS DEVELOP, CALL THE DOCTOR OR BRING THE PATIENT BACK TO THE HOSPITAL RIGHT AWAY:

1. Drowsiness, confusion, sleepiness or inappropriate speech or lethargy.
2. Vomiting
3. Unequal pupil size (black central portion of the eyes not the same size).
4. Blurred vision or seeing double.
5. Dizziness, unsteady gait, staggering.
6. Fever over 100° F (38°C).
7. Slowing of pulse (less than 50 beats per minute in adults) (less than 80 beats per minute in infants).
8. Loss of muscular strength or inability to move arms or legs.
9. Convulsions or unconsciousness.
10. Blood or colorless fluid coming from ears or nose.
11. Persistent headache.
12. Strange or unusual behavior.

INSTRUCCIONES PARA PACIENTES CON GOLPE A LA CABEZA

Cualquier persona que se haya golpeado la cabeza debe ser observado cuidadosamente después del accidente. Despierte a la persona herida cada hora durante las primeras dieciocho (18) horas. SI ALGUNO DE ESTOS SÍNTOMAS OCURRE, LLAME A SU MÉDICO O LLEVE AL PACIENTE AL HOSPITAL INMEDIATAMENTE:

1. Mucho sueño, confusión, letargo, dificultad o incoherencia al hablar.
2. Vómitos.
3. Tamaño desigual de las pupilas (la parte negra de los ojos no está del mismo tamaño).
4. Visión doble o borrosa.
5. Mareos, falta de coordinación, o tambaleo.
6. Fiebre de más de cien (100) grados F o treinta y ocho (38) grados C.
7. Pulso lento (menos de cincuenta (50) latidos por minuto en adultos, menos de ochenta (80) latidos en un bebé).
8. Reducción marcada de la fuerza de músculos o inabilidad de mover los brazos o las piernas.
9. Convulsiones o pérdida del conocimiento (inconsciencia).
10. Sangre o líquido claro saliendo de los oídos o de la nariz.
11. Dolor persistente de cabeza.
12. Comportamiento extraño o inapropiado.

In addition, the following treatment should be followed:

1. Limit your activities for 24 hours.
2. Clear liquids (no milk) for 8 hours, followed by small quantities of food for the following 24 hours.
3. Take nothing stronger than aspirin or Tylenol for headache or discomfort.

HEAD LICE

Lice may live in all hairy parts of the body. One of the most common places where they are found is the head. Eggs hatch in a week and the louse is able to reproduce in 2 weeks. The only way to get rid of them is to destroy the eggs.

Method of Control

1. Shampoo hair first in the usual manner, rinse well but do not dry.
2. Work 2 tablespoonsful of Kwell Shampoo into hair until a good lather forms.
3. Rub all hair and scalp continuously at least 4 minutes.

Además, se debe seguir este tratamiento:

1. Limite sus actividades por veinticuatro (24) horas.
2. Tome líquidos claros (evite leche) por ocho (8) horas, luego cantidades pequeñas de alimentos por las siguientes veinticuatro (24) horas.
3. No tome nada que sea más fuerte que aspirina o Tylenol para dolor de cabeza o malestar.

LOS PIOJOS

Los piojos pueden infestar cualquiera parte velluda del cuerpo. Una de las más comunes en que se encuentran es el pelo de la cabeza. El período de incubación del huevo del piojo es de una semana y el piojo es capaz de reproducirse cada dos semanas. La única manera de exterminarlos es destruir los huevos.

Método de Control

1. Aplique champú como regular al cabello y después enjuáguelo bien, pero no lo seque.
2. Aplique dos cucharadas del champú Kwell al cabello y frote hasta que haya mucha espuma.
3. Frote todo el cabello y cuero cabelludo bien durante por lo menos cuatro (4) minutos.

4. Rinse thoroughly with warm water.

5. You may then want to comb lice and eggs from hair with a fine-tooth comb. This is not necessary for cure, but may be cosmetically desirable.

6. A second application is seldom needed. If necessary, repeat treatment in 24 hours, but not more than twice in one week.

<u>Caution</u>: Avoid getting Kwell Shampoo in the eyes.

Remember

1. Follow the above instructions carefully.
2. Everyone in the family shampoos at the same time.
3. Wash clothing and bedding with soap and HOT water immediately after treatment.
4. Don't share combs, brushes, or clothing with others.

<u>Clearance for school</u>: When hair is free of lice and nits.

4. Enjuague el cabello bien con agua tibia.

5. Entonces usted querrá peinar, y sacar los piojos y huevos del pelo con un peine de dientes finos. Esto no es necesario para la curación, pero sí para su presentación personal.

6. Es raro que se necesite otra aplicación del champú Kwell. Pero si es necesario, repita el proceso en veinticuatro (24) horas, pero no más de dos veces por semana.

<u>Precaución</u>: Tenga cuidado de no dejar que el Kwell entre en los ojos.

Recuerde

1. Siga las instrucciones de arriba con cuidado.
2. Aplique el champú a toda su familia al mismo tiempo.
3. Lave la ropa personal y la ropa de cama en agua MUY CALIENTE inmediatamente al terminar el tratamiento.
4. No comparta peine, cepillo ni ropa con nadie.

<u>Permiso para la escuela</u>: Cuando ya no tenga piojos ni liendres.

HOW TO TAKE THE TEMPERATURE OF YOUR CHILD

To convert Centigrade temperature to Fahrenheit: multiply the Centigrade temperature by 9/5, then add 32.

To convert Fahrenheit temperature to Centigrade: subtract 32 from the Fahrenheit temperature, then multiply the remainder by 9/5.

Important

First, shake the thermometer to below 98° F (37° C). The child should not drink cold liquids or hot liquids for a few minutes before taking the temperature.

By Mouth

1. Put the long silver tip of the thermometer under the tongue of the child.
2. The child should close his lips carefully without biting the thermometer.
3. Keep the thermometer under the tongue of the child for two minutes.
4. Take out the thermometer.

COMO TOMAR LA TEMPERATURA DE SU NIÑO (NIÑA)

Para convertir la temperatura Centigrado a Fahrenheit: multiplique la temperatura Centigrado por nueve quintos (9/5) y añada treinta y dos (32).

Para convertir la temperatura Fahrenheit a Centigrado: reste treinta y dos (32) de la temperatura Fahrenheit y multiplique el resto por nueve quintos (9/5).

Importante

Primero, sacuda el termómetro a bajo noventa y ocho grados (98° F), o treinta y siete grados (37° C). El niño (la niña) no debe beber líquidos fríos ni calientes durante unos minutos antes de tomar la temperatura.

Por la Boca

1. Ponga la larga punta plateada del termómetro bajo la lengua del niño (de la niña).
2. El niño (la niña) debe cerrar los labios cuidadosamente sin morder el termómetro.
3. Guarde el termómetro bajo la lengua del niño (de la niña) durante dos (2) minutos.
4. Saque el termómetro.

5. Read the degree of temperature (exactly where the mercury stops).

By Rectum

1. Lubricate the silver tip of the thermometer.
2. Open the cheeks in order to see the rectum easily.

3. Insert the thermometer little by little until you can't see the silver tip, then keep it in place for two minutes.

4. Take out the thermometer.
5. Read the degree of temperature (exactly where the mercury stops).

IN CASE OF POISONING

1. Call your doctor or the Poison Control Center nearest you and follow the instructions that are given to you.
2. Take the original container of poison to the doctor or to the hospital.
3. Always have at hand the telephone number of your doctor, his home number as well as his office number, and the phone numbers of the police, the hospital and the Poison Control Center. (In the United States there are more than 500 of these centers that can give you and your doctor help in case of emergency.)

5. Lea el grado de temperatura (exactamente donde el mercurio se para).

Por el Recto

1. Lubrique la punta plateada del termómetro.
2. Abra las nalgas (posaderas) para poder ver el recto con facilidad.

3. Inserte el termómetro poco a poco hasta que no se vea la punta plateada, entonces sosténgalo en el lugar durante dos (2) minutos.

4. Saque el termómetro.
5. Lea el grado de temperatura (exactamente donde el mercurio se para).

EN CASO DE ENVENENAMIENTO

1. Llame a su médico o al Centro de Control de Envenenamientos más cercano y siga las instrucciones que le sean dadas.
2. Lleve el envase original del veneno al médico o al hospital.
3. Tenga siempre a mano el teléfono de su médico, tanto el de su casa como el de la oficina, y los teléfonos de la policía, del hospital, y del Centro de Control de Envenenamientos. (Existen en los Estados Unidos más de 500 de estos centros que pueden ofrecerle información a usted y a su médico y ayuda en caso de emergencia.)

INSERTION OF VAGINAL SUPPOSITORIES

Instructions

The plastic applicator provided with the package is specifically designed to permit proper placement of the vaginal tablet. The applicator consists of a barrel and its plunger.

Loading the Applicator

Remove protective foil wrapping from the vaginal tablet. Moisten tablet in warm water for only a second or two. To load applicator pull plunger out about one inch and place tablet into the cup end where it will fit snugly and remain in place.

Inserting the Vaginal Tablet

For proper insertion you should be lying on your back. Using either hand, grasp the barrel of the applicator firmly with the thumb and middle finger.

Do not push the plunger with the index finger until after the applicator is in the proper position in the vagina. Pointing the applicator slightly downward, insert it deeply into the vagina as far as it will comfortably go without using force.

Now, push the plunger all the way down to deposit the tablet in the vagina. Withdraw the applicator from the vagina when the tablet has been deposited.

INSERCION DE SUPOSITORIOS VAGINALES

Instrucciones

El aplicador de plástico que contiene el paquete está diseñado especialmente para permitir la aplicación correcta de la tableta vaginal. El aplicador se compone del cilindro y de su émbolo.

Para Cargar el Aplicador

Quite la envoltura de papel de aluminio que contiene la tableta vaginal. Humedezca la tableta en agua tibia por sólo uno o dos segundos. Para cargar el aplicador tire el émbolo hacia afuera unos dos centímetros y medio (una pulgada) y coloque la tableta en la taza del extremo en la que debe caber cómodamente y permanecer en su lugar.

Para Insertar la Tableta Vaginal

Para insertar la tableta correctamente la paciente debe acostarse boca arriba. Tome firmemente el cilindro del aplicador entre el pulgar y el dedo de en medio.

No empuje el émbolo con el índice sino después de que el aplicador se halle en el lugar correcto de la vagina. Dirigiendo el aplicador ligeramente hacia abajo, insértelo profundamente en la vagina, tanto como pueda entrar cómodamente, sin forzarlo.

Ahora, empuje todo el émbolo para colocar la tableta en la vagina. Retire el aplicador de la vagina una vez que la tableta ha sido depositada.

Care of the Applicator

Separate the plunger from the barrel by pulling it all the way out. Wash both sections of the applicator thoroughly under a stream of water allowing the water to flow through the barrel. Sterilization of the applicator is not necessary and extremely hot water should not be used because it may soften the plastic applicator. Dry the applicator and store it in a clean place.

Caution: During pregnancy, the applicator should be used only on the advice of a physician.

INSTRUCTIONS FOR A FECAL SAMPLE*

Important: Please read and follow all instructions carefully. Do not drink contents of either vial.

1. You have been given a kit which will help you conveniently collect the stool specimen which is required. Proper use of this kit will allow the laboratory to do a better job and cut down time-consuming and costly repeat testing.

2. This kit consists of 2 vials, both of which may contain liquid. In some kits only one vial marked "SAF FIXA-TIVE" or "PVA FIXATIVE" contains a liquid.

*Courtesy of Meridian Diagnostics, Inc.

Cuidado del Aplicador

Separe el émbolo del cilindro jalándolo hacia afuera. Lave las dos secciones del aplicador con agua corriente, haciendo que el agua fluya entre el cilindro. No es necesario esterilizar el aplicador y no debe usar agua demasiado caliente porque puede ablandecer el plástico. Seque el aplicador y guárdelo en un lugar limpio.

Advertencia: Durante el embarazo, el aplicador debe usarse sólo por recomendación de un médico.

INSTRUCCIONES PARA UNA MUESTRA FECAL

Importante: Favor de leer y seguir cuidadosamente las instrucciones que siguen. Cuidado: No beber el contenido de los frascos.

1. Se le ha entregado un equipo para recoger la muestra de heces que se pide. El uso correcto de este equipo asegurará un buen trabajo por el laboratorio y evitará repeticiones costosas.

2. Este equipo consiste en 2 frasquitos que contienen un líquido. Algunos equipos tienen solamente un frasco con letras "SAF FIXATIVE" o "PVA FIXATIVE" que contiene líquido.

3. The stool should be passed into a DRY container. Urine must not be voided into the specimen or it will void the test. At home, if a bed pan is not available, place a large plastic bag into the toilet seat opening and pass the specimen into the bag.

4. Open the vial containing the liquid. Using the collection spoon built into the lid of the vial, place small scoopfuls of stool into the vial until the liquid rises to the "Fill to Here" line. It is very important for you to sample areas which appear bloody, slimy, or watery. If the stool is formed (hard), please try to sample small amounts from each end and the middle. MIX SPECIMEN THOROUGHLY WITH COLLECTION SPOON.

5. Using the same specimen place stool in the second vial in the same way. If the second vial has no liquid in it, fill it one-third to one-half full with stool. Fill carefully.

   Note: Please tell the lab whether the stool is hard, soft, or runny.

6. Put the caps back on the vial and twist them firmly shut. Then SHAKE EACH VIAL WITH LIQUID IN IT VIGOROUSLY UNTIL IT IS WELL MIXED. Do not shake the vial marked "Empty—Clean."

7. Return the two vials to their container, label the box appropriately and send to the laboratory.

3. Las materias fecales deben ser recogidas en un recipiente SECO. No debe de orinar en la muestra porque invalida el examen. Si en casa no tienen un cómodo pongase una bolsa de plástico dentro del retrete y elimine en la bolsa.

4. Abra el frasco con el líquido. Con la cuchara pegada a la tapa llene el frasco hasta la línea con materia fecal. Es importante tomar muestras que se vean con moco, sangre o líquidos. Si el excremento está duro procure tomar pequeñas muestras de cada extremo y del centro. MEZCLE LA MUESTRA MUY BIEN CON LA CUCHARITA DE LA TAPA.

5. De la misma manera ponga excremento en el segundo frasco llenándolo la tercera parte o hasta la mitad. Llene el frasco con precaución.

   Nota: Favor de avisar al laboratorio si el excremento está duro, suave o con líquido.

6. Cierre los frascos con sus tapas, apretándolas bien y AGITE FUERTEMENTE EL FRASCO QUE TIENE LÍQUIDO HASTA QUE QUEDE BIEN MEZCLADO. No agite el frasco marcado "Empty—Clean."

7. Ponga los frascos en su caja, marque la caja, y entréguelos al laboratorio.

8. Wash hands thoroughly.

If either solution contacts skin, flush with running water; if irritation develops, consult a physician.

If ingested, dilute by drinking milk or water and call the local poison center or physician immediately.

INSTRUCTIONS FOR
BREAST FEEDING THE BABY

The most healthful, simple, natural, and inexpensive method of nursing a child is to breast feed him. The majority of mothers can nurse their children if they try and persist.

1. Before breast feeding your child, wash your hands well with soap and water. Next, wash your breasts and nipples with clear water.

2. To nurse the baby make yourself comfortable. Stretch out, or sit in a low chair so that you can support your arms. The child should be with his head higher than his stomach, so that he can swallow easily.

3. Breast feed him when the baby is hungry—generally every one, two or three (1-2-3) hours. At the end of a time period, the baby will get accustomed to his own schedule.

8. Lávese bien las manos.

Si alguna solución cae en las manos, lávelas inmediatamente con agua corriente de la llave. Si se irrita la piel consulte a un médico.

Si por accidente se tomara este líquido, se diluye tomando leche o agua y llamen al centro de veneno o a un médico inmediatamente.

INSTRUCCIONES PARA
AMAMANTAR AL BEBE

La forma más sana, simple, natural y económica de criar a un niño es amamantarlo. La mayoría de madres pueden mamar a los hijos si prueban y persisten.

1. Antes de dar el pecho a su niño, lávese las manos con agua y jabón. A continuación, lávese los pechos y los pezones con agua clara.

2. Para amamantar al bebé póngase cómoda. Tiéndase, o siéntese en una silla baja, de modo que pueda apoyar los brazos. El niño debe estar con la cabecita más alta que el estómago; así puede tragar fácilmente.

3. Déle el pecho cuando el bebé tenga hambre—generalmente cada una, dos, o tres (1-2-3) horas. Al cabo de un tiempo, el bebé se acostumbrará a su propio horario.

4. Breast feed the baby until the breast is empty, then give him the other breast until he does not want anymore. Usually the baby will nurse from 10 to 20 minutes. If one breast is sufficient, give him the other one the next time.

5. In order that your milk does not diminish, rest a lot and eat moderately. Your diet should include a selection of milk, eggs, meat, poultry, fish, fruit, vegetables, and brown bread, tortillas or cereal.

6. If your nipples bleed, crack, or hurt call your doctor.

7. The doctor will advise you if it is necessary to give your child a bottle in addition to or instead of the breast from time to time.

INSTRUCTIONS FOR THE TREATMENT OF SCABIES AND PEDICULOSIS

1. Your skin condition is caused by a small parasite. It can be transferred from one person to another by contact; hence, any or all members of your family may be affected.

4. Amamante al bebé de un pecho hasta que esté vacío, luego déle del otro hasta que no quiera más. Por lo regular, el bebé mamará de diez a veinte (10 a 20) minutos. Si con un pecho basta, la próxima vez déle del otro.

5. Para que su leche no diminuya descanse mucho y coma moderadamente. Su dieta debe incluir una selección de leche, huevos, carne, pollo, pescado, fruta, vegetales, y pan moreno, tortillas o cereal.

6. Si se le agrietan, o le sangran, o le duelen los pezones, llame al médico.

7. El médico le indicará si conviene que dé a su niño un biberón de vez en cuando o "como substituto del pecho."

INSTRUCCIONES PARA EL TRATAMIENTO DE LA SARNA Y PEDICULOSIS

1. Su enfermedad cutánea está causada por un pequeño parásito. En consecuencia, puede pasar de una persona a otra por contacto; de aquí que todos los miembros de la familia pueden estar afectados.

2. Carry out treatment carefully as follows:

For Scabies: Take a hot, soapy bath or shower, using liberal amounts of soap. Dry skin thoroughly. Next, apply a thin layer of Kwell Cream or Lotion to affected areas as well as surrounding skin. Do not miss a single portion of the skin surface or you may fail to cure your disease. Leave medication on skin for 24 hours, then wash thoroughly. Put on freshly laundered or dry-cleaned clothing. Treatment is finished. If necessary, a second or third application may be made at weekly intervals.

For Pediculosis: Take a hot, soapy bath or shower, using liberal amounts of soap. Dry skin thoroughly. Next, apply a thin layer of Kwell Cream or Lotion to hairy, infested areas. Also cover adjacent skin surface. Leave medication on for 12 to 24 hours. Then wash thoroughly and put on freshly laundered or dry-cleaned clothing. Repeat treatment in four days if necessary.

2. **El tratamiento debe realizarse cuidadosamente, en la forma siguiente:**

Para Sarna: Tome una ducha o baño jabonoso caliente, usando cantidad abundante de jabón. Después de secar la piel, apliquese la Crema o Loción Kwell a las áreas afectadas, incluyendo la piel que las rodea. No deje de cubrir ninguna porción de la superficie de la piel. o de otro modo no curará su enfermedad. Déjese la crema o loción en la piel por 24 (veinticuatro) horas. Después lávese enteramente y póngase ropas limpias o lavadas en seco. El tratamiento se ha terminado. Si es necesario puede emplearse una segunda o tercera aplicación a intervalos semanales.

Para Pediculosis: Tómese una ducha o baño jabonoso caliente, usando jabón en abundancia. Séquese la piel enteramente. Después apliquese una capa fina de Crema o Loción Kwell a las áreas cabelludas infestadas, incluyendo la piel que las rodea. Déjese la crema o loción en la piel de 12 (doce) a 24 (veinticuatro) horas. Después lávese minuciosamente y póngase ropas limpias o lavadas en seco. Repítase el tratamiento a los 4 (cuatro) días si es necesario.

3. The parasite which causes your condition may also rest in clothes which have been worn within the week before you were treated. Therefore it is necessary for your cotton clothes to be laundered, your woolens to be dry-cleaned and for you to use fresh towels, wash cloths and bed sheets after your treatment is complete. Put on freshly laundered, clean clothing after each application of Kwell Cream or Lotion.

INSTRUCTIONS FOR OUTPATIENT ANESTHESIA

1. Take nothing by mouth after midnight. Do not eat or drink anything for breakfast or lunch before coming to the hospital.

2. Do not smoke the night before or on the day of surgery, before or after the operation.

3. Notify your doctor if you develop a cold, sore throat, cough, fever, or any other illness prior to your operation.

4. Arrive at the hospital promptly for your appointment. Late arrival may necessitate cancellation of your appointment. Wear loose-fitting clothing; sleeves should be easy to roll up past the elbow.

5. Remove rings.

6. Women should remove nail polish, lipstick, and other make-up.

3. El parásito que provoca su enfermedad también puede encontrarse en las ropas utilizadas la semana antes del tratamiento. Por lo tanto es necesario que la ropa de algodón se mande a lavar, se laven en seco las lanas, y que se utilicen toalla, toallita y ropa de cama limpias después que se termine el tratamiento. Use ropas limpias y recién lavadas después de cada aplicación de Crema o Loción Kwell.

INSTRUCCIONES PARA ANESTESIA DE PACIENTES AMBULANTES

1. No tome ni coma nada después de la medianoche. No tome ni coma nada de desayuno ni almuerzo antes de venir al hospital.

2. No fume la noche anterior o el día de la operación, ni antes ni después de la misma.

3. Avise a su médico si llega con catarro, dolor de garganta, tos, calentura o cualquier otra enfermedad antes de la operación.

4. Llegue al hospital a la hora de su cita. Si llega tarde podrá ser necesario cancelar su cita. Use ropa ancha con mangas que se puedan subir arriba del codo.

5. Quítese los anillos.

6. Las mujeres no deberán llevar esmalte en las uñas, ni pintura en los labios, u otro maquillaje.

7. Come accompanied by a person who will drive you home. You will not be allowed to take a public conveyance or to drive a car. You should not drive a car, operate machinery, or ingest alcohol for 24 hours after leaving the hospital.

8. Nausea or vomiting may occur in the immediate postoperative period.

9. If difficult breathing, excessive bleeding, fever, or any other disturbing problems should develop after leaving the hospital, you should come to the hospital's emergency room immediately. Parents or guardians of children should observe the child continuously upon return home and bring the child to the emergency room immediately if any of these problems should occur.

10. You should limit activity requiring full concentration power, such as making significant personal or business decisions, since full mental alertness may not return for several hours.

INSTRUCTIONS FOR TAKING AN ENEMA

1. Equipment: enemas.

2. Position: You should lie on the left side to take the enema. NEVER take an enema while sitting on the toilet, while standing bent forward, or even while lying flat on back.

7. Venga acompanado/a de alguna persona que lo/la lleve a su casa, ya que no se le permtirá manejar su carro ni tomar transporte público. No debe manejar su carro, ni operar maquinaria ni tomar bebidas alcohólicas por 24 horas después de salir del hospital.

8. Es posible que tenga náuseas o vómitos en el período postoperativo inmediato.

9. Avise en persona a la sala de emergencia del hospital inmediatamente si llega con dificultad al respirar, si sangra excesivamente, si tiene calentura, o si tiene algún problema. Los padres o tutores de menores deben observar al niño/a constantemente y llevarlo a la sala de emergencia si llegan a tener alguno de los problemas indicados.

10. Limite sus actividades que requieran concentración tal como decisiones personales o de negocios, ya que no estará mentalmente alerta por varias horas después de la anestesia.

INSTRUCCIONES PARA LA ENEMA

1. Equipo: enemas (lavativas).

2. Posición: Usted debe acostarse al lado izquierdo para tomar la enema (lavativa). NUNCA tome una enema (lavativa) mientras esté en el retrete, mientras esté parado doblado hacia adelante, ni tampoco mientras esté acostado boca arriba.

3. Instructions: Pull off cap. Insert tube in rectum. Squeeze container to expel fluid. Discard container.

4. Take one enema the night before clinic appointment. Take the other enema two hours before coming to clinic. Do not take a cathartic (laxative) the night before. You may eat breakfast.

INSTRUCTIONS TO PATIENTS WITH EYE INJURIES

1. If the doctor puts an eye patch over your eye, leave it on as long as he instructs. This is necessary because healing will be delayed if the patch is removed too early.

2. Avoid activities that involve much eye movement. This includes sitting too close to the TV set while watching television, reading, or driving a vehicle.

3. Avoid bright lights and glaring sunshine.

4. Use all medicines and drops only as recommended.

5. If the pain gets worse or does not improve, you should return for further evaluation. The pain may increase very briefly after the anesthetic wears off, for about one hour. This is expected and should not alarm you if the increased pain does not exceed one hour.

3. Instrucciones: Arranque la tapa. Inserte el tubo en el recto. Apriete el recipiente para expeler flúido. Deseche recipiente.

4. Tome una enema la noche antes de la cita en la clínica. Tome la otra enema dos horas antes de venir a la clínica. No tome un purgante la noche anterior. Usted puede comer desayuno.

INSTRUCCIONES PARA PACIENTES CON HERIDAS O LESIONES DE LOS OJOS

1. Si el médico le aplica un parche en uno de sus ojos, déjelo puesto hasta que él se lo indique. Esto es necesario porque las heridas tardarán tiempo en curar si se quita el parche muy pronto.

2. Evite realizar las actividades que requieren el uso y movimiento del ojo herido. Esto incluye el mirar la televisión muy de cerca, el leer o el manejar un vehículo.

3. Evite luces brillantes y rayos del sol fuertes.

4. Use todas las medicinas y gotas siguiendo bien las instrucciones del médico.

5. Si el dolor aumenta o no se mejora, deberá regresar a ver a su médico para más evaluaciones. El dolor puede aumentar pocos minutos después de que la anestesia pase, más o menos por una hora. Esto es natural y no debería alarmarlo(la) si el dolor no pasa de una (1) hora.

6. Keep all appointments and if you need additional help, call the Eye Clinic at _____ or return to the Emergency Department.

6. Mantenga todas sus citas con el médico y si usted necesita ayuda adicional, llame a la Clínica para la Vista (los ojos) a _____, o regrese al Departamento de Emergencia.

INSTRUCTIONS TO FOLLOW AFTER D & C

INSTRUCCIONES QUE DEBE SEGUIR DESPUÉS DE UN RASPADO Y LIMPIEZA DEL ÚTERO (MATRIZ)

1. You should rest for about 12 hours after leaving the hospital. Drink plenty of fluids (juice, water, milk, etc.).

2. Bleeding should slow down gradually and should have stopped at the end of two weeks.

3. You may use tampons as soon as desired when necessary.

4. You may have intercourse or douche after two weeks if bleeding has stopped.

5. Talk with your doctor regarding some kind of contraceptive if repeat pregnancy is not planned.

6. If you have fever above 100.4°, severe abdominal pain or heavy vaginal bleeding, call your Gynecologist immediately.

1. Ud. debe descansar por unas doce horas después de salir del hospital. Tome bastantes líquidos (jugos, agua, leche, etc.).

2. La hemorragia disminuirá gradualmente y debe haber parado completamente al final de dos semanas.

3. Ud. puede usar tapones tan pronto como quiera cuando sea necesario.

4. Ud. puede tener relaciones sexuales o darse un lavado vaginal después de dos semanas si el flujo de sangre se ha detenido.

5. Hable con su médico acerca de algunas clases de anticonceptivos si no quiere Ud. salir embarazada (en cinta) otra vez.

6. Si tiene fiebre de más de 100° F (cien grados) o 39° C (treinta y nueve grados) con dolores abdominales fuertes o mucha hemorragia vaginal, llame a su ginecólogo inmediatamente.

7. Keep your appointment as instructed.

8. Resume usual activities (housework, shopping, job) as soon as you feel well.

INSTRUCTIONS TO REDUCE FEVER IN CHILDREN

If child's temperature is 102° F (39° C) or higher, follow these instructions to lower the fever:

1. Give:*
   a. Baby aspirin drops every 4 hours.
      (Dose: 1 gr per every year or proportionately less if under one year.)

      or

   b. Acetaminophen gtts (Baby Tylenol, Tempra or Liquiprin).
      (Dose: 1 gr/1 yr or proportionately less if under 1 year.)

      or

   c. Alternate aspirin with Acetaminophen every 2 hours if temperature remains above 102° F after first dose.

*If child refuses oral medication, can give ASA suppository (1 gr/yr).

INSTRUCCIONES PARA REDUCIR LA FIEBRE O LA CALENTURA EN NIÑOS

Si la temperatura del niño es ciento dos grados (102° F) o treinta y nueve grados (39° C) o más alta, siga las siguientes instrucciones:

1. Administre:*
   a. Aspirina de niño (gotas) cada cuatro (4) horas.
      (Dosis: un (1) gramo por cada año o proporcionalmente menos si tiene menos de un año.)

      o

   b. Acetaminophen (gotas) (Tylenol de niño, Tempra o Liquiprin).
      (Dosis: un (1) gramo por año o proporcionalmente menos, si tiene menos de un año.)

      o

   c. Alterne aspirina con Acetaminophen cada dos (2) horas si la temperatura se mantiene sobre ciento dos grados (102° F) o treinta y nueve grados (39° C) después de la primera dosis de medicina.

*Si el bebé rehusa tomar medicación por boca, se puede administrar un supositorio ASA (1 gramo por año).

2. Increase fluid intake.
3. Bathe child with warm comfortable water.
4. Clothe the child lightly—do not keep wrapped in blankets.

MEXICAN-AMERICAN DIABETIC DIET*

Recommended Foods to Eat Each Day

Milk
Units daily: 2 glasses
Choose skim milk. You may use ¼ cup of powdered skim milk.

Vegetable
Units daily: 1 serving
Choose a ½ cup serving of one of the following: carrots, peas, onions, pumpkin, beets or squash. You may use a combination to make a ½ cup serving.

*Courtesy of USV Pharmaceutical Corp.
Additional diets can be found within the Dietician section, p. 244.

2. Aumente los líquidos.
3. Bañe al niño con agua tibia.
4. Vista al niño con ropa ligera—no use frazadas ni ropa caliente.

DIETA MEXICANO-AMERICANA PARA DIABÉTICOS

Alimentos Recomendados para Uso Diario

Leche
Unidades al día: 2 vasos
Escoja leche descremada. Puede usar ¼ taza de leche descremada en polvo.

Verduras
Unidades al día: 1 porción
Escoja una porción de media taza de uno de los siguientes: zanahorias, chícharos, cebollas, calabaza, betabeles o calabacitas. Puede escoger una combinación de verduras que den una porción de ½ taza.

Fruit

Units daily: 3 servings
Select only fruits that are fresh, frozen or canned without sugar added. Choose as one serving one of the following: 1 orange or ½ grapefruit or ½ cup juice, 1 apple, pear, peach or guava, 2 apricots, ½ small mango, ⅓ papaya, ½ cup of fresh pineapple or 2 slices of canned pineapple, ¼ cataloupe, 2 fresh figs or 2 tablespoonfuls of raisins.

Bread

Units daily: 6 servings
Choose as one serving one of the following: 1 slice of bread or 1 roll, 1 tortilla, 2½ tablespoonfuls of flour or cornmeal, ½ cup of rice or beans (frijoles), ½ cup of cooked cereal, hominy or spaghetti, 1 small corn on the cob or 1 small white potato or 1 small sweet potato or yam.

Meat

Units daily: 6 ounces
Choose beef, pork, lamb, veal, chicken, turkey or fish. These are 3-ounce servings:
- 2 very small pieces of chicken
- 2 small meatballs
- 1 pork chop
- 1 small piece of fish

1 egg, ¼ cup of cottage cheese, 1 slice of cheese or luncheon meat, 1 frankfurter, 1 (5 × 2-inch) piece of tripe, ¼ cup of canned fish, or 2 tablespoonfuls of peanut butter is about a 1-ounce meat serving.

Fruta

Unidades al día: 3 porciones
Escoja solamente frutas que sean frescas, congeladas o enlatadas sin azúcar. Escoja una porción de una de las siguientes: 1 naranja, o media toronja o ½ taza de jugo, 1 manzana, pera, durazno o guayaba, 2 albaricoques, medio mango pequeño, ⅓ de papaya, ½ taza de piña fresca o 2 rebanadas de piña enlatada, ¼ de melón, 2 higos frescos o 2 cucharadas de pasas.

Pan

Unidades al día: 6 porciones
Escoja uno de los siguientes: 1 rebanada de pan o un bolillo, 1 tortilla, 2½ cucharadas de harina o de harina de maíz, ½ taza de arroz o de frijoles, ½ taza de cereal cocido, maíz machacado o espaguetis, 1 elote pequeño o 1 papa blanca pequeña o un camote pequeño.

Carne

Unidades al día: 6 onzas
Escoja carne de res, cerdo ternera, pollo, pavo o pescado. Cada uno de los siguientes son ejemplos de 3 onzas:
- 2 pequeños pedazos de pollo
- 2 albóndigas pequeñas
- 1 chuleta de cerdo
- 1 pequeño trozo de pescado

1 huevo o ¼ taza de requesón o una rebanada de queso o de pastel de carne o 1 salchicha o 1 pedazo (5 × 2 pulgadas) de tripa o ¼ taza de pescado enlatado o 2 cucharadas de crema de cacahuate equivalen aproximadamente a una porción de carne de una onza.

Fat

Units daily: 4 servings

Choose as one serving one of the following: 1 small pat of butter or margarine, 1 teaspoonful of oil or lard, 1 teaspoonful of mayonnaise, $1/8$ avocado, 1 slice of crisp bacon, 6 small nuts or 5 small olives. Be sure to count the fat used to cook foods.

"No Count" Foods

Eat these foods as desired, but in moderation: asparagus, broccoli, Brussels sprouts, cabbage, cauliflower, celery, cucumbers, lettuce, cacti leaves (nopales), mushrooms, green beans, green and red peppers, tomatoes, spinach and salad greens such as kale, mustard or beet greens, chard and collard, radishes and pimiento.

You may have coffee, tea, clear broth or bouillon, unsweetened gelatin and sour pickles. Season foods with herbs, spices, garlic, lemon and vinegar. You may use cinnamon, celery and garlic salt, paprika, cayenne, mustard, mint, parsley and vanilla.

Do Not Eat These Foods

Sugar and syrups, honey, jams and jellies, desserts with sugar—cakes, cookies, pastries, candy, sweetened condensed milk, sweetened soft drinks, sweetened fruits and beverages.

Grasa

Unidades al día: 4 porciones

Escoja una porción de uno de los siguientes: 1 rebanadita de mantequilla o margarina, 1 cucharadita de mayonesa, $1/8$ de aguacate, 1 rebanada de tocino bien cocido, 6 nueces pequeñas o 5 aceitunas pequeñas. Asegúrese de incluir la grasa usada para freír alimentos.

Alimentos Que "No Cuentan"

Puede tomar estos alimentos como guste, pero con moderación: espárragos, bróculi, coles de Bruselas, col, coliflor, apio, pepino, lechuga, nopalitos, hongos, ejotes, pimientas verdes y rojas, tomates, espinacas, y verduras para ensalada, tales como col rizada, hojas de mostaza y betabel, acelgas, rábanos y pimiento morrón.

Puede tomar café, té, caldo claro o consomé, gelatina sin azúcar y pepinos encurtidos con eneldo. Sazone sus alimentos con hierbas, condimentos, sal de ajo, limón y vinagre. Puede condimentar con canela, apio, ajo, pimentón rojo molido, pimentón, mostaza, menta, perejil y vainilla.

No Coma Estos Alimentos

Azúcar y jarabes, miel de abeja, mermeladas y jaleas, postres con azúcar, pasteles, galletas, dulces, leche condensada azucarada, refrescos endulzados, frutas, jugos y bebidas endulzadas.

Sample Menu for One Day

Breakfast

Orange juice—½ cup
Egg—1
Fried potatoes—½ cup
Tortilla—1 or 1 slice dry toast
Skim milk—½ glass
Coffee

Lunch

Vegetable soup with meat
Refried beans—½ cup with 1 slice cheese
Green salad with lemon
Tortilla—1
Apricots—2
Skim milk—½ glass
Coffee or tea

Dinner

Fried chicken—2 small pieces
Rice with tomatoes and spice—½ cup
Cooked carrots—½ cup
Apple—1
Coffee or tea

Evening snack

Taco—1
Skim milk—1 glass

Ejemplo De Menú para Un Día

Desayuno

Jugo de naranja—½ taza
Huevo—1
Papas fritas—½ taza
Tortilla— 1 o 1 rebanada de pan tostado
Leche descremada—½ taza
Café

Almuerzo

Sopa de verduras con carne
Frijoles refritos—½ taza con una rebanada de queso
Ensalada verde con limón
Tortilla—1
Albaricoques—2
Leche descremada—½ vaso
Café o té

Cena

Pollo frito—2 trozos pequeños
Arroz con jitomates y condimentos—½ taza
Zanahorias cocidas—½ taza
Manzana—1
Café o té

Bocadillo

Taco—1
Leche descremada—1 vaso

MIDSTREAM URINE COLLECTOR WITH PROTECTIVE COLLAR*

Instructions for Use (FEMALE)

1. Grasp white lid by tab and lift to remove.
2. Place white lid on flat surface with specimen cap FACE UP.

3. Open packet of three towelettes.
4. While seated on the toilet, spread labia majora (outer folds).

5. With the first towelette, wipe one side of the labia minora (inner fold) using a single downward stroke. Discard towelette.
6. With the second towelette, repeat procedure on opposite side using a single downward stroke. Discard towelette.
7. With the third towelette, cleanse meatus (center area) with a single downward stroke. Discard towelette.
8. First void in toilet. As you continue to void bring urine collector (HOLDING IT BY THE HANDLE) into "midstream" to collect urine specimen.

9. Unscrew protective collar from specimen container and discard.

*Courtesy of Bard Urological Division, C. R. Bard, Inc.

COLECTOR DE CORRIENTE PLENO PARA LA ORINA

Instrucciones para el Uso (MUJER)

1. Levante y quite la tapa blanca, tomándola de la oreja.
2. Coloque la tapa blanca sobre una superficie plana, con el casquete del recipiente para muestra MIRANDO HACIA ARRIBA.
3. Abra el paquete de tres toallitas.
4. Mientras está sentada en el retrete, separe los labios mayores (pliegues exteriores).
5. Con la primera toallita, limpie un lado de los labios menores (pliegues interiores) con una sola pasada hacia abajo. Descarte la toallita.
6. Con la segunda, repita el procedimiento del lado opuesto con una sola pasada hacia abajo. Descarte la toallita.
7. Con la tercera toallita, limpie el meato (area central) con una sola pasada hacia abajo. Descarte la toallita.
8. Orine primero en el retrete. Sin dejar de orinar coloque el recipiente para orina (SOSTENIÉNDOLO DE LA MANIJA) directamente en la "corriente" para recoger la la muestra de orina.
9. Desenrosque el aro protector del recipiente para muestra y descártelo.

10. WITHOUT TOUCHING SPECIMEN CONTAINER CAP pick up white funnel lid and screw onto specimen container.

11. Remove the white lid from cap by lifting up tab.

12. Fill in complete information on label and attach to specimen container.

Instructions for Use (MALE)

1. Grasp white lid by tab and lift to remove.

2. Place white lid on flat surface with specimen cap FACE UP.

3. Open packet of three towelettes.

4. Retract foreskin if present.

5. With the first towelette, cleanse the meatal orifice with a single downward stroke. Discard towelette.

6. Repeat step 5 with the two remaining towelettes.

7. First void in toilet. As you continue to void bring urine collector (HOLDING IT BY THE HANDLE) into "midstream" to collect urine specimen.

10. SIN TOCAR EL CASQUETE DEL RECIPIENTE PARA MUESTRA levante la tapa blanca en forma de embudo y enrosque el casquete al recipiente para muestra.

11. Quite la tapa blanca del casquete levantando la oreja.

12. Escriba en el rótulo toda la información necesaria y pegue el mismo al recipiente para muestra.

Instrucciones para el Uso (HOMBRE)

1. Levante y quite la tapa blanca, tomándola de la oreja.

2. Coloque la tapa blanca sobre una superficie plana, con el casquete del recipiente para muestra MIRANDO HACIA ARRIBA.

3. Abra el paquete de tres toallitas.

4. Retraiga la piel del pene si está presente.

5. Con la primera toallita, limpie el orificio del canal solamente una vez, comenzando desde arriba hacia abajo. Luego bote la toallita.

6. Repita el paso número 5 de la misma manera con el resto de las toallitas.

7. Orine primero en el retrete. Sin dejar de orinar coloque el recipiente para orina (SOSTENIENDOLO DE LA MANIJA) directamente en la "corriente" para recoger la muestra de orina.

8. Unscrew protective collar from specimen container and discard.

9. WITHOUT TOUCHING SPECIMEN CONTAINER CAP pick up white funnel lid and screw cap onto specimen container.

10. Remove the white lid from cap by lifting up tab.

11. Fill in complete information on label and attach to specimen container.

PROTOCOL FOR "STUFFY NOSE" IN INFANTS

The chief problem results from the fact that nasal congestion obstructs breathing when the child is nursing or sleeping. Since the infant cannot blow his nose, another cleansing method is necessary.

Mix 4 oz water with ¼ tsp. of table salt (Iodized or regular).

This solution can be kept in a jar for 1–2 days and used as necessary. Put 2 or 3 drops in one nostril—the baby will probably cough or sneeze a bit; then repeat in the other nostril.

Do not worry if a small amount gets into the eyes or if the baby swallows some. It is best to use the drops before feeding the baby. The drops can be used as often as necessary.

8. Desenrosque el aro protector del recipiente para muestra y descártelo.

9. SIN TOCAR EL CASQUETE DEL RECIPIENTE PARA MUESTRA levante la tapa blanca en forma de embudo y enrosque el casquete al recipiente para muestra.

10. Quite la tapa blanca del casquete levantando la oreja.

11. Escriba en el rótulo toda la información necesaria y pegue el mismo al recipiente para muestra.

DIRECCIONES PARA "NARIZ SOFOCADA" EN LOS BEBÉS

El problema principal resulta a consecuencia que la congestión nasal obstruye respirar cuando el niño o niña está siendo alimentado o al dormir. Ya que el niño o niña no puede sonarse la nariz, otra manera es necesaria.

Mezcle cuatro (4) onzas de agua con una y cuarta (1¼) cucharita de sal de mesa (Iodizada o regular).

Esta solución se puede mantener en un frasco por uno a dos (1 a 2) días y usarse como sea necesario. Ponga dos o tres (2 o 3) gotas en una fosa—el bebé probablemente toserá o estornudará un poco; en seguida repita en la otra fosa.

No se preocupe si una cantidad le cae dentro de los ojos o si el bebé traga un poco de la solución. Es mejor usar las gotas antes que se le dé alimentación a su bebé. Las gotas se pueden usar como sea necesario.

PSORIASIS

Use of Anthialin

1. Apply Anthialin only to psoriasis. Do not apply it to skin that does not have psoriasis.
2. Pat the Anthialin with cornstarch to keep it from smearing on your skin.
3. You must remove the Anthialin in 4 to 10 hours. If it is left on too long, it may burn your skin.
4. You must remove Anthialin <u>paste</u> with mineral oil. It will not wash off with soap and water. Anthialin <u>ointment</u> will wash off with soap and water.
5. After removing the Anthialin, take a tar bath and shampoo. You must take a tar bath and shampoo every day.

INSTRUCTIONS FOR SELF-ADMINISTRATION OF INSULIN

1. It is very important to keep very clean.
2. Wash your hands.
3. Roll the bottle of insulin between your hands in order to mix.
4. Do not shake the bottle.

PSORIASIS

El Uso de la Antialina

1. Aplique Antialina solamente a la psoríasis. No la aplique en la piel que no tenga la psoríasis.
2. Aplique la Antialina con almidón para que no se unte en la piel.
3. Debe quitar la Antialina después de 4 a 10 horas. Si la deja mucho tiempo la Antialina puede quemarle la piel.
4. Debe quitar la <u>pasta</u> de la Antialina con aceite mineral. No se debe lavar con jabón y agua. El <u>ungüento</u> de la Antialina se lavará solamente con jabón y agua.
5. Después de quitarse la Antialina, báñese con brea (alquitrán) y champú. Debe bañarse con brea y champú diariamente.

INSTRUCCIONES PARA INYECTARSE A SÍ MISMO LA INSULINA

1. Es muy importante mantenerse muy limpio.
2. Lávese las manos.
3. Haga rodar la botella de insulina entre las manos para mezclarla.
4. No agite la botella.

5. Wipe off the top of the bottle with alcohol and cotton. Keep the needle sterile.
6. Set the plunger at the mark showing your dosage.
7. Then push the needle through the rubber top of the bottle and inject the air from the syringe into the bottle.
8. Invert the bottle.
9. Keep the needle below the surface of the solution.
10. Draw out your dosage of insulin into the syringe.
11. Push out air bubbles from the syringe and place syringe on the boxtop.
12. Wipe the skin with alcohol at the site of the injection.

13. Stretch the skin or pinch it up with fingers spread about 3 inches apart.
14. Insert the needle quickly under the skin.
15. Pull the plunger back slightly.
16. If blood shows in the syringe, pull needle out and use a new site.
17. If no blood shows, push the plunger slowly until all the insulin is gone from the syringe.
18. Place cotton with alcohol over the site, press slightly, and pull out the needle.
19. Take your insulin at the same time every day or as the doctor orders it.

5. Limpie la tapa de la botella con algodón mojado en alcohol. Mantenga la aguja esterilizada.
6. Mueva el émbolo hasta la marca que corresponda a la dosis.
7. Después inserte la aguja por la tapa de goma de la botella e inyecte el aire de la jeringuilla dentro de la botella.
8. Invierta la botella.
9. Mantenga la aguja bajo la superficie de la solución.
10. Extraiga la dosis de insulina dentro de la jeringuilla.
11. Saque el aire de la jeringuilla y póngala sobre la caja del frasco.
12. Limpie o frote la piel con algodón mojado en alcohol en el sitio de la inyección.

13. Estire la piel o pellízquela con sus dedos puestos distantes a unas tres pulgadas.
14. Inserte la aguja rápidamente bajo la piel.
15. Jale el émbolo un poco hacia atrás ligeramente.
16. Si sale sangre, saque la aguja y use otro sitio.

17. Si no sale sangre, apriete el émbolo suavemente hasta que se haya terminado toda la insulina en la jeringuilla.
18. Ponga algodón con alcohol sobre el sitio, apriete la piel ligeramente, y extraiga la aguja.
19. Póngase la insulina a la misma hora todos los días, o según se lo indique su doctor.

TREATING DIARRHEA IN YOUR CHILD

Diarrhea means loose, liquid, soft, watery or more frequent bowel movements. Diarrhea can be caused by infection, poison in the intestinal tract, allergy, or other causes. It can also indicate illness in other parts of the body, such as the ear or the throat. If others in your family have diarrhea, you can expect your child to have it too.

Most causes of diarrhea can be treated as follows without the use of medication:

1. Put your child at rest in bed.
2. Give him nothing by mouth for 3 hours.
3. Then start feeding him with small amounts at frequent intervals (a baby can have ½ to 1 oz every half hour), beginning with the first foods on the list below and moving down the list as the diarrhea improves. At first, give no milk or solid food.
   a. Clear liquids (including jello or diluted jello water, weak tea, 7-Up or other favorite soda pop, ice chips, clear juice, or sherbet).
   b. Clear broth soups.
   c. Skim milk.
   d. Banana, half a canned pear, or applesauce.
   e. Cottage cheese.
   f. Oatmeal, soda crackers, or dry toast (no butter).
   g. Strained baby meats or stewed chicken.
   h. Soft-boiled eggs.

TRATANDO LA DIARREA EN SU NIÑO

Diarrea significa que hay movimientos intestinales en forma de líquido o de arrojo muy suelto. La diarrea es causada por una infección, veneno en el estómago, alergia, o por cualquier otro motivo. Puede indicar enfermedad en otra parte del cuerpo, como el oído o la garganta. Si otras personas en su familia tienen diarrea, es probable que su niño se va a contagiar también.

En muchos casos se puede tratar la diarrea sin medicina haciendo lo siguiente:

1. Acueste a su niño a descansar en la cama.
2. Durante tres (3) horas no le dé nada por boca.
3. Después de las tres (3) horas déle con frecuencia cantidades pequeñas (un bebé puede tomar media a una (½ a I) onza cada media (½) hora) empezando con las comidas que van primeras en la lista y las comidas que siguen según mejore la diarrea. Al principio no se debe dar leche ni comida sólida.
   a. Líquido claro (incluyendo gelatina, té no fuerte, 7-Up (Siete Up) u otro refresco, hielo triturado, jugo claro o sorbete).
   b. Caldo claro.
   c. Leche desnatada (descremada).
   d. Plátano, media pera de lata, o puré de manzana.
   e. Requesón.
   f. Avena, galletas, o pan tostado sin mantequilla.
   g. Carne para bebés, o pollo cocido.
   h. Huevos pasados por agua (huevos tibios).

4. The physician may prescribe medication or a special diet if the child has severe cramps, much blood in the stools, or if the diarrhea continues for several days.

5. If the child is obviously losing weight, looks increasingly pale or tired, and especially if his tongue is dry, he may be becoming dehydrated. CALL your physician. However, if he is making tears and urinating frequently, he is probably all right. The most important part of the treatment is to keep as much liquid going in by mouth as is being lost with the diarrhea.

6. Do not give fried, greasy or fatty foods or whole milk until the diarrhea has completely cleared for at least two days.

THE MOST COMMON MISTAKE IN TREATING DIARRHEA AND VOMITING AT HOME IS TO FORCE THE CHILD TO EAT SOLID FOODS AND HEAVY LIQUIDS. WHEN THIS IS DONE, THE BODY USES ITS OWN WATER TO FLUSH OUT THIS MATERIAL, WHICH DRIES OUT THE BODY EVEN MORE. DON'T MAKE THIS MISTAKE!

4. El médico puede recetar medicina o dar una dieta especial si el niño tiene calambres severos, mucha sangre en las evacuaciones, o si sigue la diarrea por más de tres días.

5. Si el niño está perdiendo peso, se ve más pálido o cansado, y especialmente si tiene la lengua seca, es posible que esté deshidratado. LLAME a su médico. Sin embargo, si tiene lágrimas cuando llora y está orinando con frecuencia, es probable que esté bien. Lo más importante del tratamiento es darle tanto líquido por boca como está perdiendo con la diarrea.

6. No le dé comidas grasosas y leche entera hasta dos días después de que se haya terminado la diarrea.

EL ERROR MÁS FRECUENTE EN EL TRATAMIENTO DE LA DIARREA Y DE VOMITÓS EN CASA ES DE FORZAR AL NIÑO A COMER SÓLIDOS Y LIQUÍDOS PESADOS. CUANDO LE DA AL NIÑO ESTAS COSAS EL CUERPO TIENE QUE UTILIZAR SU PROPIA AGUA PARA DIRIGIRLAS Y RESULTA QUE RESECA AÚN MÁS EL CUERPO. ¡FAVOR DE NO COMETER ESTE ERROR!

WARNING SIGNS OF HYPOGLYCEMIA

LAS SEÑALES DE ADVERTENCIA DE LA HIPOGLICEMIA

1. fatigue
2. sudden hunger
3. exhaustion
4. drowsiness
5. tremulousness
6. dizziness
7. nervousness

1. fatiga
2. hambre repentina
3. agotamiento
4. somnolencia
5. temblores vibratorios
6. vértigo
7. nerviosidad

8. weakness
9. sweating
10. double vision
11. headache
12. nausea
13. palpitations

8. debilidad
9. sudores
10. visión doble
11. dolor de cabeza
12. náusea
13. palpitaciones

2-3 GRAMS SODIUM DIET

1. Do not use SALT in cooking or at the table.

2. Do not use the following seasonings that contain salt or sodium in cooking or at the table:

bouillon cubes*	Accent (monosodium glutamate)
ketchup*	
prepared mustard	meat tenderizer
horseradish	seasoned salt
chili sauce	garlic salt powder
soy sauce	onion salt powder
hot sauce	celery salt powder
Worcestershire sauce	prepared meat sauces and gravy mixes
barbecue sauce	
	steak sauce

*Unsalted brand may be used.

DIETA DE 2-3 GRAMOS DE SODIO

1. No use SAL en la mesa ni al cocinar.

2. No use los siguientes condimentos que contienen sal o sodio para cocinar o en la mesa:

cuadritos de caldo*	"Accent" (monosodio glutamate)
catsup*	
mostaza en pomo	polvo para ablandar carne
salsa de rábano picante	sal sazonada
salsa de chile	polvo de sal de ajo
salsa de soya	polvo de sal de cebolla
salsa picante	polvo de sal de apio
salsa Worcestershire	salsa de carne en paquete o en lata
salsa de barbacoa	
	salsa para bistec

*Marcas sin sal pueden usarse.

3. Do not use highly salted foods such as salted crackers*, salted pretzels*, salted nuts*, salted popcorn*, potato chips*, corn chips*.

4. Avoid as much as possible commercially canned or packaged soups*, salad dressings*, cocoa powder, frozen dinners, quick-cooking cereals, and prepared mixes such as cakes, cookies, biscuits, potatoes, and puddings.

5. Avoid all canned vegetables*, vegetable juices*, and pickled foods such as olives, relish, sauerkraut, pickles, and pimientos.

6. Avoid as much as possible:
   a. salted and smoked meats—ham, bacon, salt pork, cold cuts, frankfurters, sausage, koshered meats.

   b. salted and smoked fish—anchovies, salted cod, herring, mackerel, canned tuna*, canned salmon*, lox, whitefish, canned sardines*.

7. Avoid smoked or processed cheeses, cheese spreads, buttermilk.

8. Certain salt substitutes may be used only if recommended by a physician or nutritionist.

9. Check with a nutritionist before using food labeled as "dietetic."

*Unsalted brand may be used.

---

3. No use alimentos salados como galletas saladas*, pretzels salados*, nueces saladas*, palomitas ("popcorn") saladas*, papitas fritas*, o tostaditas de maíz* (corn chips).

4. Evite lo más posible usar alimentos preparados comercialmente en lata o en caja como: sopas*, aderezos para ensalada*, cacao en polvo, comidas congeladas (TV dinners), cereales pre-cocidos, y mezclas para pasteles, galletas, bizcochos, papas, pudines y flanes.

5. Evite todos vegetales enlatados*, jugos de vegetal* y encurtidos, como aceitunas, pepinos condimentados, sauerkraut, pepinillos, y pimientos marrones.

6. Evite lo más posible:
   a. carnes saladas y ahumadas—jamón, tocino, puerco salado, carnes para sándwiches (entremeses), salchichas, embutidos, comidas "Kosher."
   b. pescados salados y ahumados—anchoas, bacalao, arenque, macarela, atún en lata*, salmón en lata*, lox, pescado blanco, sardinas en lata*.

7. Evite quesos procesados y ahumados, quesos para untar, leche agria (leche de mantequilla).

8. Ciertos substitutos de sal pueden usarse si el médico o su nutricionista los recomienda.

9. Consulte a la nutricionista antes de usar productos que digan "de dieta."

*Marcas sin sal pueden usarse.

General Recommendations

1. Eat three regular meals daily.
2. Try to eat your main meal at lunch time.
3. Exercise regularly.

Sample Meal Plan

Breakfast

fruit or fruit juice
egg (optional)
cereal

bread
butter or margarine
milk
coffee or tea

Lunch

meat, fish or poultry
cooked vegetable
potato or substitute
bread

butter or margarine
milk
coffee or tea
fresh fruit or juice

Dinner

meat, fish or poultry
salad
bread

butter or margarine
milk
coffee or tea
fresh fruit or juice

Recomendaciones Generales

1. Coma tres (3) comidas regulares al día.
2. Trate de que el almuerzo sea la comida principal.
3. Haga ejercicios regularmente.

Menu Ejemplar

Desayuno

fruta o jugo de fruta
huevo (si desea)
cereal

pan
mantequilla o margarina
leche
té o café

Almuerzo

carne, pescado, o aves
vegetal cocido
papa o substituto
pan

mantequilla o margarina
leche fresca
té o café
fruta fresca o jugo

Comida

carne, pescado, o aves
ensalada
pan

mantequilla o margarina
leche fresca
té o café
fruta fresca o jugo

DOUCHING

What Is a Douche?

It is the cleaning of the vagina with a solution to stop infection.

How Is It Prepared?

Put two tablespoons of white vinegar in a quart of warm water. The water and the container should be very clean. Put the mixture of water and vinegar in a douche bag with a hose. (You can buy it in the drug store.) Close the hose with the valve that comes with the bag or with your hands.

The Correct Way to Take a Douche

TAKE A SEATED POSITION ON THE COMMODE, or a horizontal position in the bath tub in the desired position. Gently introduce the nozzle of the hose into the vagina about 2 inches. Raise the douche bag about 2 feet above the vagina and take off the valve so the liquid can enter the vagina. Let the solution run until the bag is empty. Remove the nozzle gently from the vagina, wash the bag and nozzle and put them away until they are needed again.

A douche should be taken not more than twice a week or according to your doctor's instructions.

TOMANDO UN LAVADO

¿Qué Es un Lavado?

Es la limpieza de la vagina con una solución para quitar infección.

¿Cómo Se Prepara?

Ponga dos cucharadas de vinagre blanco en un cuarto de agua tibia. El agua y el envase deben estar bien limpios. Ponga la mezcla de agua y vinagre en una bolsa con manguera. (Se puede comprar en la farmacia.) Cierre la manguera con la válvula que viene con la bolsa o con sus propias manos.

La Técnica Correcta para Tomar un Lavado

SIÉNTESE EN EL RETRETE, o acuéstese en la tina. En la posición deseada, introduzca suavemente la lanza de la manguera en la boca de la vagina unas dos pulgadas. Levante la bolsa unos dos pies de altura sobre la vagina y quite la válvula para que entre la solución en la vagina. Deje que la solución corra hasta que la bolsa esté vacía. Quite la lanza suavemente de la vagina, lave bien la bolsa y la lanza y guárdelas hasta la próxima vez.

Hágase un lavado no más de dos veces a la semana o según las instrucciones de su médico.

WHAT TO DO FOR A HIGH FEVER

Fever is any temperature over 100° F. It can be treated with cool bathing or giving aspirin or medicines like Tempra, Tylenol, Liquiprin, etc.

Infants and children from 9 months to 3 years tend to get very high fevers from mild infections. Any temperature that is over 102° F should be brought down. At that level your child will not feel well and may have a convulsion or fit.

Any infant of less than 3 months who has a fever of more than 101.5°F or 38.5°C should be examined by a doctor as soon as possible.

Do not use any aspirin or other medicines under the age of 6 months. Use only cool bathing. After this age you may give 1 normal baby aspirin (1¼ grains) for each year of age every four hours for as long as the temperature is above 102°F.

If the temperature does not come down with aspirin or if your baby is under 6 months of age, it is best to place your child in a tub and sponge or wipe off the hot skin with cool water. This will not be pleasant, but it will make him feel better in the long run and will not make the illness worse. As the air dries, the water cools the skin.

LO QUE DEBE HACER EN CASO DE FIEBRE ALTA

Calentura es cualquier fiebre de más de ciento (100° F) o treinta y siete (37.7°C). Se puede tratar con baños frescos o aspirina o medicinas como Tempra, Tylenol, Liquiprin, etcétera.

Los bebés y los niños de nueve (9) meses a tres (3) años de edad pueden tener fiebre muy alta como consecuencia de infecciones leves. Cualquier calentura de más de ciento dos (102° F) debe bajarse. A ese nivel, la criatura no se siente bien y posiblemente tendrá convulsiones o ataques.

Cualquier bebé de menos de tres meses con fiebre (calentura) de más de ciento uno punto cinco (101.5°F) o treinta y ocho punto cinco (38.5°C) debe ser examinado por un médico lo más pronto posible.

No use aspirina ni ninguna otra medicina si el bebé es menor de seis meses. Solamente báñelo en agua fresca. Mayores de esta edad pueden tomar una aspirineta normal de uno y un cuarto (1¼) grano por cada año de edad cada cuatro (4) horas durante el período de calentura de más de ciento dos (102° F) o treinta y nueve (39° C).

Si la calentura no baja con aspirineta o si el bebé es menor de seis (6) meses, lo mejor es meterlo en una tina de agua templada y enfriar la piel con una esponja. Esto le resultará desagradable al niño, pero con el tiempo se sentirá mejor y además no empeorará la enfermedad. Al evaporarse el agua de la piel, enfría la piel.

When the skin is cool, dry him off and take his temperature again. If it is still high, place him back in the tub and do it again. It may take two or three washings to get the temperature below 102° F. Once his temperature is down, check it again in 3 to 4 hours.

Dress the child lightly. Do not cover him with heavy blankets, etc. when fever is present.

Fluids should be offered frequently.

If the fever persists for more than 12–24 hours, or if the child is acting very ill, contact your physician. If your own physician is unavailable, call the Emergency Department.

Cuando la piel esté fresca, séquelo y tómele otra vez la temperatura. Si todavía está alta, métalo otra vez en la tina. Es posible que se necesiten dos o tres baños para poder bajar la temperatura a menos de ciento dos (102° F) o treinta y nueve (39° C). Después de que la temperatura haya bajado, tómesela de nuevo a las tres o cuatro horas.

Póngale ropa ligera al niño. No lo cubra con frazadas pesadas cuando haya fiebre.

Déle líquidos frecuentemente.

Si la fiebre sigue por más de doce a veinticuatro (12 a 24) horas o si el niño se ve muy enfermo, póngase en contacto con su médico. Si no está disponible llame al Departamento de Emergencia.

SECTION D

Procedures

AMNIOCENTESIS*

1. Amniocentesis is a test whereby we can ascertain whether your baby has any genetic abnormalities.
2. It is especially useful for women who are over the age of 36 and therefore have an increased risk of having a Down's syndrome baby or an otherwise genetically damaged baby.
3. It is useful if there is any history of genetic problems in the family.
4. We will put a needle through your abdomen, into the uterus, and withdraw a small amount of fluid from around the baby.
5. There is a less than 1% chance of injuring the baby in this process.

LABORATORY PROCEDURES

Patient Check-In

1. Do you have written instructions from your doctor?
2. May I have your identification card?
3. Please sign here so that we can bill Medi-Cal.

4. Please have a seat, and your name will be called.

AMNIOCENTESIS

1. Amniocentesis es una prueba por la cual se puede asegurar si su niño tiene anormalidades genéticas.
2. Es útil especialmente para las mujeres que tienen más de 36 (treinta y seis) años de edad y por lo cual llevan más riesgo de tener un niño con el Síndrome de Down o un niño genéticamente dañado de otro modo.
3. Es útil en caso de que haya historia de problemas genéticos en la familia.
4. Le pondremos una aguja por el abdomen hasta el útero, y le sacaremos un poco de flúido de alrededor del niño.
5. Hay menos de 1% (un por ciento) de probabilidad de dañar al bebé con este proceso.

PROCEDIMIENTOS DE LABORATORIO

Inscripción Registro del Paciente

1. ¿Tiene instrucciones escritas de su médico?
2. Favor de darme su tarjeta de identidad.
3. Favor de firmar aquí para que podamos hacer la cuenta para Medi-Cal.
4. Favor de sentarse. Llamaremos su nombre.

*Conversation useful for explaining the ultrasound procedure can be found on pp. 129–130.

Preliminary Questions and Requests

1. May I see the doctor's orders? (for outpatients)

2. Did you have breakfast?
3. Have you eaten since midnight?
4. This test must be done on an empty stomach.

5. Eat something and come back in 2 hours.
6. Eat a good breakfast with orange juice, toast, eggs, and coffee or milk, and come for the test 1 hour later.

Specimen Collection

<u>Venipuncture</u>

1. I have to draw some blood.
2. I need to take a little blood from your arm.
3. Have you ever had a blood test before?
4. Don't be afraid.
5. This will hurt just a little.
6. Roll up your sleeve.
7. Stretch out your arm.
8. Make a fist.
9. First I will tie this tourniquet around your arm.

Preguntas Preliminares y Pedidos

1. ¿Puedo ver las instrucciones del médico? (para pacientes ambulantes)
2. ¿Tomó desayuno?
3. ¿Ha comido desde la medianoche?
4. Este análisis tiene que hacerse con el estómago vacío. Esta prueba tiene que hacerse con el estómago vacío.
5. Coma algo y regrese en dos horas.
6. Coma un buen desayuno con jugo de naranja, pan tostado, huevos, y café o leche, y venga para el análisis (la prueba) una hora más tarde.

Colección de Espécimen (Muestra)

<u>Venipuntura</u>

1. Tengo que sacar un poco de sangre.
2. Necesito sacar un poco de sangre de su brazo.
3. ¿Ha tenido alguna vez una prueba de sangre?
4. No tenga miedo.
5. Esto le va a doler un poquito.
6. Súbase la manga.
7. Extienda el brazo.
8. Haga un puño.
9. Primero ataré este torniquete alrededor de su brazo.

10. You will feel a small prick. It will not hurt much.
11. Try to hold still. Hold your arm still.
12. Open your hand.
13. Press here with your fingers (to stop the bleeding).
14. Bend your arm (to put pressure on the puncture site to help stop the bleeding).
15. Are you dizzy?
16. Lean forward and put your head between your legs for a few minutes.
17. I can't find the vein.
18. I'm sorry, but I have to stick you once more.
19. I was not able to get enough blood the first time.
20. Your doctor will tell you the results.
21. We are waiting for the results of the lab work.

Heel-Stick and Finger-Stick Blood Drawing

1. I need to take a few drops from your finger.
2. I need to take a few drops of blood from your baby's heel.
3. Remove the baby's shoe and sock.
4. Hold the child.

Urine Collection

1. Can you collect a sample of urine in this?
2. Go to the bathroom.

10. Sentirá un piquete. No le va a doler mucho.
11. Trate de estar tranquilo. No mueva el brazo.
12. Abra la mano.
13. Apriete aquí con los dedos (para dejar de sangrar).
14. Doble el brazo (para poner presión en la punción y para ayudar a que pare la sangre).
15. ¿Está usted mareado?
16. Inclínese hacia adelante, poniendo la cabeza entre las piernas por unos minutos.
17. No puedo encontrar la vena.
18. Lo siento, pero tengo que pincharle otra vez.
19. No pude obtener bastante sangre la primera vez.
20. Su médico le dirá los resultados.
21. Estamos esperando los resultados del laboratorio.

Sangre del Talón y de los Dedos

1. Necesito sacarle unas gotas de su dedo.
2. Necesito sacar unas gotas de sangre del talón del bebé.
3. Quítele al bebé el zapato y el calcetín.
4. Sostenga al niño (a la niña).

Colección de la Orina

1. ¿Puede darme una muestra de orina en este frasco?
2. Vaya al baño (retrete).

3. Bring a urine specimen.

4. Bring the specimen in this.

5. I will tape this bag for a urine specimen on the baby.

6. Remove the baby's diaper.

Sputum Specimen

1. Bring me a specimen of your sputum.

2. Take this and use it for spitting.

Stool Specimen

1. Take a laxative tonight.

2. Bring me a stool specimen.

Bleeding-Time Test

1. Have you had a bleeding-time test before?

2. I'm going to do a bleeding-time test.

3. I will make a small cut on your arm.

4. Have you ever had bleeding problems?

Throat Culture

1. You have a complaint of a sore throat.

2. You have a temperature of 100° F.

3. Your tonsils are swollen, red, and with pus.

4. I am going to do a throat culture.

3. Traiga una muestra de orina.

4. Traiga la muestra en esto.

5. Voy a ponerle al bebé esta bolsa para una muestra de orina.

6. Quítele el pañal al bebé.

Espécimen del Esputo

1. Tráigame una muestra de su esputo.

2. Llévese esto y úselo para escupir.

Espécimen del Excremento

1. Tome un purgante esta noche.

2. Tráigame una muestra de su excremento.

Examen-Tiempo de Sangría

1. ¿Ha tenido un examen de tiempo de sangría antes de esto?

2. Voy a hacerle una prueba de tiempo de sangría.

3. Le haré una incisión pequeña en el brazo.

4. ¿Ha tenido alguna vez problemas con sangría?

Cultivo de la Garganta

1. Ud. se queja de dolor de garganta.

2. Ud. tiene temperatura de 100° (cien) F.

3. Sus anginas están hinchadas, rojas y con pus.

4. Le voy a hacer un cultivo de la garganta.

5. This is a curette.

6. I am going to swab your tonsils and the back of your throat with the cotton end.

7. It may feel uncomfortable, and you may want to gag. That is a normal reflex.

8. Then I'll put it back into the container and send it to the laboratory.

9. They will see if any bacteria, especially streptococcus, grows on it.

10. We will know in 24–48 hours. If it is positive we will give you some medicine—penicillin.

11. If not, it's most likely a virus and it will take 7–10 days to resolve.

12. Also, it will help to gargle with warm salt water (½ tsp salt + 1 qt warm water).

13. Take aspirin or acetaminophen (Tylenol) every 4 hours for fever.

14. Drink plenty of liquids and eat three meals as well as you can.

15. Sucking on throat lozenges will help the discomfort of swallowing.

16. I will call you with the results of the test.

17. Please see me tomorrow if the symptoms change.

5. Esta es una cureta.

6. Le voy a frotar las amígdalas y la parte trasera de la garganta con algodón.

7. Le sentirá incómodo, y sentirá que se atraganta. Este es reflejo normal.

8. Repondré la cureta en el envase y la mandaré al laboratorio.

9. La examinarán para ver si hay bacteria, especialmente si le crece estreptococo.

10. Sabremos dentro de 24 (veinticuatro) a 48 (cuarenta y ocho) horas. Si es positivo le daremos medicina—penicilina.

11. Si no, es posible que sea un virus, y que dure de 7 (siete) a 10 (diez) días para resolver.

12. También ayudará a hacer gárgaras con agua tibia salada (½ (media) cucharadita de sal a 1 (un) cuarto de agua tibia).

13. Tome aspirina o acetaminofena (Tylenol) cada 4 (cuatro) horas para la calentura.

14. Tome bastantes líquidos y coma tres comidas al día lo mejor que pueda.

15. Chupar pastillas para la garganta ayuda el malestar al tragar.

16. Le llamaré acerca de los resultados del examen.

17. Favor de verme mañana si cambian los síntomas.

Postural Drainage

1. You will lie on your side with head downwards. This will help to drain your lung.
2. We will position you like this and then tap your lungs from the back.
3. We will press down as you exhale.
4. We will pat your back in a cupping motion.
5. There are 13 positions in all.
6. We will encourage you to cough.

Drenaje Pulmonar

1. Póngase de lado y con la cabeza hacia abajo. Esto le facilitará el drenaje del pulmón.
2. Lo pondremos de esta manera, y le daremos unos golpes ligeros en la espalda.
3. Le apretaremos el pecho mientras usted exhala el aire.
4. Le daremos unas palmadas en la espalda.
5. Hay un total de 13 (trece) posiciones diferentes.
6. Lo estimularemos para que tosa.

TESTS/PROCEDURES VOCABULARY

VOCABULARIO PARA EXÁMENES Y PROCEDIMIENTOS

1. allergy test
2. analysis
3. arteriogram
4. barium test
5. blood count

6. blood test
7. cardiac catheter
8. cardiogram
9. checkup, medical

1. prueba para alergias
2. análisis
3. arteriograma
4. prueba de bario
5. recuento (conteo) globular
6. análisis (prueba) de sangre
7. cateter cardíaco
8. cardiograma
9. reconocimiento (chequeo) médico

10. chest x-ray

11. cholecystogram
12. culture
    a. the throat
    b. the nose
    c. the ear
13. electrocardiogram
14. electroencephalogram
15. electromyography

10. radiografía (rayos equis) del pecho (de los pulmones)
11. un colecistograma
12. cultivo de
    a. la garganta
    b. la nariz
    c. el oído
13. electrocardiograma
14. electroencefalograma
15. electromiografía

16. encephalogram
17. examination
18. eye test

19. gastroscopy
20. hearing test
21. intermittent positive-pressure breathing machine
22. laboratory
23. myelogram
24. oxygen therapy
25. pregnancy test

16. encefalograma
17. reconocimiento, examen
18. examen de la vista (de los ojos)
19. gastroscopia
20. examen de audición
21. aparato para la respiración por presión intermitente positiva
22. laboratorio
23. mielograma
24. terapia de oxígeno
25. prueba de embarazo (examen de preñez)

26. postural drainage
27. skin test

28. specimen
29. sputum test
30. tuberculin test
31. ultrasonic nebulizer therapy
32. upper gastrointestinal (GI) series
33. urinalysis
34. Wasserman test
35. x-rays

26. drenaje pulmonar
27. prueba cutánea (epidérmica)
28. muestra (espécimen)
29. análisis de esputo
30. prueba de tuberculina
31. terapia vaporizadora ultrasónica
32. serie gastrointestinal superior
33. análisis de orina
34. prueba de Wasserman
35. radiografís (rayos equis)

SECTION E

Therapies

OCCUPATIONAL THERAPY

1. Copy this design.
2. This splint will help stretch your muscles out. It is important to wear it.
3. Do it yourself.
4. Use both hands.
5. Use your right/left hand.
6. Put your
   a. right leg in first.
   b. left leg in first.
   c. right arm in first.
   d. left arm in first.
7. Move the wheelchair close to the bed.
8. Lock your brakes.
9. Scoot forward.
10. Reach for the bell.
11. Stand up and turn.
12. Reach behind you for the arm of the chair.
13. Sit down.
14. This will help you to strengthen your muscles.
15. This will help you to see things better.
16. Push yourself up in bed.
17. Push yourself up to a sitting position.

TERAPIA OCUPACIONAL

1. Copie este diseño.
2. Este entablillado le ayudará a estirar los músculos. Es importante usarlo.
3. Hágalo para sí mismo(a).
4. Use Ud. las dos manos.
5. Use la mano derecha/izquierda.
6. Ponga
   a. la pierna derecha primero.
   b. la pierna izquierda primero.
   c. el brazo derecho primero.
   d. el brazo izquierdo primero.
7. Mueva la silla de ruedas cerca de la cama.
8. Ponga los frenos.
9. Muévase hacia adelante.
10. Alcance el timbre.
11. Párese y vuélvase.
12. Alcance por detrás el brazo de la silla.
13. Siéntese.
14. Esto le ayudará a fortificar los músculos.
15. Esto le ayudará a ver mejor.
16. Empújese hacia arriba en la cama.
17. Empújese y siéntese.

18. Lift/hike up your hips.
19. Show me your _____.
20. Put these in order.
21. Calm down.
22. Don't
    a. hit.
    b. bite.
    c. spit.
    d. kick.
    e. swear.
23. Raise your arm.
24. Do you understand?
25. Keep your hands to yourself.

PHYSICAL THERAPY

1. Roll over and sit up over the edge of the bed.
2. Stand up slowly. Put weight only on your right/left foot.

3. Move the cane, then step with opposite leg.
4. Move the walker first, then take a step with your right foot, then with your left foot.
5. Put more weight on your hands.
6. Step through with the heel.

18. Levante las caderas.
19. Enséñeme su _____.
20. Ponga estos en orden.
21. Cálmese.
22. No
    a. dé golpes.
    b. muerda.
    c. escupa.
    d. patee.
    e. diga malas palabras.
23. Levante el brazo.
24. ¿Entiende?
25. Mantenga las manos a sí mismo(a).

TERAPIA FÍSICA

1. Voltéese y siéntese sobre el borde de la cama.
2. Párese despacio. Ponga peso sólo en la pierna derecha/izquierda.

3. Mueva el bastón, luego dé un paso con la otra pierna.
4. Mueva el andador primero, y dé un paso con la pierna derecha, luego con la pierna izquierda.
5. Ponga más peso en las manos.
6. Pase por aquí con el talón.

7. Lift your head up.

8. Take a step to the side.

9. Step back until you feel the wheelchair at the back of your legs.

10. Reach back and sit down.

11. Turn to your left.

12. Turn to your right.

13. Does the pain radiate to your left leg?

14. Hold your leg up. Don't let me push it down.

15. Stand up and walk.

16. Straighten your leg.

17. Bend your knee.

18. Move the walker forward.

19. Step with left then right leg.

Neuromuscular Exam

1. This is a test of your sensation. Close your eyes and tell me if this feels sharp or dull.

2. Relax and let me move you. Close your eyes and tell me whether I am moving your arm (leg) toward me or toward you.

7. Levante la cabeza.

8. Dé un paso al lado.

9. Dé un paso hacia atrás hasta que sienta la silla de ruedas detrás de las piernas.

10. Alcance hacia atrás y siéntese.

11. Doble a la izquierda.

12. Doble a la derecha.

13. ¿Le corre el dolor a la pierna izquierda?

14. Levante la pierna. No me deje movérsela hacia abajo.

15. Párese y camine.

16. Enderece la pierna.

17. Doble la rodilla.

18. Mueva el andador hacia adelante.

19. Dé un paso con la pierna izquierda, luego con la pierna derecha.

Examen Neuromuscular

1. Este es un examen de su sensación. Cierre los ojos y dígame si esto le siente puntiagudo o sin punta.

2. Relájese y déjeme moverlo/la. Cierre los ojos y dígame si estoy moviendo su brazo (pierna) hacia mí o hacia Ud.

3. This is a test to see how strong you are. Hold this position as hard as you can. Don't let me move you. Hold!

4. Take in a deep breath—as big as you can. Then blow it all out into the mouthpiece.

5. Push/pull.

6. Up/down.

7. In/out.

8. Slow/fast.

9. Rest.

10. Cough.

11. Scoot.

12. Right/left.

13. Roll.

14. Sit up.

15. Kneel.

16. Get on your hands and knees.

17. Get on your stomach.

18. Lift up your arms.

19. Hard/easy (push).

3. Esta es una prueba para ver qué tan fuerte es Ud. Mantenga esta posición lo más tieso posible. No me deje moverlo/la. ¡Manténgala!

4. Aspire lo más profundo que pueda. Luego expírelo todo en la boquilla.

5. Empuje/jale.

6. Arriba/abajo.

7. Adentro/afuera.

8. Despacio/aprisa.

9. Descanse.

10. Tosa.

11. Muévase pronto adelante.

12. Derecha/izquierda.

13. Revuélvase (dése vuelta).

14. Siéntese.

15. Arrodíllese.

16. Póngase en manos y rodillas.

17. Póngase de estómago.

18. Levante los brazos.

19. Fuerte/suave (empuje).

RADIATION THERAPY

1. The first day the technologist will take an x-ray to determine the treatment area, show the doctor the x-ray for his approval, and mark the area.

2. These marks need to be kept on because they will be used every day to show the correct area to be treated.

3. Please do not use soap, creams, deodorant, or perfume in the treatment area, during treatment, or for a short while afterward.

4. Keep the treatment area covered when in the sun.

5. Soap, creams, deodorant, perfume, and sun can all irritate the treatment area, and they may cause a bad reaction to the radiation.

6. The treatments are painless and take about 1 minute.

7. Some patients will need to have a weekly blood test (the technologist will let you know).

8. Please tell the technologist any other problems you have so that the problems can be dealt with and resolved.

TERAPIA DE RADIACIÓN

1. El primer día, el técnico tomará un rayos equis para determinar el área del tratamiento, le enseñará al doctor para aprobación y marcará el área.

2. Estas marcas necesitan ser guardadas porque se usan todos los días para enseñar el área correcta que debe ser tratada.

3. Favor de no usar jabón, cremas, desodorantes, ni perfume en el área de tratamiento, durante los tratamientos, ni por un rato después.

4. Mantenga cubierta el área de tratamiento cuando esté en el sol.

5. Jabón, cremas, desodorantes, perfume y el sol pueden irritar el área de tratamiento, y pueden causar una mala reacción a la radiación.

6. Los tratamientos no le duelen y duran un minuto.

7. Algunos pacientes necesitarán tener una prueba de sangre cada semana (el técnico le avisará).

8. Si tiene otros problemas avise al técnico para que podamos tratarlos y mejorarlos.

RESPIRATORY THERAPY

General

1. I need to give you a breathing treatment.
2. Take a deep breath and hold it for 2 seconds, then breathe out normally.
3. Take a deep breath and cough strongly.
4. Spit out what you can. Do not swallow it.
5. I'm going to clap on your chest to loosen the secretions in your lungs. Roll on your side.
6. Blow into this bottle.
7. This is medication for your lungs.
8. Take a big breath in.
9. Keep breathing deeply.
10. We need to clear the tube.
11. It will make you cough.

Intermittent Positive Pressure Breathing

1. This machine is designed to aid your breathing capabilities.

2. The machine pushes air into your lungs with gentle pressure.

TERAPIA RESPIRATORIA

General

1. Necesito darle un tratamiento para respirar.
2. Respire profundamente, mantenga la respiración por dos segundos y luego exhale normalmente.
3. Respire profundamente y tosa fuerte.
4. Escupa lo que pueda. No trague.
5. Le voy a dar palmadas en el pecho para soltar las secreciones en sus pulmones. Póngase de lado.
6. Sople en la botella.
7. Esto es medicación para sus pulmones.
8. Inhale fuerte.
9. Siga respirando profundamente.
10. Necesitamos limpiar el tubo.
11. Le hará toser.

Respiración por Presión Intermitente Positiva

1. Se ha diseñado esta máquina para ayudarle con su capacidad de respiración.

2. Esta máquina forza el aire en los pulmones con presión suave.

3. When your lungs reach a certain pressure the machine shuts off and allows exhalation.

4. You initiate the next step with a light sipping motion through the mouthpiece as you would sip a straw.

5. In order for the machine to work properly, you must keep your lips sealed around the mouthpiece so that no air escapes.

6. Please do not breathe through your nose.

7. Breathe only through the mouthpiece, taking all of your air from the machine for each breath and exhaling only through the tube.

8. After inhalation try to maintain air in your lungs by closing the glottis in the lower throat like you do when coughing.

9. Try not to puff out your cheeks when you inhale.

Maximum Inspiratory Flow Rate

1. I need to try a breathing test with you.

2. This is a test which measures the force with which you inhale.

3. You should breathe as deeply as possible.

4. It is important to give a strong effort with each test so our results will be accurate.

3. Cuando los pulmones lleguen a cierta presión la máquina se apaga y le permitirá exhalar.

4. Ud. mismo inicia el próximo paso cuando hace una moción por la boquilla como si chupara por un popote (pitillo).

5. Para que la máquina funcione bien, debe tener los labios bien cerrados alrededor de la boquilla para que el aire no escape.

6. No respire por la nariz, por favor.

7. Respire solamente por la boquilla respirando todo el aire de la máquina para cada aliento y exhalando solamente por el tubo.

8. Después de inhalar trate de mantener el aire en los pulmones cerrando la glotis en la garganta inferior como si estuviera tosiendo.

9. Trate de no resoplar cuando inhale.

Grado de Máxima Fuerza Inspiratoria

1. Tengo que hacerle una prueba respiratoria.

2. Esto es una prueba que mide la fuerza con la cual Ud. inhala.

3. Ud. debe (de) respirar lo más profundo que pueda.

4. Es importante hacer un esfuerzo con cada prueba para que nuestros resultados sean precisos.

5. Breathe normally for a few minutes, blow out all of your air, and then take in as deep a breath as possible.
6. Keep going. More. Relax. Very good. Thank you.

Maximum Expiratory Flow Rate

1. I am going to measure how fast you can blow air out of your lungs.
2. Take a deep breath in.
3. Blow out as hard and as fast as you can until your lungs feel like they are empty.

Vital Capacity Maneuver

1. I need to measure how much air you can blow out with your best effort.
2. You must take in as deep a breath as possible and then exhale maximally.
3. Sit up straight and do not cross your legs.
4. As you breathe, concentrate on expanding your rib cage.
5. When you blow out the air, use all of your strength.
6. Take a big breath in. Now blow out as fast and fully as you are able. Very good, thank you.

5. Respire normalmente por unos minutos, sople fuera todo el aire y respire lo más profundo que pueda.
6. Siga. Más. Descanse. Muy bien. Gracias.

Grado de Máxima Fuerza Expiratoria

1. Voy a medir qué rápido puede soplar el aire de sus pulmones.
2. Aspire profundamente.
3. Sople lo más fuerte y lo más rápido posible hasta que sus pulmones se le sientan como vacíos.

Maniobra Vital de Capacidad

1. Necesito medir cuánto aire Ud. puede soplar con su mayor esfuerzo.
2. Debe aspirar lo más profundo que pueda y exhalar todo lo que pueda.
3. Siéntese recto y no cruce las piernas.
4. Mientras que esté respirando siga expandiendo la caja torácica costal.
5. Cuando sople el aire use toda la fuerza.
6. Aspire profundamente. Ahora sople lo más rápido y completamente que pueda. Muy bien, gracias.

Intubation and Mechanical Ventilation

1. We will have to place a tube into your throat for breathing.

2. Please try to cooperate and do not be frightened.
3. This tube will pass through the mouth into the throat.
4. The machine will give you a breath every 4 or 5 seconds.

5. Try to synchronize your breaths with the machine breaths and do not oppose the machine-given breaths.
6. Relax and expand your rib cage with the delivered volume.

7. When you fight the machine or cough a loud alarm will sound like a buzzer.

Manual Resuscitation, Suction, and Lavage

1. We need to insert a suction catheter into your breathing tube to clear any secretions that may narrow the airway.

2. Manual resuscitation (bagging) consists of squeezing the bag of oxygen, thus forcing air out of the bag and into your lungs.

Intubación y Ventilación Mecánica

1. Tendremos que insertar un tubo en la garganta para que pueda respirar.

2. Trate de cooperar y no tenga miedo.
3. Este tubo pasará por la boca hasta la garganta.
4. La máquina le dará un aliento cada 4 o 5 (cuatro o cinco) segundos.

5. Trate de sincronizar su respiración con la respiración de la máquina y no esté en contra la respiración de la máquina.
6. Relájese y agrande su caja toráxica con cada cantidad de aire entregada.

7. Cuando se oponga usted a la máquina o tosa una alarma sonará como un zumbador.

Resuscitación Manual, Succión y Lavado

1. Tenemos que meter una sonda de succión en su tubo de respiración para sacar (extraer) cualquier secreción que pueda estrechar la vía respiratoria.

2. Resuscitación manual consiste en apretar la bolsa de oxígeno, así forzando el aire fuera de la bolsa hacia el interior de sus pulmones.

SPEECH THERAPY—PRESCHOOL SPEECH QUESTIONNAIRE

Name of Child _____ Birthdate _____

Address _____ Telephone _____
      Street   Zip

Describe the problem _____
_____
_____
_____

When and how was the problem first noticed? _____
_____

What have you done to help solve the problem? _____
_____

Has your child received or is your child receiving speech therapy? _____ When? _____

With whom? _____
          Name   Address

Is your child being seen for other types of therapy? _____

By a medical specialist? _____

With whom? _____
          Name   Address

CUESTIONARIO DEL HABLA PREESCOLAR

Nombre del Niño _____ Fecha de Nacimiento _____

Dirección _____ Teléfono _____
         Calle   Zona Postal

Describa el problema _____
_____
_____
_____

¿Cuándo y cómo fue descubierto el problema primero? _____
_____

¿Qué ha hecho para resolver el problema? _____
_____

¿Ha recibido o está recibiendo su niño/niña terapia de habla?
_____ ¿Cuándo? _____

¿Con quién? _____
           Nombre   Dirección

¿Hay otros tipos de terapia con que estén tratando al niño/a la niña? _____ ¿Por un especialista médico? _____

¿Con quién? _____
           Nombre   Dirección

Is a language other than English/Spanish spoken in the home?___

Does the child understand simple commands? _____

Does the child hear well? _____

How much of the child's speech can the mother/father understand?   All   Most   Some   Little

How much speech can other adults understand?

All   Most   Some   Little

If vocabulary is limited, list words frequently used: _____

_____

Is your child attending nursery school? _____ What days? _____

Name _____

Address _____

How does your child react to his/her speech or hearing problem? _____

If the child is enrolled in therapy, who would be able to help at home? _____

Name of parents or guardians: _____

Father: _____   Mother: _____

Employer: _____   Employer: _____

Phone: _____   Phone: _____

Marital status (married, separated, etc.) _____

¿Se habla en su casa otra lengua además del inglés/español? ___

¿Entiende el niño/la niña los mandatos simples? _____

¿Oye bien el niño/la niña? _____

¿Cuánto del lenguaje del niño/la niña puede entender la madre/el padre?   Todo   Casi todo   Algo   Poco

¿Cuánto del lenguaje pueden entender otros adultos?

Todo   Casi todo   Algo   Poco

Si el vocabulario está limitado, dé una lista de las palabras muy usadas: _____

¿Asiste a un pre-kinder su niño(a)? _____ ¿Cuáles días? _____

Nombre del pre-kinder _____

Dirección _____

¿Cómo reacciona su hijo(a) a su problema de lenguaje o de audición? _____

Si el niño/la niña se matriculara en terapia; quién lo/la ayudaría en casa? _____

Nombres de los padres o de los tutores: _____

Padre _____   Madre _____

Dónde trabaja _____   Dónde trabaja _____

Teléfono _____   Teléfono _____

Estado Civil (casado, separado, viudo, soltero) _____

List names and birthdates of
other children in the family: Birthdate

_____

_____

_____

_____

_____

Have any other members of the family had speech problems?
Please describe: _____

_____

_____

_____

* * * * *

Describe any behavior of the child that is a problem _____

_____

What rewards (treats, special privileges) does the child like?

_____

What special fears does the child have? _____

_____

Does the child dress him/herself? _____

Dé una lista de los nombres y las fechas de nacimiento
de los otros niños en la familia: Fecha de Nacimiento

_____

_____

_____

_____

_____

¿Han tenido otros miembros de la familia problemas de lenguaje? Dé los detalles: _____

_____

_____

_____

* * * * *

¿Qué conducta del niño/de la niña ha sido un problema? _____

_____

¿Qué recompensas le gustan al niño/a la niña? _____

_____

¿Qué temores/miedos tiene el niño/la niña? _____

_____

¿Se viste solo el niño/la niña? _____

Is the child toilet trained? _____

When was training during the day complete? _____

At what age did your child master the following skills? (If you guess, please place a question mark after your answer.)

   Sat without support _____

   Walked alone _____ Babbled _____

   Spoke first word (on his own) _____

   Spoke two- to three-word combinations _____

Does your child have difficulty swallowing? _____

chewing? _____ blowing? _____

Does your child gag? _____

choke? _____ drool? _____

     * * * * *

What problems did the mother have during labor or delivery?

_____

Birth weight: _____

Did your child have evidence of difficulties at birth (feeding, breathing, injury)? _____

_____

_____

¿Está entrenado el niño/la niña para ir solo(a) al baño? _____

¿Cuándo terminó esta educación para durante el día? _____

¿A qué edad logró el niño/la niña las siguientes habilidades? (Si usted sólo adivina, ponga un signo de interrogación después de la respuesta.)   Se sentó sin apoyo _____

   Caminó solo _____ Balbuceó _____

   Dijo su primera palabra (por sí mismo) _____

   Dijo frases de dos o tres (2-3) palabras _____

¿Tiene dificultad al tragar su niño(a)? _____

¿en masticar? _____ ¿al soplar? _____

¿Se le atraganta la garganta? _____

¿se sofoca? _____ ¿babea? _____

     * * * * *

¿Cuáles problemas tuvo la madre durante labor o parto? _____

_____

Peso cuando nació: _____

¿Tuvo el niño/la niña dificultades cuando nació (de alimentarse, de respirar, de lesión)? _____

_____

_____

Has your child had surgery, serious accidents, hospitalization?
_____ If so, please explain _____
_____
_____

About how many colds per year has your child had?_____
_____

List illnesses and diseases that your child has had:
_____ Date _____
_____ Date _____
_____ Date _____
_____ Date _____

List any allergies _____
_____

Is your child on medication?_____ If so, what? _____
_____

Name of family doctor or pediatrician:
_____

Address: _____

¿Ha tenido el niño/la niña cirugía, serios accidentes, hospitalización? _____ Si afirmativo, favor de explicar _____
_____
_____

¿Aproximadamente cuántos resfriados por año ha tenido su niño(a)? _____

Haga lista de las enfermedades que ha tenido el niño/la niña:
_____ Fecha _____
_____ Fecha _____
_____ Fecha _____
_____ Fecha _____

Haga lista de alergias, si tiene _____
_____

¿Toma su niño(a) medicina ahora? _____ ¿Cuál? _____
_____

Nombre del pediatra o del médico de familia:
_____

Dirección: _____

SECTION F

Consent Forms

PERMIT FOR OUT-
PATIENT ANESTHESIA

PERMIT FOR OUTPATIENT ANESTHESIA

Permission is hereby granted for premedication and anesthesia for out-patient surgery. I have read, have understood, and will comply with the written directions furnished to me. Although I will have my surgery as an out-patient, I understand that I may have to be admitted to the hospital after the operation. I will not drive home or use a public conveyance. Someone will take me home. I realize that I may not be fully mentally alert for several hours after the operation, and I will avoid any decision or activity postoperatively that depends on full concentration power or mental judgment to ensure safe completion of that activity. My answers to all questions are true to the best of my knowledge, and I have not withheld any information.

Witness: _____ Patient: _____

Date: _____ Guardian: _____

AUTORIZACIÓN PARA ANESTESIA DE PACIENTE AMBULANTE

Por la presente doy permiso para medicinas previas y anestesia para cirugía de paciente ambulante. He leído, entiendo, y cumpliré con las instrucciones escritas que se me han dado. Entiendo que podrá ser necesario internarme en el hospital después de la operación. No manejaré ni usaré transporte público. Alguien me llevará a mi casa. Entiendo que mis facultades mentales pueden ser afectadas por unas cuantas horas después de la anestesia, por lo cual evitaré cualquier decisión o actividad de la cual dependa mi completa concentración o juicio mental. Mis contestaciones a todas las preguntas son verdaderas, según he entendido, y no he retenido ninguna información.

Testigo: _____ Paciente: _____

Fecha: _____ Tutor: _____

SECTION G

Offices and Records

INDUSTRIAL MEDICAL RECORD

STRICTLY PRIVATE

(Answer all questions in your own handwriting)

NAME: (Last, First, Middle Initial)		Home Telephone	Male	Female	Date of Birth
ADDRESS: (Number, Street, Apartment No., City, State, Zip Code)					
Notify in case of EMERGENCY	Work Telephone	Home Telephone	Relationship to you	POSITION APPLIED for:	
Family PHYSICIAN Name	Physician's Address				
Reason for last visit to your Doctor				Date of visit	

#	HAVE YOU EVER HAD	No	Yes	Reference line number and EXPLAIN EVERY Yes answer	Yes	No	#	HAVE YOU EVER HAD
1	glasses						11	ringing in the ear
2	eye trouble other than glasses						12	punctured ear drum
3	contact lenses						13	work wearing ear protection
4	broken nose						14	frequent headaches
5	sinus infection						15	head injury
6	hay fever						16	skull fracture
7	throat trouble						17	brain concussion
8	bad hearing						18	dizzy spells
9	ear trouble						19	fainting spells
10	running ear						20	convulsions

INSCRIPCIÓN INDUSTRIAL MÉDICA

EN ABSOLUTA CONFIANZA

(Conteste todas las preguntas escritas por sí mismo/a)

NOMBRE: (Apellido, Nombre, Inicial)	Teléfono de hogar Varón Mujer Fecha de Nacimiento

DIRECCIÓN: (Número, Calle, Apartamento, Ciudad, Estado, Zona)

En caso de EMERGENCIA notifique a	Teléfono de Empleo Teléfono de Hogar	Parentesco de Ud. EMPLEO SOLICITADO:	

Nombre del MÉDICO de la Familia	Dirección del Médico

Razón de la última consulta con el Médico	Fecha de la consulta

#	ALGUNA VEZ HA TENIDO	No	Sí	Escriba el número de la referencia EXPLIQUE cada respuesta de Sí	Sí	No	#	ALGUNA VEZ HA TENIDO
1	gafas, anteojos						11	zumbido en el oído
2	molestia de los ojos que no sea gafas						12	oído perforado
3	lentes de contacto						13	empleo necesitando protección para los oídos
4	la nariz quebrada						14	dolores frecuentes de la cabeza
5	infección del seno nasal						15	daño a la cabeza
6	catarro asonático, fiebre del heno						16	fractura del cráneo
7	problemas de la garganta						17	concusión del cerebro
8	problemas de audición						18	mareos o vértigo
9	problemas de los oídos						19	desmayos
10	supuración del oído						20	convulsiones

#	HAVE YOU EVER HAD	No	Yes	Reference line number and EXPLAIN EVERY Yes answer	Yes	No	#	HAVE YOU EVER HAD
21	epilepsy						44	allergy to insects
22	meningitis						45	allergy to food
23	a stroke						46	frequent nausea
24	paralysis						47	frequent vomiting
25	nervous attacks						48	ulcers
26	mental trouble						49	stomach trouble
27	neurologic disorder						50	chronic indigestion
28	a goiter						51	abdominal pain
29	rheumatic fever						52	appendicitis
30	breast trouble						53	gall bladder trouble
31	chronic chest condition						54	jaundice
32	lung disease						55	bowel troubles
33	shortness of breath						56	colitis
34	a feeling of tightness in chest						57	hemorrhoids
35	asthma						58	kidney trouble
36	night sweats						59	urinary bladder trouble
37	tuberculosis						60	rupture or hernia
38	silicosis						61	painful or swollen joints
39	chronic cough						62	rheumatism
40	coughing up of blood						63	arthritis
41	heart trouble or heart attack						64	a knee injury
42	high blood pressure						65	swollen ankles
43	allergy to medication						66	foot trouble or painful feet

#	ALGUNA VEZ HA TENIDO	No	Sí	Escriba el número de la referencia EXPLIQUE cada respuesta de Sí	Sí	No	#	ALGUNA VEZ HA TENIDO
21	epilepsia						44	alergia a insectos
22	meningitis						45	alergia a ciertos alimentos
23	ataque fulminante, derrame						46	náuseas frecuentes
24	parálisis						47	vómitos frecuentes
25	ataques de nervios						48	úlceras
26	problemas mentales						49	problemas del estómago
27	desorden neurológico						50	indigestión crónica
28	bocio, buche						51	dolor abdominal
29	fiebre reumática						52	apendicitis
30	problemas de los pechos						53	problemas de la vesícula biliar
31	padecimiento crónico del pecho						54	ictericia
32	enfermedad de los pulmones						55	problemas de los intestinos
33	dificultad en respirar						56	colitis
34	sentido de opresión en el pecho						57	hemorroides
35	asma						58	problemas de los riñones
36	sudores durante la noche						59	problemas de la vejiga urinaria
37	tuberculosis, tisis						60	ruptura, padecer de hernia
38	silicosis						61	coyunturas dolorosas o inflamadas
39	tos crónica						62	reumatismo
40	arrojo de sangre al toser						63	artritis
41	padecer, o ataque del corazón						64	lesión de rodilla
42	presión alta						65	tobillos hinchados
43	alergia a medicación						66	problemas de los pies

#	HAVE YOU EVER HAD	No	Yes	Reference line number and EXPLAIN EVERY Yes answer	Yes	No	#	HAVE YOU EVER HAD
67	back trouble						79	work with lasers
68	spine trouble						80	work with ultraviolet radiation
69	broken bones; dislocations						81	work with x-radiation
70	skin trouble						82	work with beta or gamma radiation
71	alcoholism						83	work with neutrons
72	diabetes						84	work with heat stress
73	malaria						85	work with noise
74	anemia or other blood condition						86	work with vibrations
75	growths or tumors						87	work in dust areas
76	any chronic ailment						88	work with chemicals (list)
77	a prosthesis						89	work with metals (list)
78	work with microwaves						90	Do you smoke? How much?

#	ALGUNA VEZ HA TENIDO	No	Sí	Escriba el número de la referencia EXPLIQUE cada respuesta de Sí	Sí	No	#	ALGUNA VEZ HA TENIDO
67	problemas de la espalda						79	trabajo relacionado a rayos laser
68	problemas de la espina						80	trabajo relacionado a rayos ultravioleta
69	quebraduras de hueso, deslocaciones						81	trabajo relacionado a los rayos X
70	problemas del cutis (de la piel)						82	trabajo relacionado a radiación Beta o Gama
71	alcoholismo						83	trabajo relacionado a los neutrones
72	diabetes						84	trabajo relacionado a fuerza térmica
73	malaria						85	trabajo relacionado a ruido
74	anemia u otros problemas de la sangre						86	trabajo relacionado a vibraciones
75	lobanillos o tumores						87	empleo en áreas donde hace polvo
76	alguna enfermedad crónica						88	trabajo con substancias químicas (alístelas)
77	una prostesis						89	trabajo con metales (alístelos)
78	trabajo relacionado a microondas						90	¿Fuma usted? ¿Cuánto?

INJURY TO EMPLOYEE, REPORT

IF INJURY IS FATAL OR SERIOUS TELEPHONE DIVISION OFFICE   ANSWER EACH QUESTION

Name of Injured Employee _____ Social Security No. _____

Male ☐   Female ☐   Wages _____ per Hour Day   Regular ☐   Seasonal ☐   Other ☐
                                                      Week Month

Address (Street and Number) _____ City _____ State _____

Age _____ How Long Employed _____ Days Worked/Week _____ Married? _____ Children? _____

Occupation When Injured _____ General Duties _____ Dept. _____

Date of Injury _____ Time _____ M. Date of Disability _____ Time _____ M.

Date First Reported _____ To Whom _____ Did Injury Cause Loss of Time _____

Date Returned to Work _____ Probable Period of Disability _____

Where Did Accident Happen _____

How Did Accident Happen (Employee's Statement, If Possible) _____

_____

_____

Describe Injury Fully (Including Parts of Body) _____

_____

_____

Date Medical Aid First Rendered _____ Name of Doctor _____ Name of Hospital _____

This Notice Prepared By _____ Date _____ Time _____ M.

REPORTE DE DAÑO AL EMPLEADO

SI EL DAÑO ES FATAL O SERIO LLAME POR TELÉFONO A LA OFICINA DE LA DIVISIÓN   **CONTESTE CADA PREGUNTA**

Nombre del Empleado Dañado _____ Número de Seguro Social _____

Varón ☐   Hembra ☐   Salario _____ por: Hora   Día   Regular ☐   De Estación ☐   Otro ☐
                                                        Semana Mes

Dirección (Calle y Número) _____ Ciudad _____ Estado _____

Edad _____ Cuánto Tiempo Lleva Empleado _____ Días Trabajados por Semana _____ ¿Casado? _____ ¿Hijos? _____

Ocupación Cuando fue Herido _____ Deberes Generales _____ Dept. _____

Fecha del Daño _____ Hora _____ M. Fecha de Incapacidad _____ Hora _____ M.

Fecha en que fue Reportado _____ ¿A Quién? _____ ¿Causó Pérdida de Tiempo el Daño? _____

Fecha en que Regresó al Trabajo _____ Período Probable de Incapacidad _____

¿Dónde Ocurrió el Accidente? _____

¿Cómo Ocurrió el Accidente? (En Palabras del Empleado, Si Posible) _____

_____

_____

Describa el Daño Completamente (Incluya Partes del Cuerpo) _____

_____

Fecha en que Ayuda Médica le fue Dada Primero _____ Nombre del Médico _____ Nombre del Hospital _____

Esta Noticia fue Preparada por _____ Título _____ Fecha _____

EMPLOYEE'S STATEMENT

How Could Accident Have Been Prevented _____

_____

_____

Prepared By _____ Date _____ Time _____ M.

Names and Addresses of Two Witnesses of Accident _____

_____

_____

DECLARACIÓN DEL EMPLEADO

¿Cómo se habría podido prevenir el accidente? _____

_____

_____

Escuchado por _____ Fecha _____ Hora _____

Nombres y Direcciones de dos testigos del accidente _____

_____

_____

ADMISSIONS DESK

1. What is the patient's complete and correct name?

2. What is the address and zip code of the patient?

3. What is the Social Security number?

4. What is the patient's telephone number?

5. What is the sex of the patient?

6. What is the date of birth?

7. How old is the patient?

8. In what city, state, and country was the patient born?

9. What is the religion of the patient?

10. What is the marital status of the patient?
    a. Married?
    b. Single?
    c. Divorced?
    d. Widowed?
    e. Separated?
    f. Name of spouse?

11. What is the patient's occupation?

12. What is the address and telephone number of the patient's employer?

13. Give me the name of the patient's nearest relative.

CAJA DE INGRESOS

1. ¿Cuál es el nombre completo y correcto del (de la) paciente? (¿Cómo se llama el/la paciente?)

2. ¿Cuál es la dirección y la zona postal del (de la) paciente?

3. ¿Cuál es el número del Seguro Social?

4. ¿Cuál es el número de teléfono del (de la) paciente?

5. ¿Cuál es el sexo del paciente?

6. ¿Cuál es la fecha de nacimiento?

7. ¿Qué edad tiene el/la paciente?

8. Dígame el nombre de la ciudad, del estado y del país donde nació el/la paciente.

9. ¿Cuál es la religión del (de la) paciente?

10. ¿Cuál es su estado civil?
    a. ¿Casado/a?
    b. ¿Soltero/a?
    c. ¿Divorciado/a?
    d. ¿Viudo/a?
    e. ¿Separado/a?
    f. ¿Nombre del esposo/de la esposa?

11. ¿Cuál es su ocupación (empleo)?

12. ¿Cuál es la dirección y el número de teléfono del patrón del/de la paciente?

13. Dígame el nombre del pariente más cercano del/de la paciente.

14. What is his/her relationship with the patient?
15. What is his/her address and telephone number?
16. To whom should we send the bill?
17. Does the patient have insurance?
    a. Blue Cross/Blue Shield?
    b. Kaiser?
    c. Medi-Cal?
    d. Medicaid?
    e. Medicare?
    f. Champus
18. What is the number of the policy?
19. What is the complete name of the policy holder?
20. Is this the patient's first time in the hospital?
21. Was the patient admitted to the hospital within the last 6 months?
22. Was the patient admitted because of an accident?
23. When and where did the accident occur?
24. Was the patient admitted from another hospital?
25. Was the patient admitted from home?
26. Was the patient admitted from an extended-care facility?

27. What was the admission's diagnosis?
28. Does the patient want a private room, a semiprivate room, or a ward?

14. ¿Cuál es su parentesco con el/la paciente?
15. ¿Cuál es su dirección y el número de teléfono?
16. ¿A quién debemos mandar la cuenta?
17. ¿Tiene el paciente algún seguro?
    a. ¿Cruz Azul/Escudo Azul?
    b. ¿Kaiser?
    c. ¿Medi-Cal?
    d. ¿Medicaid?
    e. ¿Medicare?
    f. ¿Champus?
18. ¿Cuál es el número de la póliza?
19. ¿Cuál es el nombre completo del retentor de la póliza?
20. ¿Es ésta la primera vez del/de la paciente en el hospital?
21. ¿Fue admitido(a) el/la paciente al hospital dentro de los últimos seis meses?
22. ¿Ingresaron al/a la paciente a causa de un accidente?
23. ¿Cuándo y dónde ocurrió el accidente?
24. ¿Fue ingresado(a) el/la paciente de otro hospital?
25. ¿Fue ingresado(a) el/la paciente de su casa?
26. ¿Fue ingresado(a) el/la paciente de una institución de cuidado prolongado?
27. ¿Cuál fue la diagnosis al ingresar?
28. ¿Quiere el/la paciente un cuarto privado, semiprivado, o una sala?

29. What is the name of the patient's physician?
30. Does the patient consent to and authorize all treatments, surgical procedures, and administration of all anesthetics which in the judgement of the physician may be considered necessary for the diagnosis or treatment of this case while he/she is a patient in _____ Hospital?
31. Sign here.

MEDICAL OFFICE

1. Do you have an appointment? At what time?
2. Who referred you to this office?
3. The doctor will be here in a few minutes. Please sit down.
4. Do you have insurance? Do you have a welfare card?
5. Have you seen the doctor before? When?
6. The doctor's fees per visit are $_____.

7. We will send the bill to your home by mail.
8. Who is your family doctor?
9. Where does it hurt?
10. How have you treated this?
11. How long have you had it?

29. ¿Cuál es el nombre del médico particular del de la paciente?
30. ¿Da el/la paciente su consentimiento y autorización para todos los tratamientos, procedimientos quirúrgicos, y administración de todas las anestesias que juzgue necesarias su médico para la diagnosis o tratamiento de este caso mientras que esté en _____ Hospital?
31. Firme aquí.

OFICINA DEL MÉDICO

1. ¿Tiene una cita? ¿A qué hora?
2. ¿Quién le recomendó que viniera a esta oficina?
3. El doctor vendrá dentro de poco. Tome asiento, por favor.
4. ¿Tiene seguro? ¿Tiene una tarjeta para "welfare?"
5. ¿Ha visto al médico antes? ¿Cuándo?
6. Los honorarios del doctor por visita son de $_____ (dólares).
7. Le mandaremos la cuenta por correo a su casa.
8. ¿Quién es el doctor de su familia?
9. ¿Dónde le duele?
10. ¿Cómo se lo ha curado?
11. ¿Desde cuándo lo tiene?

12. When did the accident happen? Did they take x-rays? Where are they?

13. Have you had an operation previously?

14. Have you had an illness of the
    a. eyes?
    b. mouth?
    c. throat?
    d. nose?

15. Are you allergic to any drugs?

16. I will now take your blood pressure, temperature, respirations and pulse.

17. What time is best for your next appointment?

MEDICAL RECORDS

1. Tell me the complete and correct name of your child.

2. On what day, month and year was he/she born?

3. At what time was the child born?

4. What is the sex?

5. In what county was the child born?

6. What is your complete and correct maiden name?

7. How old are you?

8. Date of birth?

9. Place of birth?

12. ¿Cuándo sucedió el accidente? ¿Le tomaron rayos equis? ¿Dónde están?

13. ¿Ha tenido una operación antes?

14. ¿Ha estado enfermo
    a. de los ojos?
    b. de la boca?
    c. de la garganta?
    d. de la nariz?

15. ¿Es usted alérgico a algunas medicinas?

16. Ahora le voy a tomar su presión, temperatura, respiraciones y pulso.

17. ¿Cuál es la mejor hora para su próxima cita?

REGISTROS MÉDICOS

1. Dígame el nombre completo y correcto de su niño/niña.

2. ¿En que día, mes, y año nació?

3. ¿A qué hora exacta nació?

4. ¿Cuál es su sexo?

5. ¿En qué país nació el niño/la niña?

6. Dígame su nombre de soltera completo y correcto.

7. ¿Cuántos años tiene Ud?

8. ¿Fecha de nacimiento?

9. ¿Cuál es su lugar de nacimiento?

10. What is your exact address?

11. How do you spell your name?

12. Tell me the name and address of your doctor.

13. What is your relationship to the patient?

14. What is the number of your green card?

15. Do you have medical insurance?

16. What is the name of your insurance company?

17. Sign here.

10. ¿Cuál es su dirección exacta?

11. ¿Cómo se deletrea su nombre?

12. Dígame el nombre y dirección de su médico.

13. ¿Qué parentesco tiene con el/la paciente?

14. ¿Cuál es el número de su tarjeta verde?

15. ¿Tiene Ud. seguros médicos?

16. ¿Cuál es el nombre de su aseguranza? (seguro médico)

17. Firme aquí.

SECTION H
Equipment and Supplies

GENERAL HOSPITAL EQUIPMENT AND SUPPLIES*

EQUIPO Y ARTÍCULOS GENERALES

1. adhesive tape	1. la cinta adhesiva	21. emergency kit	21. el botiquín de emergencia
2. band	2. la cinta	22. exercise bar	22. la barra de ejercicios
3. bandage	3. la venda	23. faucets	23. los grifos, las llaves
4. bath bench	4. la banquita para el baño	24. flashlight	24. la linterna
5. bath lift	5. el elevador de baño	25. floor	25. el suelo, el piso
6. bathmat	6. el tapete de baño	26. fluoroscope	26. el fluoroscopio
7. bathtub	7. la tina	27. flusher	27. la manija de excusado, el mango
8. bed	8. la cama		
9. bedpan	9. la chata, el bacín, el cómodo, el orinal, el pato, la bacinica, la bacinilla	28. gauze	28. la gasa
		29. glass	29. el vaso
10. blanket	10. la cobija, la frazada, la manta	30. grab bar	30. la barra de agarrarse
		31. hamper	31. el cesto de ropa
11. call bell	11. el timbre	32. hypodermic	32. el hipodérmico
12. cane	12. el bastón	33. light (to call the nurse)	33. la luz (para llamar a la enfermera)
13. cardiograph	13. el cardiógrafo		
14. catheter	14. el catéter, la sonda	34. medicine cabinet	34. el botiquín
15. commode	15. la silleta, el sillico	35. microscope	35. el microscopio
16. cotton	16. el algodón	36. mirror	36. el espejo
17. crank	17. la manivela	37. night table	37. la mesita
18. crutches	18. las muletas	38. operating table	38. la mesa de operaciones
19. curtains, draw curtain	19. las cortinas, la cortina separadora	39. ophthalmoscope	39. el oftalmoscopio
		40. overbed	40. la mesita auxiliar para la cama
20. electrocardiograph	20. el electrocardiógrafo	41. pillow	41. la almohada

*A list of equipment and supplies for infants can be found on p. 107.

42. pillow case
43. pitcher
44. quad cane
45. raised toilet seat

46. reflex hammer
47. safety grips

48. safety pin
49. safety side rails
50. safety toilet frame

51. sheet
52. shower
53. side rails
54. sink
55. sitzbath
56. soap
57. sphygmomanometer
58. stethoscope
59. straw
60. stretcher

42. la funda
43. la jarra
44. el andén
45. el asiento elevado para el excusado
46. el martillo de reflejos
47. los agarraderos de seguridad
48. el alfiler de seguridad
49. las barandas de seguridad
50. el marco de seguridad del excusado
51. la sábana
52. la ducha, la regadera
53. las barandas de seguridad
54. el lavamanos
55. el baño de asiento
56. el jabón
57. el baumanómetro
58. el estetoscopio
59. el popote, la pajilla
60. la camilla

61. syringe
62. thermometer
63. toilet
64. toilet frame, safety

65. toilet paper
66. tongue depressor

67. toothbrush
68. toothbrush holder

69. towel
70. walker

71. washcloth
72. wastebasket
73. wheelchair
74. whirlpool bath

75. window
76. x-ray

61. la jeringa, la jeringuilla
62. el termómetro
63. el excusado, el retrete
64. el marco de seguridad del excusado
65. el papel higiénico
66. el pisalengua, el bajalengua
67. el cepillo de dientes
68. el soporte de cepillos de dientes
69. la toalla
70. el apoyador para caminar, el andador
71. el paño para lavarse
72. el cesto
73. la silla de ruedas
74. el baño de remolino, el agitador de agua
75. la ventana
76. la radiografía, los rayos-equis

MEDICAL, LABORATORY, AND PROCEDURAL SUPPLIES

ARTÍCULOS PARA MEDICINA, LABORATORIO, Y PROCEDIMIENTO

1. adhesive tape
2. ankle support
3. arch supports

4. artificial limb
5. band
6. bandage
7. Band-Aid
8. binder
9. birth control pill
10. bottle (formula)
11. blood plasma
12. blood transfusion
13. booster shot
14. brace
15. cane
16. cold pack
17. compress (hot)
18. corn plaster
19. crutch
20. curettage
21. douche
22. dropper
23. elastic bandage

1. la cinta adhesiva
2. la tobillera
3. los soportes para el arco del pie
4. el miembro artificial
5. la cinta
6. la venda
7. la curita
8. el vendaje abdominal
9. la píldora anticonceptiva
10. el biberón, el tetero
11. el plasma sanguíneo
12. la transfusión de sangre
13. la inyección secundaria
14. el braguero
15. el bastón
16. el emplasto frío
17. la compresa (caliente)
18. el emplasto para callos
19. le muleta
20. el curetaje, el raspado
21. la ducha
22. el gotero
23. la venda elástica

24. enema
    enema bag

25. first aid
26. flask
27. foam
28. gargle
29. gauze
30. hearing aid

31. heat therapy
32. hot water bag
33. hypodermic injection
    hypodermic needle
    hypodermic syringe
34. ice pack
35. injection
    a. intramuscular
    b. intravenous
    c. subcutaneous
36. intrauterine device (IUD)
    intrauterine loop
    intrauterine ring
    intrauterine shield

24. la enema, la lavativa
    la bolsa para enema, la lavativa
25. los primeros auxilios
26. el frasco
27. la espuma
28. la gárgara
29. la gasa
30. el aparato para la sordera
31. la termoterapia
32. la bolsa de agua caliente
33. la inyección hipodérmica
    !a aguja hipodérmica
    la jeringuilla hipodérmica
34. la bolsa de hielo
35. la inyección
    a. intramuscular
    b. intravenosa
    c. subcutánea
36. el dispositivo intrauterino
    la espiral intrauterina
    el anillo intrauterino
    el escudo intrauterino

37. jelly	37. la jalea	51. steam	51. el vapor
38. kit	38. el botiquín	52. support	52. el apoyo
39. loop (IUD)	39. el lazo	53. syringe (disposable)	53. la jeringa (disponible)
40. massage	40. el masaje	54. tampon	54. el tampón
41. pacemaker	41. el marcapaso	55. tongue depressor	55. el pisalengua
42. pill (birth control)	42. la píldora (anticonceptiva)	56. tourniquet	56. el torniquete
43. radiation shield	43. el blindaje contra la radiación	57. traction	57. la tracción
		58. transfusion	58. la transfusión
radiation therapy	la radioterapia	59. vaccination	59. la vacuna
44. ring (IUD)	44. el anillo	60. walker	60. el andador, el apoyador para caminar
45. salt water	45. el agua salada		
46. shield (IUD)	46. el escudo	61. wheel chair	61. la silla de ruedas
47. sling	47. el cabestrillo	62. x-ray	62. la radiografía (el rayo equis)
48. splint	48. la tablilla		
49. spray	49. la rociada	x-ray therapy	la radioterapia
50. sprayer	50. el rociador		

PHYSICAL AND OCCUPATIONAL THERAPY EQUIPMENT

EQUIPO PARA TERAPIA FÍSICA Y OCUPACIONAL

1. cane	1. el bastón	7. ice pack	7. la bolsa de hielo
2. cast shoe	2. el zapato de yeso	8. garments for burns	8. los ajustadores (soportadores) para quemaduras
3. crutches	3. las muletas		
4. forceps	4. las pinzas		
5. goniometer	5. el goniómetro	9. pinch meter	9. el medidor del pellizcar
6. hot pack	6. la compresa caliente	10. slide board	10. la tabla resbaladora

11. sling
12. splints

    a. resting splint
    b. stretch splint
    c. cock-up splint
    d. dynamic splint

13. walker

11. el cabestrillo
12. las tablillas,
    los entablillados
    a. la tablilla de apoyo
    b. la tablilla para estirar
    c. la tablilla para levantar
    d. la tablilla para mover

13. el andador

14. weights
    a. pulleys
    b. dumbbells
    c. cuff weights
    d. bench press

15. wheel chair
    a. par course

    b. strengthening/endurance
       training

14. las pesas
    a. las poleas
    b. las pesas de gimnasia
    c. las pesas de puño
    d. banco de pesas

15. la silla de ruedas
    a. los ejercicios en silla de
       ruedas
    b. el entrenamiento para
       promover fuerzas y
       tolerancia

SECTION I

For Other Medical Personnel

DIETITIAN

1. I am your dietitian.
2. Do you have any problems chewing?
3. Do you have any food allergies?
4. Do you wear dentures?
5. Do they fit properly?
6. Do you need your food mechanically softened or pureed?
7. Do you have your menu filled out for tomorrow?
8. Do you need help with your menu?
9. Do you follow a diet at home?
10. Do you cook for yourself?
11. Have you had a weight problem most of your life?
12. Have you gained or lost any weight in the past 6 months?
13. Do you know what your present diet is, and why you are on that diet?
14. Is a family member who speaks English coming to visit you today?
15. How is the food?
16. Do you want snacks between meals?
17. For the next 3 days you will be on a calorie count (nutritional analysis) to see how many calories you are eating.

LA DIETISTA

1. Yo soy su dietista.
2. ¿Tiene problemas al mascar (masticar)?
3. ¿Tiene alergias a ciertos alimentos?
4. ¿Usa dentaduras artificiales?
5. ¿Le vienen bien?
6. ¿Necesita comida mecánicamente ablandada o en puré?
7. ¿Tiene su menú listo para mañana?
8. ¿Necesita ayuda con el menú?
9. ¿Lleva dieta en casa?
10. ¿Cocina para sí mismo/a?
11. ¿Ha tenido problema de peso casi toda su vida?
12. ¿Ha ganado o perdido peso en los últimos 6 (seis) meses?
13. ¿Sabe cuál es su dieta actual y por qué está en esa dieta?
14. ¿Lo/la visitará hoy algún miembro de su familia que habla inglés?
15. ¿Cómo está la comida?
16. ¿Gusta comer algo fuera de horas de las comidas?
17. Durante los siguientes 3 (tres) días estará en cuenta de calorías (análisis nutricional) para ver cuántas calorías consume.

18. Are you hungry?
19. Are you full?
20. Is there something we can bring you?

Bases Excess–Intravenous Pyelogram (B.E.–I.V.P.) or Excretory Urogram Test Diet

Purpose

To provide a limited quantity of food restricted in both residue and fat as a preparatory measure for the B.E-I.V.P. test on the next day.

Characteristics

1. The noon meal for the day preceding the test consists of the following foods:

a. clear juice	½ cup
b. bouillon or clear broth	1 cup
c. sliced turkey or chicken, trimmed	3 ounces
d. plain jello	½ cup
e. white bread or toast	2 slices
f. nonfat milk	1 cup
g. salt	

2. The evening meal is composed of clear liquids (bouillon, clear juice, tea, and gelatin dessert).

18. ¿Tiene hambre?
19. ¿Está satisfecho/a?
20. ¿Hay algo que le podemos traer?

Dieta para Exceso de Base–Pielograma Intravenoso o para Examen de Urograma Excretorio

Propósito

Para proveer una cantidad limitada de comida restringida en ambos residuo y grasa como medida preparataria para el examen B.E. (exceso de base)-I.V.P. (examen de urograma excretorio) del día siguiente.

Características

1. La comida del mediodía para el día antes de la prueba consiste en los siguientes alimentos:

a. jugo claro	½ taza
b. caldo claro	1 taza
c. tajadas de pavo o pollo, sin grasa o pellejo	3 onzas
d. gelatina sola	½ taza
e. pan blanco o tostado	2 rebanadas
f. leche descremada	1 taza
g. sal	

2. La comida de la noche consiste en líquidos claros (caldo, jugo claro, té, y gelatina).

3. After the evening meal only water may be given until midnight.

4. Nothing by mouth (NPO) after midnight when the urogram is scheduled before 11:00 a.m. If the urogram is scheduled after 11:00 a.m., a breakfast having less than one (1) cup fluids is given as follows:

a. black coffee	½ cup
b. clear juice	¼ cup
c. poached egg	1 egg
d. white toast or	1 slice/
English muffin	½ muffin
e. clear jelly	
f. sugar and salt	

Motor Meal Test Diet

Purpose

This test is used to show how the stomach empties physiologically after a meal has been taken. A conventional gastrointestinal series may appear normal but when the motor meal is used, disorders may appear.

3. Después de la comida de la noche se puede dar sólo agua hasta la medianoche.

4. Nada por boca después de la medianoche cuando se tantea el urograma antes de las once de la mañana. Si el urograma está planeado después de las once de la mañana, un desayuno que consiste de menos de una taza de flúidos se da como sigue:

a. café solo	½ taza
b. jugo claro	¼ taza
c. huevo escalfado o tibio	1 huevo
d. pan blanco tostado o	1 tajada
pan inglés tostado	½ pieza
e. jalea clara	
f. azúcar y sal	

Dieta para Prueba de Comida Motor

Propósito

Esta prueba se usa para demostrar cómo se vacía el estómago fisiológicamente después de que se haya consumido una comida. Una serie convencional gastrointestinal puede parecer normal pero cuando se usa una comida motor, pueden aparecer desórdenes.

Characteristics

The meal used includes the following foods:

1. 120 grams fibrous meat (not ground).
2. Cooked cereal, cream, sugar.
3. Soft-cooked egg.
4. 2 slices toast and margarine.
5. 8 ounces milk.

Sample Menu

1. Orange juice.
2. Oatmeal, nondairy creamer, sugar.
3. 120 gm ham.
4. Toast and margarine.
5. 8 ounces low-fat milk.
6. Coffee.
7. Salt and pepper.

No Added Salt Diet

The No Added Salt Diet consists of regular foods except for those having a very high sodium content.

Características

La comida puede incluir los siguientes elementos:

1. 120 (ciento veinte) gramos de carne fibrosa (no molida).
2. Cereal cocido, crema, azúcar.
3. Huevo tibio.
4. 2 (dos) tajadas de pan tostado con margarina.
5. 8 (ocho) onzas de leche.

Menú Ejemplar

1. Jugo de naranja.
2. Avena, crema (no de leche), azúcar.
3. 120 (ciento veinte) gramos de jamón.
4. Pan tostado con margarina.
5. 8 (ocho) onzas de leche baja en grasa (descremada).
6. Café.
7. Sal y pimienta.

Dieta Sin Sal Adicional

La Dieta Sin Sal Adicional consiste en alimentos regulares excepto ésos que contienen una cantidad muy alta de sodio (sal).

Guidelines

1. No special foods are required for this diet.
2. Approximately _____ tsp salt per day may be used in cooking, but do not add salt at the table.
3. Salt substitutes may be used with the doctor's permission.

Foods to Avoid

1. Meats and meat products.
   a. Salty or smoked meats, such as bacon, bologna, corned beef, chipped beef, frankfurters, ham, luncheon meats, salt pork, or sausage.
   b. Commercially prepared dishes such as casseroles, frozen dinners or entrees, Mexican, Chinese, or Italian dishes.

   c. Salty canned or smoked fish, such as anchovies, caviar, salted and dried cod, herring, sardines, or tuna.
   d. Cheese, except cottage cheese or cream cheese. Limit buttermilk to 1 cup (8 oz) per day.

2. Vegetables
   a. Sauerkraut, pickles, or others prepared in brine.

   b. Excessive amounts of canned vegetables.
   c. Regular canned tomato or V-8 juice.
3. Snack foods—potato chips, pretzels, corn chips, salted popcorn, or salted crackers.

Normas

1. No se requieren alimentos especiales para esta dieta.
2. Aproximadamente _____ cucharitas de sal al día se pueden usar al cocinar, pero no añada sal en la mesa.
3. Substitutos para la sal se pueden usar con el permiso del médico.

Alimentos Que Se Deben Evitar

1. Carnes y productos de carne
   a. Carnes saladas o ahumadas, tal como tocino, salchichón, carne en salmuera, carne seca, salchichas, jamón, carnes frías, puerco salado, o chorizo.
   b. Platos preparados comercialmente tal como caserolas, comidas congeladas, platillos mexicanos, chinos o italianos.
   c. Pescado salado, enlatado o ahumado, tal como anchoas, caviar, bacalao salado y seco, arenque, sardinas o atún.
   d. Queso, excepto requesón o queso de crema. Limite leche agria (leche de mantequilla) a una taza (ocho onzas) al día.

2. Legumbres
   a. Chucruta, encurtidos u otras legumbres preparadas en salmuera.
   b. Cantidades excesivas de legumbres enlatadas.
   c. Jugo enlatado de tomate o Jugo V-8.
3. Comidas entremedias—papas fritas, roscas saladas, tostados de maíz, rosetas (palomitas) de maíz con sal, o galletas saladas.

4. Miscellaneous
   a. Commercially canned or dried soups or bouillon cubes; commercially canned gravies.
   b. Commercial salad dressings other than oil and vinegar or mayonnaise. Low-sodium salad dressings may be used.
   c. Olives, pickles, or relishes.
   d. Limit commercially baked products containing baking powder or baking soda to two small servings per day (biscuits, muffins, quick breads, cakes, cookies, and so on).
5. Flavorings
   a. Condiments: catsup, mustard (may use dried), relishes, steak sauces, soy sauce, horseradish prepared with salt, barbecue sauce. (Many of these products are available salt free.)
   b. Spices: monosodium glutamate, garlic, onion or celery salt (powder may be used).
   c. Meat tenderizers and meat extracts.
   d. Seasoning mixes: packaged dry mixes for beef stew, beef stroganoff, chili, sloppy joe, spaghetti and similar dishes.

4. Misceláneo
   a. Sopas o caldos enlatados o cubitos de caldo, salsas o jugos de carne enlatados.
   b. Salsas de ensalada más que aceite y vinagre o mayonesa. Se pueden usar salsas de ensalada bajas en sodio (sal).
   c. Aceitunas, pepinos curtidos, encurtidos.
   d. Limite productos de panadería que contengan levadura química o carbonato a dos porciones pequeñas al día (bizcochos, bollos, panes ligeros, pasteles, galletitas, y otros productos semejantes).
5. Aderezos
   a. Condimentos: salsa de tomate, mostaza (se pueden usar la seca), encurtidos, salsas para bistec, salsa soy, rábano picante preparado con sal, salsa de barbacoa. (Muchos de estos productos se pueden obtener sin sal.)
   b. Especias: monosodio glutamate, sal de ajo, de cebolla o de apio (se pueden usar en polvo).
   c. Ablandadores para carnes, y extractos de carne.
   d. Mezclas para sazonar: mezclas secas en paquete para cocidos, para cocido stroganoff, de chile, para picadillo, para espaguetis y para otros platillos semejantes.

If desired, you may substitute any of the following for ¼ tsp. salt:

A-1 Sauce	2 tablespoons
Barbecue sauce	3 tablespoons
Catsup	3 tablespoons
Prepared mustard	
Yellow and brown type	4 tablespoons
Horseradish and German	2 tablespoons
Soy sauce	½ tablespoon
Lemon pepper	$^3/_4$ teaspoon
Monosodium glutamate	1 teaspoon
Garlic or onion salt	$^1/_3$ teaspoon

Liquid Diets

A liquid diet consists of clear fluids that leave minimal residue and can be absorbed easily. Foods included are fluid or become fluid at body temperature. A clear liquid diet is nutritionally inadequate and should be used only for a short period of time.

Suggested Uses

Before or after operations; during very acute conditions in which regular foods are not tolerated.

Si gusta, usted puede substituir cualquiera de los siguientes por ¼ (cuarta) cucharita de sal:

Salsa A-1	2 (dos)	(2) cucharas
Salsa de barbacoa	3 (tres)	(3) cucharas
Salsa de tomate	3 (tres)	(3) cucharas
Mostaza preparada		
Tipo amarillo y moreno	4 (cuatro)	(4) cucharas
Rábano picante y alemán	2 (dos)	(2) cucharas
Salsa soy	½ (media)	cuchara
Pimienta con limón	¾ (tres cuartos de)	cucharita
Monosodio glutamate	1 (una)	cucharita
Sal de ajo o de cebolla	$^1/_3$ (un tercero de)	cucharita

Dietas de Líquidos

Una dieta de líquido consiste en líquidos que dejan residuo mínimo, y que el cuerpo puede absorber con facilidad. Los alimentos incluidos son fluídos o se hacen fluídos con la temperatura del cuerpo. Una dieta de líquido no es adecuada para satisfacer las necesidades del cuerpo y no se debe seguir por mucho tiempo.

Usos Sugeridos

Antes o después de una operación; durante una condición o estado grave o serio cuando el cuerpo no puede soportar comida sólida.

Foods Included (all others are not recommended)

1. Clear broths, bouillon, consommes.
2. Clear flavored gelatin.
3. Popsicles.
4. Tea, coffee, carbonated beverages.
5. Clear fruit-flavored beverages such as Kool-Aid.
6. Clear and strained fruit juices as tolerated.
7. Sugar, honey, clear syrups.
8. Hard clear candies.
9. Salt.

Sample Menu

Morning
  Apple juice
  Broth
  Gelatin, flavored
  Coffee
  Sugar

Morning snack
  Cranberry juice

Noon
  Strained grape juice
  Consommé
  Gelatin, flavored
  Hard clear candy
  Tea

Alimentos Incluidos (todos otros no son recomendados)

1. Caldos claros.
2. Agua de gelatina.
3. Sorbetes en paleta (Popsicles).
4. Té, café, aguas gaseosas.
5. Refrescos claros de sabores frutas, como Kool-Aid.
6. Jugos de fruta colados y claros.
7. Azúcar, miel.
8. Dulces que son duros y claros.
9. Sal.

Muestra de un Menú

Por la mañana
  Jugo de manzana
  Caldo
  Gelatina de sabor
  Café
  Azúcar

Tentempiés por la mañana
  Jugo de arándano

Al mediodía
  Jugo de uva
  Consomé
  Gelatina de sabor
  Dulces
  Té

Afternoon snack
   Popsicle

Evening
   Gingerale
   Strained orange juice
   Gelatin, flavored
   Hard clear candy
   Coffee

Bedtime snack
   Gelatin, flavored
   Tea

Tentempiés por la tarde
   Sorbete en paleta (Popsicle)

Por la noche
   7-Up
   Jugo claro de naranja
   Gelatina de sabor
   Dulces
   Café

Tentempiés antes de acostarse
   Gelatina de sabor
   Té

Coronary Care Unit (CCU) Diet

1. A CCU diet consists of low-fat and low-cholesterol foods.

2. 3 eggs per week (no more).

3. Fish, poultry, veal, or lean meats, but no more than one red meat per day.

4. Non-fat milk instead of whole milk.

5. Decaffeinated instead of caffeinated coffee.

6. No ice, ice cream, or sherbet while on CCU. Nothing very cold or very hot to stimulate the heart.

Dieta de Cuidado Cardíaco (del Corazón)

1. La dieta de cuidado cardíaco (CCU) consiste en alimentos de poca grasa y poco colesterol.

2. 3 (tres) huevos por semana (no más).

3. Pescado, aves (pollo), ternera, o carnes sin grasa, pero no más de 1 (una) carne por día.

4. Leche desnatada en vez de leche entera.

5. Café decafeinado en vez de café entero.

6. Mientras en dieta CCU no tome hielo, helados o nieve. Nada demasiado frío o demasiado caliente que estimule el corazón.

Bland Diet

1. A bland diet consists of six small feedings.
2. No coffee, tea, alcoholic beverages, cola, strong spices, fried foods, or raw vegetables or fruit.
3. Same diet is followed for patient with ulcers but raw vegetables and fruit may be added to the patient's tolerance.
4. If citrus or tomato juice is not tolerated, ascorbic acid supplementation may be necessary.

Protein-Restricted Diet

Purpose

To restrict protein

Characteristics

Any level of protein restriction may be ordered. The following diet is for severe restriction (0–3 grams).

1. This diet is used as a temporary measure in the treatment of hepatic coma or acute renal failure. It is inadequate in almost all nutrients. Calories that are provided in the form of carbohydrate and fat may be inadequate when total fluid is limited.

Dieta Blanda

1. La dieta blanda consiste en 6 (seis) comidas pequeñas.
2. Nada de café, té, bebidas alcohólicas, coca, especias fuertes, comida frita, ni lugumbres o frutas crudas.
3. La misma dieta se usa para el paciente con úlceras pero se pueden añadir legumbres y frutas así como el paciente las tolere.
4. Si no se toleran jugos cítricos o jugo de tomate, será necesario suplir el ácido ascórbico.

Dieta de Proteína Limitada

Propósito

Para limitar la proteína

Características

Cualquier nivel de restricción de proteína se puede ordenar. La dieta siguiente es para restricción severa (0–3 gramos).

1. Esta dieta se emplea como medida temporaria en el tratamiento de coma hepática o de agudo colapso renal. Es inadecuada en casi todos los nutricios. Las calorías que se proveen en forma de carbohidrato y grasa pueden ser inadecuadas cuando se limita el flúido en total.

2. The only foods allowed are:
   a. sugar
   b. syrup
   c. carbonated beverages
   d. Kool-Aid
   e. concentrated glucose solutions (approximately 60 calories per ounce)
   f. sugar candy
   g. butterballs
   h. coffee
   i. tea
   j. specially prepared low protein products made with wheat starch (for example, cookies, pudding, rusks)

3. These foods provide a minimum of sodium. The potassium value varies with the inclusion of coffee and tea.

Low-Residue Diet

Purpose

To reduce the amount of residue in the lower bowel and to decrease fecal output

2. Los únicos alimentos permitidos son:
   a. azúcar
   b. almíbar
   c. bebidas carbonadas (gaseosas)
   d. Kool-Aid
   e. soluciones concentradas de glucosa (aproximadamente 60 calorías por onza)
   f. dulces de azúcar
   g. bombones de azúcar y mantequilla (butterballs)
   h. café
   i. té
   j. productos de baja proteína especialmente preparados, hechos con almidón de trigo (por ejemplo, galletas, pudín, panecillos tostados)

3. Estos alimentos proveen un mínimo de sodio. El valor del potasio varía con la inclusión de café o té.

Dieta Baja en Residuo

Propósito

Para reducir la cantidad de residuo en el intestino inferior y para disminuir la producción fecal

Characteristics

1. Dietary fiber is reduced by using refined cereal grains, whole well-cooked tender vegetables, cooked or canned fruits (without any skins or seeds), and tender meats. Strained fruits and strained vegetables are not stipulated because of their unacceptability.
2. Fried or spicy foods may be included, unless bland modification is ordered.
3. Milk and milk products, such as cheese, are not restricted.
4. Foods that may contribute to elevated cholesterol or triglycerides are limited.

Foods to Exclude

1. Less tender, fibrous meats; frankfurters or other sausage in a casing
2. Raw egg
3. All raw vegetables
4. Potato skins
5. Prunes; seeds and coarse skins of fruits
6. Prune juice
7. Whole-grain cereals; bran flakes; all-bran; granola
8. Breads: whole wheat, rye, pumpernickel, raisin, or any containing seeds
9. Crackers: any containing whole-grain flours

Características

1. La fibra dietaria se reduce con el use de granos de cereales refinados, legumbres enteras pero bien cocidas, frutas cocidas o enlatadas (sin ningún pellejo ni semillas), y carnes tiernas. Frutas y legumbres coladas no son estipuladas a causa de su inaceptabilidad.
2. Se pueden incluir alimentos fritos o picantes, a menos que no se exija modificación blanda.
3. Leche y productos de leche, tal como queso no son restringidos.
4. Alimentos que pueden contribuir colesterol elevado o triglicéridos son limitados.

Alimentos que se Deben Evitar

1. Carnes menos tiernas y con fibra. Salchichas u otra carne en envoltura.
2. Huevo crudo
3. Todas legumbres crudas
4. Cáscaras de papas
5. Ciruelas pasas; semillas y pellejos toscos de frutas
6. Jugo de ciruela pasa
7. Cereales de grano entero; hojuelas de afrecho (bran flakes); afrecho puro (all-bran); granola
8. Panes: de trigo entero, de centeno, pan negro (pumpernickel) de pasas o cualquiera que contengan semillas
9. Galletas: cualesquiera que contengan harina de grano entero

10. Brown rice and wild rice

11. Nuts, olives

12. Soups made with dried peas or beans

13. Desserts containing coconut, nuts, raisins, or other dried fruits

14. Candies containing coconut, nuts, or dried fruits

15. Olives and pickles

10. Arroz moreno y arroz silvestre

11. Nueces y aceitunas

12. Sopas preparadas con chícharos (guisantes) secos o con frijoles secos

13. Postres que contienen coco, nueces, pasas, u otras frutas secas

14. Dulces que contienen coco, nueces o frutas

15. Aceitunas y encurtidos

Foods

Alimentos

1. the meals
   (the three meals)
2. proteins
3. calories
4. vitamins

1. las comidas
   (las tres comidas)
2. las proteínas
3. las calorías
4. las vitaminas

Meats

1. beef
2. pork

3. lamb, sheep

4. chicken, hen, turkey
5. meatball
6. steak
7. chop

Carnes

1. la carne de res, de vaca
2. la carne de puerco,
   de cerdo
3. la carne de borrego,
   de carnero
4. el pollo, la gallina, el pavo
5. la albóndiga
6. el bistec, el biftec
7. la chuleta

5. meats
6. fish, seafood
7. vegetables

8. grains, cereals

5. la carne, las carnes
6. el pescado, los mariscos
7. los vegetales, las verduras, legumbres
8. los cereales

8. lamb chop

9. pork chop

10. veal chop

11. ham
12. bacon
13. sausage

8. la chuleta de cordero,
   la costilla de cordero
9. la chuleta de cerdo, de
   puerco, de lechón
10. la chuleta de ternera,
    la costeleta de ternera
11. el jamón
12. el tocino
13. el chorizo

Seafoods	Mariscos
1. clam	1. la almeja
2. tuna fish	2. el atún
3. cod fish	3. el bacalao
4. shrimp, jumbo shrimp	4. el camarón, la gamba, el langostino
5. crab	5. el cangrejo

6. lobster	6. la langosta
7. filet of sole	7. el lenguado
8. halibut	8. el halibut
9. oyster	9. la ostra
10. flounder	10. el rodaballo
11. salmon	11. el salmón

Milk and Dairy Products	Leche y Productos Lácteos
1. milk, cow's	1. la leche de vaca
2. milk, goat's	2. la leche de cabra
3. raw milk	3. la leche cruda
4. boiled milk	4. la leche hervida
5. low-fat milk	5. la leche desgrasada
6. skim milk	6. la leche descremada

7. powdered milk	7. la leche en polvo
8. evaporated milk	8. la leche evaporada
9. condensed milk	9. la leche condensada
10. cream	10. la crema
11. cheese	11. el queso
12. cottage cheese	12. el requesón

Vegetables	Legumbres, Vegetales, Verduras
1. avocado	1. el aguacate (la palta)
2. beans green beans/ string beans	2. las habichuelas (los frijoles); las habichuelas (las judías verdes, los ejotes)
3. Brussels sprouts	3. los coles de Bruselas
4. cabbage	4. la col, el repollo
5. carrot	5. la zanahoria
6. cauliflower	6. la coliflor
7. celery	7. el apio
8. corn	8. el maíz
9. garlic	9. el ajo

10. lettuce	10. la lechuga
11. lentils	11. las lentejas
12. onion	12. la cebolla
13. pea	13. el guisante, el chícharo
14. pepper, green	14. el chile verde, el pimiento verde
15. potato mashed potatoes	15. la papa, patata el puré de papas
16. tomato	16. el tomate, el tomatillo el jitomate
17. sweet potato	17. el camote
18. yam	18. el camote amarillo

Fruits

1. apple
2. apricot
3. banana
4. blackberry
5. cherry
6. cranberry
7. grapefruit
8. lemon
9. lime

Frutas

1. la manzana
2. el albaricoque
3. el plátano, la banana
4. el moro
5. la cereza
6. el arándano
7. la toronja
8. el limón
9. la lima

10. orange
11. peach
12. pineapple
13. plum
14. prune
15. raspberry
16. strawberry
17. tomato

10. la naranja
11. el durazno, el melocotón
12. la piña
13. la ciruela
14. la ciruela pasa
15. la frambuesa
16. la fresa
17. el tomate

Bread, Flour, and Grains

1. bread
   white bread
   toast
2. cake
3. cereal
4. corn meal
5. cupcakes
6. flour, rice
   flour, wheat

Pan, Harinas y Granos

1. el pan
   el pan blanco
   el pan tostado
2. el pastel
3. el cereal
4. la harina de maíz
5. los pastelitos
6. la harina de arroz
   la harina de trigo

7. rice
8. rolls, French
   rolls, sweet
9. spaghetti
10. tortilla, corn
    tortilla, white flour
11. wheat germ

7. el arroz
8. el pan francés
   el pan dulce, los bizcochos
9. los fideos
10. la tortilla de maíz
    la tortilla de harina
11. el gérmen de trigo

Lard and Fats

1. butter
2. lard
   lard, beef

Manteca y Grasas

1. la mantequilla
2. la manteca de puerco
   el unto de res, el sebo

3. oil
   oil, cooking
   oil, olive
4. peanut butter

3. el aceite
   el aceite para cocinar
   el aceite de oliva
4. la crema de cacahuate,
   mantequilla de maní

Sugar, Sweets, and Desserts

1. cake
2. candy
3. cookie
4. cupcake
5. custard
6. ice cream

Drinks

1. beer
2. coffee
3. juice
   lemon juice
   orange juice

Miscellaneous

1. egg
   omelet, or Mexican
   "torta de huevo"
2. fried
3. hors d'oeuvres

Typical Spanish Dishes

1. roast chicken
2. roast chicken with rice
3. rice dish with meat, seafood, vegetables

Azúcar, Dulces y Postres

1. el pastel, la torta, la tarta
2. los dulces
3. la galleta, la galletita
4. el bizcocho, el pastelito
5. el flan, las natillas
6. el helado

Bebidas

1. la cerveza
2. el café
3. el jugo (zumo)
   el jugo de limón
   el jugo de naranja

Misceláneo

1. el huevo
   la tortilla (la torta)
   de huevos
2. frito
3. los bocaditos, el
   entremés

Platillos Típicos Españoles

1. el pollo asado
2. el pollo asado con arroz
3. la paella

7. jam
8. jelly
9. nougat
10. pie
11. sugar
    brown sugar
    raw sugar

4. lemonade
5. milk
6. tea (cup of tea)
7. wine

4. menu
5. pepper (seasoning)
6. salad
7. salt
8. sauce or gravy
9. soup

4. chick peas
5. cold vegetable soup
6. suckling pig
7. Spanish stew

7. la mermelada, la conserva
8. la jalea
9. el turrón
10. el pastel
11. el azúcar
    el azúcar moreno
    el azúcar crudo

4. la limonada
5. la leche
6. el té (taza de té)
7. el vino

4. la lista, el menú
5. la pimienta
6. la ensalada
7. la sal
8. la salsa
9. la sopa

4. los garbanzos
5. el gazpacho
6. el lechón
7. el cocido

Nutritional Problems and Diseases

1. Diabetes
2. Obesity
3. Malnutrition, person with malnutrition
4. Excessive carbohydrate intake
5. Excessive sugar intake
6. Cholesterol
7. Hypoglycemia

HOSPITAL VOLUNTEERS*

1. Hello, Good morning, good afternoon, good evening.
2. How are you feeling?
3. My name is _____. I am a hospital volunteer.
4. What is your name?
5. Can I help you in any way?
6. These flowers are for you.
7. Would you like to speak with the chaplain?
8. Of what religion are you?

Problemas y Enfermedades de la Nutrición

1. La diabetes
2. La obesidad, la gordura
3. La desnutrición, desnutrido(a)
4. El exceso de carbohidratos
5. El exceso de azúcares
6. El colesterol
7. La hipoglicemia

VOLUNTARIOS DEL HOSPITAL

1. Hola. Buenos días, buenas tardes, buenas noches.
2. ¿Cómo se siente usted?
3. Me llamo _____. Soy un(a) voluntario(a) del hospital.
4. ¿Cómo se llama usted?
5. ¿En qué puedo ayudarle?
6. Estas flores son para usted.
7. ¿Quisiera usted hablar con el capellán?
8. ¿Cuál es su religión?

*For additional phrases and conversational leads, see Useful Words and Phrases, beginning on p. 314 in the Language Necessities section.

MEDICAL SOCIAL WORKERS

1. I am one of the hospital social workers. You asked to see me?

2. How can I help you?

3. I am the social worker
   a. on this floor.
   b. on this service.
   c. on this unit.
   d. who will be working with you and the rehabilitation team.

4. Your doctor has asked me to see you
   a. about your plans for discharge.
   b. about your concerns.
   c. about your home situation. Do you live alone? Will someone be available to help you? Family composition?

5. Would you prefer to speak in English or Spanish?

6. Please repeat that, I don't quite understand.

7. Do you know where you are?

8. Do you know that you are in a hospital?

9. Does your family know you are here?

10. Do you want to contact anyone?

11. Where were you living before you came into the hospital?

TRABAJADORES SOCIALES MÉDICOS

1. Soy uno de los trabajadores sociales del hospital. ¿Ud. quería verme?

2. ¿En qué puedo ayudarle?

3. Soy el/la trabajador(a) social
   a. en este piso.
   b. en este servicio.
   c. en esta unidad.
   d. que va a trabajar con usted y con el equipo de rehabilitación.

4. Su médico me ha pedido que le vea
   a. sobre sus planes para cuando salga de aquí.
   b. sobre sus problemas.
   c. sobre su situación en casa. ¿Vive solo? ¿Habrá alguien disponible para ayudarle? ¿Miembros de la familia?

5. ¿Prefiere hablar en español o en inglés?

6. Favor de repetir eso. No entiendo.

7. ¿Sabe dónde está usted?

8. ¿Sabe que usted está en un hospital? ¿Sabe por qué está aquí?

9. ¿Sabe su familia que usted está aquí?

10. ¿Quiere ponerse en contacto con alguien?

11. ¿Dónde vivía usted antes de que viniera al hospital?

12. Will you be able to return there?

13. Why can't you return there?

14. Is there someone who can transport you (bring you) to your appointments? Take you home?

15. Will you need help at home?

16. Your doctor believes it would be best to have a visiting nurse (public health nurse) come by and see you to make sure you are managing all right.

17. Do you understand what activities you are to avoid?

18. Do you understand what you are able to do?

19. Do you have a community social worker?

20. Do you think alcohol has been a major problem for you?

21. Have you ever been to an alcohol-recovery home?

22. Have you seen a psychiatrist before?

23. Have you ever been in a psychiatric facility?

24. Do you have a conservator or someone to help manage your finances?

25. Have you made any funeral arrangements?

26. What do you want to do about your discharge?

27. What do you want to do about your situation?

28. What do you hope to accomplish by that?

12. ¿Podrá usted regresar allí?

13. ¿Por qué no puede regresar allí?

14. ¿Hay alguien que pueda llevarle a sus citas? Llevarle a casa?

15. ¿Va a necesitar ayuda en casa?

16. Su médico cree que sería mejor tener una enfermera visitante (enfermera de Salud Pública) que venga a verle para asegurar que usted maneja bien.

17. ¿Entiende cuáles actividades usted debe evitar?

18. ¿Entiende lo que puede hacer?

19. ¿Tiene un trabajador social de la comunidad?

20. ¿Cree que el alcohol ha sido un problema mayor para usted?

21. ¿Ha ido alguna vez a una casa de recuperación del alcoholismo?

22. ¿Ha visto a un psiquíatra antes de esto?

23. ¿Ha estado alguna vez en una casa psiquiátrica?

24. ¿Tiene un conservador o alguien que pueda ayudarle con sus finanzas?

25. ¿Ha hecho algunos arreglos funerarios?

26. ¿Qué quiere hacer tocante a su salida de aquí?

27. ¿Qué quiere hacer tocante a su situación?

28. ¿Qué espera realizar con esa decisión?

29. Your doctor has recommended temporary convalescent placement. How do you feel about going to a nursing home until you are strong enough to go home?

30. Do you understand the severity of your child's illness?

31. Does your child understand what is wrong with him/her?

32. Have you talked to your child about his/her illness?

33. How is he/she reacting?

34. Do you feel comfortable talking with your child about what's happening to him/her?

35. Do you remember the accident? Who was involved?

36. How do you feel about what happened?

37. How do you think your family feels about what happened?

38. Do you think your life will be much different?

39. Are you ready for those changes?

40. How do you feel about this pregnancy?

41. How do your family/friends feel about your being pregnant?

42. Are you still involved with the father of the baby?

43. Does he know you are pregnant? Will you let him know? How has he reacted?

44. Are you planning to keep the baby or put it up for adoption?

29. Su doctor ha recomendado colocación temporaria de convaleciente. ¿Qué piensa Ud. de ir a una casa para convalecientes hasta que esté bastante fuerte para regresar a casa?

30. ¿Entiende la severidad de la enfermedad de su niño(a)?

31. ¿Entiende su niño(a) lo que le pasa?

32. ¿Ha hablado con su niño(a) sobre su enfermedad?

33. ¿Cómo reacciona?

34. ¿Se siente a gusto hablando con su niño(a) sobre lo que le está pasando?

35. ¿Recuerda el accidente? ¿Qué pasó?

36. ¿Cómo se siente sobre lo que pasó?

37. ¿Cómo cree usted que se siente su familia sobre lo que pasó?

38. ¿Cree usted que su vida será muy diferente?

39. ¿Está listo(a) para esos cambios?

40. ¿Qué piensa Ud. de este embarazo?

41. ¿Qué piensa su familia/sus amigos de que está embarazada?

42. ¿Todavía tiene tratos con el padre del bebé?

43. ¿Sabe él que usted está embarazada? ¿Le avisará Ud. a él? ¿Cómo ha reaccionado él?

44. ¿Piensa Ud. quedarse con el bebé o darlo(la) para adopción?

45. How have you felt during this pregnancy?

46. As part of this service for your pregnancy, a public health nurse will be out to see you.

47. Where were you working prior to your accident?

48. Do you think you'll be able to return to the same job?

49. Does your spouse work?

50. What type of income will you have?

51. What type of insurance do you have?

52. Have you applied for any type of aid/assistance?

53. Have you applied for State Disability?

54. Have you applied for Social Security Disability?

55. You will need to contact your local Social Security Office to find out what might be available for you now that you have a long-term disability.

56. Medi-Cal and Medicaid applications are available from our eligibility workers.

57. You can also find out from them what else you might be eligible for, such as food stamps, General Assistance, homemaker services.

58. Do you have any questions about what the doctor has told you?

59. Have you any questions about what I've said?

60. Please telephone me if you have other comments or concerns.

61. Here is my name and where I can be reached.

45. Cómo se ha sentido durante este embarazo?

46. Como parte de este servicio para su embarazo, una enfermera de Salud Pública vendrá a verla.

47. ¿Dónde trabajaba antes de su accidente?

48. ¿Cree Ud. que pueda regresar al mismo trabajo?

49. ¿Trabaja su esposo(a)?

50. ¿Qué tipo de ingresos tendrá?

51. ¿Qué clase de seguro tiene?

52. ¿Ha solicitado algún tipo de ayuda?

53. ¿Ha solicitado del Estado por Incapacidad?

54. ¿Ha solicitado del Seguro Social por Incapacidad?

55. Ud. tendrá que ponerse en contacto con su oficina local del Seguro Social para averiguar lo que pudiera estar disponible para Ud., ahora que tiene una incapacidad de largo plazo.

56. Solicitudes de Medi-Cal y Medicaid están disponibles de nuestros trabajadores de elegibilidad.

57. Ud. también puede informarse por medio de ellos para qué más será elegible, como estampillas para comida, Asistencia General, servicios caseros.

58. ¿Tiene algunas preguntas de lo que le ha dicho su médico?

59. ¿Tiene algunas preguntas de lo que he dicho?

60. Favor de telefonearme si tiene otros comentarios o problemas.

61. Aquí tiene mi nombre y dónde puede llamarme.

SWITCHBOARD

1. This is the operator. May I help you?
2. What can I do for you?
3. Do you want to make a call?
4. Is the call local or long distance? Is it collect or billed to your home?
5. Please hang up, dial the area code and then the number. For local calls, dial 9 and the number.

6. Stay on the line, and I will give you a long-distance operator.
7. Please have your nurse help you with your call.

8. What number do you want?
9. What room number do you want?
10. What is the patient's name?

11. Is it about a bill?
12. The line is busy. Please call back.
13. The patient has been discharged.
14. Sorry. I cannot hear you.
15. I will get someone to help you.

CUADRO DE DISTRIBUCIÓN

1. Esta es la operadora. ¿En qué puedo ayudarle?
2. ¿En qué puedo servirle?
3. ¿Quiere hacer una llamada?
4. ¿Es local o de larga distancia la llamada? ¿Es una llamada cobrada o que le mandemos la cuenta a su casa?
5. Por favor, cuelgue, marque el código del área y luego el número. Para llamadas locales, marque 9 (nueve) y luego el número.
6. Por favor, espere un momento y le comunicaré con una operadora de larga distancia.
7. Por favor, que le ayude su enfermera con su llamada telefónica.
8. ¿Qué número quiere?
9. ¿Qué número de cuarto quiere?
10. ¿Cómo se llama el enfermo (la enferma). ¿Me puede decir el nombre del enfermo (de la enferma)?
11. ¿Se trata de una cuenta?
12. La línea está ocupada. Llame de nuevo.
13. Al enfermo (a la enferma) se le ha dado de alta.
14. Lo siento. No puedo oírle.
15. (In person) Traeré a una persona.
    (On phone) Buscaré a una persona que le pueda ayudar.

16. Sorry, I cannot understand you.
17. Do you have the correct number?
18. Speak more slowly, please.

16. Lo siento, pero no le comprendo.
17. ¿Tiene usted el número correcto?
18. Hable más despacio, por favor.

AIDES AND HOMEMAKER SERVICE

1. Would you like help with a bath?
2. Would you like something to eat—breakfast, lunch, snack?
3. Would you like something to drink? Water, juice (orange, pineapple, grapefruit, prune, cranberry, apple)?
4. Can I make a meal for you today for you to eat tomorrow?
5. May I do your laundry?
6. Do you feel hot/cold?
7. Are you comfortable?

AYUDANTES Y SERVICIO CASERO

1. ¿Quisiera ayuda con un baño?
2. ¿Quisiera algo que comer—desayuno, almuerzo, merienda (bocadito)?
3. ¿Quisiera algo que beber? ¿Agua, jugo (de naranja, de piña, de toronja, de ciruela pasa, de arándano, de manzana)?
4. ¿Puedo prepararle una comida para que Ud. pueda comerla mañana?
5. ¿Puedo lavar su ropa?
6. ¿Tiene calor/frío?
7. ¿Está usted cómodo(a) (a gusto)?

VISITING NURSES

1. How is your appetite?
2. How many glasses of liquid do you drink each day?
3. How do you feel?
4. When was your last bowel movement?

ENFERMERAS VISITANTES

1. ¿Cómo está su apetito?
2. ¿Cuántos vasos de líquido toma Ud. cada día?
3. ¿Cómo se siente?
4. ¿Cuándo fue su última evacuación?

5. I'm going to come to see you at _____.

6. I am the nurse.

7. I am the physical therapist.

8. I will help you to move more easily.

9. Do you understand?

10. Please try to be more active and do as we did today when I am not here.

11. I will return _____.

12. Is there pain, and where?

13. Please do as I am doing.

14. That was very good. Thank you.

15. Relax. I'm not going to hurt you.

5. Vengo a verle a la/las _____.

6. Soy la enfermera.

7. Soy el/la terapista físico(a).

8. Le voy a ayudar a moverse más fácilmente.

9. ¿Entiende usted?

10. Favor de tratar de ser más activo y de hacer lo que hicimos hoy cuando yo no esté aquí.

11. Voy a regresar _____.

12. ¿Hay dolor, y dónde?

13. Favor de hacer lo que hago yo.

14. Eso fue muy bueno. Gracias.

15. Relájese. No le voy a lastimar.

GENERAL HOSPITAL PHRASES

Determining Patient Needs

May I help you?

Do you feel better today?

Did you sleep well?

Are you sleepy?

The doctor will examine you now.

You should remain in bed today.

FRASES GENERALES DEL HOSPITAL

Determinando las Necesidades del (de la) Paciente

¿Puedo ayudarle?

¿Se siente mejor hoy?

¿Durmió bien?

¿Tiene usted sueño?

El doctor le examinará ahora.

Ud. debe guardar cama hoy.

We want to get you up now.	Queremos que se levante ahora.
You may take a bath.	Puede bañarse.
You may take a shower.	Puede tomar una ducha.
I am going to give you a sponge bath now.	Le voy a dar un baño de esponja ahora.
Have you noticed any bleeding from	¿Ha notado alguna hemorragia
the rectum?	del recto?
the vagina?	de la vagina?
the mouth?	de la boca?
I must check for bleeding.	Debo revisar si está sangrando.
Do you still have any numbness?	¿Todavía siente adormecimiento?
This shot will make you sleep.	Esta inyección le hará dormir.
Do you have an earache?	¿Tiene dolor de oído?
Do you have a sore throat?	¿Tiene dolor de garganta?
Do you have a cough?	¿Tiene tos?
Do you have chest pain?	¿Tiene dolor de pecho?
Do you have a headache?	¿Tiene dolor de cabeza?
Do you have a backache?	¿Tiene dolor de espalda?
Do you have any drug allergies?	¿Es usted alergico(a) algún medicamento?
Do you urinate too frequently?	¿Orina con demasiada frecuencia?
Do you have burning when you urinate?	¿Siente ardor al orinar?
Your infection is clearing nicely.	Se está aliviando muy bien su infección.
I want to see your dressing.	Quiero ver su vendaje.
I need to change your dressing.	Necesito cambiar su vendaje.
What medications are you taking now?	¿Qué medicamentos está tomando ahora?

Your cholesterol level is high.	El nivel de su colesterol es alto.
Your triglyceride level is high.	El nivel de su triglicérido es alto.
You must follow a diet to lose weight.	Debe seguir una dieta para perder peso.
Do you need the bedpan?	¿Necesita el bacín (la chata)?
I'm going to put the bedpan on the bed.	Voy a poner el bacín sobre la cama.
Do you need toilet paper?	¿Necesita papel de baño (papel higiénico)?
Are you constipated?	¿Está usted estreñido(a)/constipado(a)?
Do you need a sleeping pill?	¿Necesita una pastilla para dormir?
Do you need a laxative?	¿Necesita un laxante/purgante?

Talking to the Patient's Family

Hablando con la Familia del (de la) Paciente

He/she is recuperating.	El/ella se está recuperando(a).
He/she is unconscious.	El/ella está inconsciente.
There is nothing else we can do.	No podemos hacer más.
He/she feels sore all over.	El/ella se siente adolorido(a) por todas partes.
The patient is getting worse.	El/la paciente se pone más enfermo(a)/peor/más grave.
The patient is getting better.	El/la paciente está mejor.
The patient is in a lot of pain.	El/la paciente tiene mucho dolor.
The patient is out of danger.	El/la paciente está fuera de peligro.
The operation turned out well.	La operación salió bien.
The patient is not expected to live.	No se cree que el/la paciente vaya a vivir.
The patient has been taken to intensive care.	El/la paciente ha sido llevado(a) a la Sala de Cuidado Intensivo.

Obtaining Information

You are in the hospital. You had an accident.

Do you have pain? Where?

Do you know where you are?

What day is it?

What time is it?

What is your problem (complaint)?

Where does it hurt?

Point to where it hurts.

Tell me when you feel pain.

How long have you had this?

Are you in pain?

Would you like some medication for the pain?

Are you dizzy?

Are you having pain?

Are you nauseated?

What does the pain feel like?

Is it a sharp pain or a dull pain?

Obteniendo Información

Ud. está en el hospital. Tuvo un accidente.

¿Tiene usted dolor? ¿Dónde?

¿Sabe dónde está?

¿Qué día es hoy?

¿Qué hora es?

¿Cuál es su problema?
¿De qué se queja usted?

¿Dónde le duele?

Séñale dónde le duele.
Enséñeme dónde le duele.

Dígame cuando sienta dolor.
Avíseme cuando sienta dolor.

¿Desde cuándo tiene esto?
¿Cuánto tiempo hace que tiene esto?

¿Tiene dolor?

¿Quisiera usted medicina para el dolor?

¿Tiene vértigo? ¿Está mareado(a)?

¿Siente dolor?

¿Siente náuseas?

¿Cómo es el dolor?

¿Es un dolor agudo o suave (sordo)?

Does the pain move or radiate?	¿Se extiende/le corre el dolor?
Is it constant?	¿Es constante?
Does the medicine ease the pain?	¿Le alivia el dolor la medicina?
This is a call light. Press the button if you need anything.	Esta es la luz para llamar a la enfermera. Apriete el botón si necesita algo.
I have oxygen for you in this mask. It will help you to breathe easier.	Tengo oxígeno para usted en esta mascarilla. Le ayudará a respirar más fácilmente.
I have to catheterize you.	Tengo que cateterizarle.
I have to give you an enema.	Tengo que ponerle una enema/lavativa.
I have to shave you.	Tengo que rasurarle.
Please put out your cigarette.	Por favor apague su cigarro.
There is no smoking here.	No se puede fumar aquí.
Open your mouth (very wide) (wider).	Abra la boca (muy abierta) (más abierta).
Continue.	Continúe/Siga.
Do you need to pass gas?	¿Necesita usted echar aire? (pasar gas?)
Please try to relax.	Por favor, trate de relajarse.
Are you comfortable?	¿Está usted a gusto/cómodo(a)?
Don't hold your breath.	No mantenga la respiración.
Breathe normally.	Respire normalmente.
Just a few more minutes.	Sólo unos minutos más.
Sniff.	Huela.
The technician must draw blood from your arm.	El técnico tiene que sacarle un poco de sangre de su brazo.
I am going to start an intravenous infusion.	Le voy a empezar un suero.

You will feel a little needle prick.

Sentirá un piquete (pinchazo).

This is medication to relieve your pain.

Esta es medicina para aliviarle el dolor.

Put the pill under your tongue and let it dissolve.

Ponga la pastilla bajo la lengua y deje que se disuelva.

I must give you an injection in the hip.

Tengo que ponerle una inyección en la cadera.

Please roll onto your left side.

Favor de ponerse de costado izquierdo.

Has your pain gone away?

¿Se ha ido (ha desaparecido) su dolor?

I'm going to help you.

Le voy a ayudar.

These electrodes will monitor your heartbeat.

Estos electrodos analizarán los latidos de su corazón.

Take a deep breath, slowly and deeply.

Respire profundo, lenta y profundamente.

Turn to your side.

Póngase de costado.

Flex your knees and raise your buttocks.

Flexione las rodillas y levante las nalgas.

Call when you have to go to the toilet.

Llame cuando tenga que ir al baño.

Press the button when you want a nurse.

Apriete el botón cuando quiera una enfermera.

I must draw some blood for a test.

Debo sacarle un poco de sangre para un análisis.

I am going to give you an injection.

Voy a ponerle una inyección.

I am going to give you a tuberculin skin test.

Voy a hacerle una prueba de tuberculina.

I need to put this tube through your nose, down your throat, into your stomach.

Necesito insertar este tubo por su nariz, por la garganta hasta el estómago.

This is to keep you from vomiting.

Esto es para impedir que vomite.

Fluid Intake/Outtake

You may not eat or drink anything yet, because you may vomit.

You may take a small amount of chipped ice.

What did you drink today?

We must measure how much you drink.

The doctor wants you to drink more fluids.

I want to take your temperature.

The doctor wants you to stay in bed. You must not get up and walk around.

You must lie flat.

I must check your IV.

Your IV is not running. I must fix it.

Please save your urine for us to check.

Please let us know when you have a bowel movement.

We need a specimen. Please save it.

You have fluid in your lungs.

Please take deep breaths and cough strongly to help prevent pneumonia.

Practice on this machine. Try to get all the balls to the top as you take a deep breath.

Have your bowels moved?

Consumo de Líquidos/Pérdidas de Líquidos

Usted no puede comer ni beber nada todavía porque puede vomitar.

Usted puede tomar un poco de hielo triturado.

¿Qué bebió hoy?

Debemos medir cuánto bebe.

El doctor quiere que beba más líquidos.

Quiero tomarle la temperatura.

El doctor quiere que guarde cama. No debe levantarse ni caminar.

Debe extenderse completamente.

Debo examinar (revisar) su suero.

Su suero no funciona. Debo arreglarlo.

Favor de conservar su orina para que la analicemos.

Favor de avisarnos cuando se le haya movido el vientre.

Necesitamos una muestra. Guárdela por favor.

Ud. tiene líquido en los pulmones.

Por favor, respire profundo y tosa fuerte para ayudar a prevenir la pulmonía.

Practique en esta máquina. Trate de poner todas las bolas en la parte de arriba al respirar profundo.

¿Se le ha movido el vientre?

Have you passed gas?	¿Ha pasado gas?
I want you to try and urinate.	Quiero que trate de orinar.

Useful Phrases for the Nursing Supervisor

Frases Útiles para el (la) Supervisor(a) de Enfermeras(os)

Please get the patient up.	Favor de despertar al paciente.
I want this patient turned every 2 hours, and kept off his/her back.	Quiero que usted voltee a este/a paciente cada dos horas y que no esté en la espalda.
Soak this patient's feet in warm water for 20 minutes.	Remoje los pies de este/a paciente en agua tibia por 20 (veinte) minutos.
Keep the patient's heels off the bed.	Alce los talones del/de la paciente.
I want this patient to have more fluids today—offer water frequently.	Quiero que este/a paciente tome más flúidos hoy. Ofrézcale agua con frecuencia.
Bathe this patient carefully. His/Her skin is very fragile.	Bañe a este/a paciente con cuidado. Su piel está muy frágil.
Pad this wheelchair well—otherwise the patient will hurt him/herself.	Almohadille esta silla de ruedas bien. De otro modo el/ella se dañará.
Clean the patient's teeth (dentures) after meals.	Limpie los dientes (la dentadura postiza) del/de la paciente después de las comidas.
Walk this patient at least two times today.	Camine con este/a paciente por lo menos dos veces hoy.
This patient is incontinent. Check her frequently and keep her dry.	Este/a paciente tiene incontinencia. Revísele con frecuencia y manténgalo/a seco/a.
Please use a small amount of shampoo and be sure to rinse her hair very well.	Favor de usar una pequeña cantidad de champú y enjuáguele el pelo bien.
Keep the finger and toe nails short and clean.	Mantenga las uñas de las manos y de los pies cortas y limpias.

Language Necessities

THE ALPHABET

Names of Letters

EL ALFABETO

Nombres de las Letras

Name		Pronunciation	Name		Pronunciation
a	(ah)	ah	n	ehnay	ĕnĕ
b	(be)	bā	ñ	(eñe)	ĕn yĕ
c	(ce)	cā	o	oh	ō
ch	(che)	chā	p	(pe)	pā
d	(de)	dā	q	coo	cū
e	(e)	ā	r	ehray	ĕrĕ
f	(efe)	ĕfĕ	rr	ehrray	ĕrrĕ (roll r's)
g	(ge)	hāy	s	ehsay	ĕsĕ
h	(hache)	hăche	t	(te)	tā
i	(i)	ē	u	oo	ū (oo)
j	(jota)	hōtă	v	(ve chica)	vā
k	kah	că	w	(doble ve)	dōbleh vā
l	eh lay	ĕlĕ	x	(equis)	ĕk ēs
ll	(elle)	ĕh yā	y	(i griega)	(ĭ griēgă) ē grē ā gă
m	ehmay	ĕmĕ	z	(zeta)	zātă

K and W are not Spanish letters and are found only in foreign words in Spanish use, such as kilogramo and Wáshington.

Spelling

1. How do you spell your name?
2. How do you spell your last name?
3. How do you spell your street?
4. How do you spell your doctor's name?
5. How do you spell the name of the city where you were born?

Deletreo

1. ¿Cómo se deletrea su nombre?
2. ¿Cómo se deletrea su apellido?
3. ¿Cómo se deletrea su calle?
4. ¿Cómo se deletrea el apellido de su médico?
5. ¿Cómo se deletrea el nombre de la ciudad donde usted nació?

Pronunciation

A sounds like <u>a</u> in <u>father</u> and is pronounced like a clipped <u>ah</u>.

abortar (to abort) **el abdomen** (the abdomen) **la cama** (the bed)
ayudar (to help) **la amígdala** (the tonsil) **la bata** (the robe)

B has the sound of <u>b</u> in <u>book</u> when it begins a breath group or sentence and when it follows <u>m</u> or <u>n</u>.

el bacín (the basin) **el brazo** (the arm) **el hombre** (the man)
la boca (the mouth) **bañar** (to bathe)

The sound of **B** becomes softened when it is located between vowels.

la cabeza (the head) **el rebozo** (the shawl) **el aborto** (the abortion)

The Spanish **B** and **V** have the same sound.

C has a hard sound, as in <u>come</u> when it occurs before a, <u>o</u>, or <u>u</u> or before a consonant.

la cama (the bed) **la cuna** (the cradle) **el cuello** (the neck) **la cara** (the face)

C before an e or i has an s sound.

la **medicina** (the medicine)   **ciego** (blind)   la **receta** (the prescription)   la **cintura** (the waist)
el **cerebro** (the brain)

CH has the sound of ch in child.

el **muchacho** (the boy)   **chupar** (to suck)   la **noche** (the night)   la **chaqueta** (the jacket)
la **chica** (the girl)

D is a hard dental sound at the beginning of a word.

la **debilidad** (the weakness)   los **dientes** (the teeth)   el **doctor** (the doctor)   **mandar** (to order)
el **dolor** (the pain)

D has a soft or th sound as in them between vowels.

el **lado** (the side)   el **médico** (the doctor)   el **dedo** (the finger)
el **cuidado** (the care)   el **codo** (the elbow)   **mojado** (wet)

E sounds like the e in pet.

el **pecho** (the chest)   el **pelo** (the hair)   la **enfermedad** (the illness)   el **papel** (the paper)
eructar (to belch)   el **bebé** (the baby)   la **espalda** (the back)   el **estómago** (the stomach)
equilibrio (equilibrium)   la **mesa** (the table)   **estornudar** (to sneeze)   **empujar** (to push)

F has the same sound as in English.

la **fiebre** (the fever)   **frío** (cold temperature)   la **fecha** (the date on the
fumar (to smoke)   **flaco** (skinny)   calendar)

G before a, o, or u has a hard sound as in get.

gordo (fat)   las **gafas** (the eyeglasses)   el **gargajo** (the phlegm)   el **gato** (the cat)
el **guante** (the glove)

G before an e or i has a guttural h sound as in the German ach!

la **gente** (the people)　　la **vagina** (the vagina)　　las **alergias** (the allergies)　　los **gemelos** (the twins)

Occasionally a silent u will precede the e or i to indicate that the G is hard, as in go.

pagué (I paid)　　el **hormigueo** (the itch)

To keep the u sound in the -gue or -gui combination, a dieresis (¨) is placed over the u as in:

la **vergüenza** (the shame)　　el **ungüento** (ointment)

H is a silent letter.

humano (human)　　hinchar (to swell)　　las **hormonas** (the hormones)
el **hueso** (the bone)　　el **hígado** (the liver)　　el **huevo** (the egg)

I is a short sound as in machine.

irritable (irritable)　　la **incisión** (the incision)　　el **instrumento** (the instrument)
incómodo (uncomfortable)　　mi (my)

J sounds like a hard English h, a guttural h sound as in the German ach!

la **jeringa** (the syringe)　　las **orejas** (the ears)　　el **juanete** (the bunion)
los **ojos** (the eyes)　　la **aguja** (the needle)　　trabajar (to work)

(K) is not part of the Spanish alphabet. It is used only in words of foreign origin, and it has the same pronunciation as in English.

el **kilo** (the kilogram)　　el **kilómetro** (the kilometer)

L is the same as in English.

la **lengua** (the tongue)　　la **píldora** (the pill)　　el **líquido** (the liquid)
las **lágrimas** (the tears)　　los **labios** (the lips)　　la **luz** (the light)

LL sounds like y in the word yes.

los **tobillos** (the ankles)　　llorar (to cry)　　la **cuchillada** (the gash)
las **costillas** (the ribs)　　la **espaldilla** (the shoulder blade)　　la **mejilla** (the cheek)

M is the same as in English.

morir (to die)   **las manos** (the hands)   **la médula** (the marrow)   **el muslo** (the thigh)

N is pronounced like <u>m</u> before <u>b</u>, <u>f</u>, <u>p</u>, <u>m</u>, and <u>v</u>.

enfermo (sick)   **la enfermera** (the nurse)   **un brazo** (an arm)   **un viejo** (an old man)
un pulmón (a lung)

N otherwise has a nasal sound.

la náusea (the nausea)   **nervioso** (nervous)   **la nariz** (the nose)   **nacer** (to be born)

Ñ has the English sound of <u>canyon</u> or <u>onion</u>.

los riñones (the kidneys)   **el puño** (the fist)   **estreñido** (constipated)   **el sueño** (the dream, sleep)
el señor (Mr., the gentleman, sir)

O sounds like the <u>o</u> in <u>born</u>.

la obesidad (the obesity)   **la oreja** (the ear)   **emocional** (emotional)
el muslo (the thigh)   **no** (no)   **el pelo** (the hair)

O followed by a consonant sounds like the English <u>o</u> in <u>or</u>.

orinar (to urinate)   **el ombligo** (the navel)   **el órgano** (the organ)

P is the same as in English.

la parálisis (the paralysis)   **el pañal** (the diaper)   **poco** (little, referring to
la pulmonía (the pneumonia)   **el papá** (the dad)   quantity)

There are several silent **P**s, as in:

la psicología (psychology)   **la psiquíatra** (the psychiatrist)   **la psicoterapia** (psychotherapy)

Q appears only before <u>ue</u> or <u>ui</u>. The <u>u</u> is always silent and the **Q** has a <u>k</u> sound.

quejar (to complain)   **tranquilo** (tranquil)   **la quijada** (the jaw)
la izquierda (the left)   **los bronquios** (the bronchia)   **el queso** (the cheese)

R is trilled in the initial position.

la roncha (the rash)   **la reumatismo** (rheumatism)   **las rodillas** (the knees)   **el resfriado** (cold in the nose)
la nariz (nose)

R is slightly trilled in the middle of a word.

primo (cousin)   **varicela** (chickenpox)   **la hernia** (the hernia)   **operar** (to operate)

RR is strongly trilled.

el carro (the car)   **el catarro** (cold in the head)   **la diarrea** (diarrhea)
la gonorrea (gonorrhea)   **el perro** (the dog)

S has the <u>ess</u> sound in English.

la saliva (the saliva)   **toser** (to cough)   **el sarampión** (the measles)   **la causa** (the cause)
el sudor (the sweat)   **la sangre** (the blood)   **la vista** (the sight, vision)

S before <u>b</u>, <u>d</u>, <u>g</u>, <u>l</u>, <u>m</u>, <u>n</u>, and <u>v</u> has the <u>z</u> sound as in toys.

el asma (asthma)   **los dientes** (the teeth)   **la desgana** (the loss of appetite)

T is similar to English but is dental.

el té (the tea)   **tragar** (to swallow)   **las tijeras** (the scissors)
el teléfono (the telephone)   **tranquilo** (tranquil)   **este** (this)

U sounds like the English <u>u</u> in <u>rule</u>.

último (last in a series)   **usar** (to use)   **la unión** (the union)   **único** (only)

V has the same sound as <u>b</u>.

el vértigo (the dizziness)   **vestirse** (to get dressed)   **la verruga** (the wart)
el vientre (the belly)   **vaginal** (vaginal)   **aliviarse** (to get well)

(W) is not part of the Spanish alphabet. It is used only in foreign words and is pronounced as it is in English.

Wáshington

X has the English x sound before a consonant.

explicar (to explain)   **la extensión** (the extension)   **excelente** (excellent)   **el extranjero** (the alien)

Y sounds like the English y in yes.

yo (I)   **yodo** (iodine)   **yeso** (cast)   **yerno** (son-in-law)

When **Y** follows n, it has the sound as in the English judge.

inyección (injection)   **inyectar** (to inject)

When it stands alone, it sounds like the Spanish i.

y (and)

Z always has the s sound.

el zumbido (buzzing)   **embarazada** (pregnant)   **el corazón** (the heart)   **izquierdo** (left)
el brazo (the arm)   **zurdo** (left-handed)   **el zapato** (the shoe)   **la matriz** (womb)

ACCENTUATION

To pronounce Spanish words properly requires accenting or stressing the correct syllable. The following rules apply and should be memorized:

1. If a word ends in a vowel (a, e, i, o, u), n, or s the stress will be on the next-to-last syllable.

me-sa (table)   **ca-be-za** (head)   **re-ga-lo** (gift)   **a-rri-ba** (up, upstairs)
si-lla (chair)   **de-do** (finger)   **cam-bian** (they change)   **do-sis** (dose)
le-che (milk)

2. If a word ends in a consonant other than n or s the stress is on the last syllable.

us-ted (you)   **re-loj** (clock)   **a-li-viar** (to alleviate)   **pa-red** (wall)
ca-mi-nar (to walk)   **se-ñal** (sign)   **pul-gar** (thumb)   **ciu-dad** (city)
a-bor-tar (to abort)

3. If the word does not conform to either of the above rules it must have a written <u>accent mark</u> on the <u>stressed</u> syllable.

lá-piz (pencil)	**fá-cil** (easy)	**in-di-ges-tión** (indigestion)	**nú-me-ro** (number)
ár-bol (tree)	**sa-ram-pión** (measles)	**úl-ti-mo** (last)	**ca-fé** (coffee)
ma-má (Mom)			

4. The accent mark is also used to distinguish a few words that have the same spelling but different meanings. The pronunciation is the same.

te—you (object)	**de**—of	**si**—if	**el**—the
té—tea	**dé**—give (command)	**sí**—yes	**él**—he

5. The combination of a strong and weak vowel (a diphthong) forms one single syllable, unless a written accent mark is used over the weak vowel, in which case the weak vowel carries its own syllable.

co-ca-í-na (cocaine)	**die-ta** (diet)	**dia-rio** (daily)	**o-ír** (to hear)
pa-ís (country)	**ca-fe-te-rí-a** (cafeteria)	**cuar-to** (room)	**sue-ro** (IV)
bai-le (dance)	**mí-o** (mine)	**le-í-do** (read)	**pei-ne** (comb)

DIPHTHONGS

In Spanish there are weak and strong vowels: **U** and **I** are weak vowels, **A, E,** and **O** are strong vowels. A diphthong consists of a strong and a weak vowel, a weak and a strong vowel, or two weak vowels, pronounced together.

ue sounds like <u>we</u> in <u>wet</u> in English.   Examples: **bueno, sueño, fuerte.**

ia sounds like <u>yah</u> in English.   Examples: **Julia, malaria, arteria.**

io sounds like <u>yo</u> in <u>yore</u> in English.   Examples: **Julio, radiografías.**

ie sounds like <u>ye</u> in <u>yet</u> in English.   Examples: **piel, diente.**

iu sounds like <u>ew</u> in <u>hew</u> in English.   Examples: **ciudadano, diurético**

ua sounds like <u>wa</u> in English.   Examples: **enjuagar, guante.**

ai sounds like <u>ai</u> in <u>aisle</u> in English.	Examples: **caigo, hay.**
ui sounds like the word <u>we</u> in English.	Examples: **cuidado, suicidio.**
ei sounds like <u>a</u> in the word <u>ate</u> in English.	Examples: **peine, seis.**
oi sounds like <u>oy</u> in <u>toy</u> in English.	Examples: **oigo, hoy.**
uo sounds like <u>uo</u> in <u>quota</u> in English.	Examples: **cuota, duodécimo.**
eu sounds like Spanish <u>e</u> then Spanish <u>u</u>.	Examples: **terapéutico, neurólogo.**
au sounds like <u>ou</u> in <u>our</u> in English.	Examples: **pausa, causa.**

SYLLABICATION

Dividing words into syllables makes it much easier to pronounce them. Following are rules for word division.

1. A word has as many syllables as it has diphthongs and vowels.
2. Every syllable ends in a vowel except when the vowel is followed by two different consonants.
3. A syllable usually starts with a consonant. However, every strong vowel carries its own syllable. The strong vowels are <u>a</u>, <u>e</u>, and <u>o</u>; the weak vowels are <u>i</u> and <u>u</u>.
4. A single consonant between two vowels goes with the following vowel. <u>ch</u>, <u>ll</u>, and <u>rr</u> are considered single consonants.
5. When two consonants come together they are usually in separate syllables. The following <u>cannot</u> be separated:

   <u>br</u>, <u>cr</u>, <u>dr</u>, <u>fr</u>, <u>gr</u>, and <u>tr</u>; and <u>bl</u>, <u>cl</u>, <u>fl</u>, <u>gl</u>, and <u>pl</u>.

6. Examples:

se-ño-ra (Mrs., Madam)	**mu-cha-cha** (girl)	**bar-bi-lla** (chin)	**a-pa-ra-to** (apparatus)
ni-ño (boy)	**ma-no** (hand)	**en-se-ñar** (to show)	**in-tra-mus-cu-lar** (intramuscular)
pe-rro (dog)	**can-tar** (to sing)	**An-to-nio** (Anthony)	**pa-dre** (father)
sa-rro (tartar)	**lec-ción** (lesson)	**es-ter-nón** (sternum)	**es-pe-cial** (special)

e-jer-ci-cio (exercise)
ca-ma (bed)
en-fer-mo (sick)
ja-bón (soap)
dien-te (tooth)

to-bi-llo (ankle)
li-ni-men-to (liniment)
a-rri-ba (upstairs)
ac-ci-den-te (accident)
ra-dio-gra-fí-as (X-rays)

pro-fun-do (deeply)
de-fec-to (defect)
pe-dia-tra (pediatrician)
pre-o-cu-pa-do (worried)
ci-ru-gía (surgery)

ca-té-ter (catheter)
za-pa-ti-llas (slippers)
ma-re-a-do (dizzy)
cual-quier (any)

DAYS OF THE WEEK

LOS DÍAS DE LA SEMANA

MONDAY	lunes	FRIDAY	viernes
TUESDAY	martes	SATURDAY	sábado
WEDNESDAY	miércoles	SUNDAY	domingo
THURSDAY	jueves		

MONTHS OF THE YEAR

LOS MESES DEL AÑO

JANUARY	enero	JULY	julio
FEBRUARY	febrero	AUGUST	agosto
MARCH	marzo	SEPTEMBER	septiembre
APRIL	abril	OCTOBER	octubre
MAY	mayo	NOVEMBER	noviembre
JUNE	junio	DECEMBER	diciembre

COLORS   **LOS COLORES**

black	**negro, negra**	orange	**anaranjado**
blue	**azul**	pale	**pálido**
brown	**moreno(a), pardo(a), café**	pink	**rosado**
clear	**claro(a), light (in color tone)**	purple	**púrpura, morado**
cranberry	**arándano(a)**	red	**rojo(a)**
dark	**oscuro(a)**	silver	**plateado(a)**
gold	**dorado(a)**	transparent	**transparente**
gray	**gris**	white	**blanco(a)**
green	**verde**	yellow	**amarillo(a)**
maroon	**marrón**		

A BRIEF OVERVIEW OF SPANISH GRAMMAR

Nouns

Gender of Nouns

1. Nouns ending in a are generally feminine and require the definite article la meaning the or the indefinite article una meaning a or an.

    Examples:
    la (una) mesa   the (a) table

2. Nouns ending in o are generally masculine and require the definite article el meaning the or the indefinite article un meaning a or an.

    Example:
    el (un) libro   the (a) book

Plural of Nouns

1. To make a noun plural add s if the word ends in a vowel and es if the word ends in a consonant. The definite article el becomes los; la becomes las. The indefinite article un becomes unos; una becomes unas.

2. Examples:

a. el médico, los médicos	the doctor, the doctors	c. la enfermera, las enfermeras	the nurse, the nurses
b. un señor, unos señores	a gentleman, some gentlemen	d. una infección, unas infecciones	an infection, some infections

Diminutives

1. Diminutives are commonly used among native speakers as signs of endearment and to make nouns denote objects smaller in size. The most common diminutive endings are ito (ita) and illo (illa). To form the diminutive, drop the final vowel of the noun and add the ending.

casa, casita	house, little house	hijo, hijito	son, little son (endearment)

2. When a diminutive is formed, c becomes qu. Z becomes c, and g becomes gu before ito and illo. (When qu or gu comes before e or i, the u is silent.)

a. Paco, Paquito	Frank, Frankie	d. la mano, la manita	the hand, the tiny hand
b. chica, chiquita	girl, little girl	e. el perro, el perrito	the dog, the puppy
c. un poco, un poquito	a little bit, a tiny bit		

3. Nouns ending in a consonant add cito (cita), or ecito (ecita), and cillo (cilla), or ecillo (ecilla):

a. joven, jovencito	a. youth, youngster	c. pueblo, pueblecito	c. town, little town
b. flor, florecita	b. flower, little flower	d. un momento, un momentillo	d. a moment, a little moment

4. Some uses of the diminutive can have a favorable or an unfavorable meaning depending on what the speaker intends:

a. Mamá, Mamacita	a. Mom, Mommy	c. pobre, pobrecito	c. poor one, poor little thing
b. Papá, Papacito	b. Dad, Daddy		

Adjectives

Forms of Adjectives

1. Most adjectives end in <u>o</u> in Spanish. The adjective must agree with the noun it modifies in gender and number. The four forms are:

<u>o</u> (masculine singular)   <u>os</u> (masculine plural)   <u>a</u> (feminine singular)   <u>as</u> (feminine plural)

Examples:

a. **un dolor agudo**   a. a sharp pain   c. **los uniformes blancos**   c. the white uniform
b. **una comida deliciosa**   b. a delicious meal   d. **las tarjetas blancas**   d. the white card

2. Some adjectives end in a consonant. These are made plural, by adding <u>es</u>, but they do not change in form to show gender.

Examples:

a. **una bata azul**   a. a blue robe   f. **unas batas azules**   f. some blue robes
b. **un vestido azul**   b. a blue dress   g. **unos vestidos azules**   g. some blue dresses
c. **un muchacho joven**   c. a young boy   h. **unos muchachos jóvenes**   h. some young boys
d. **una muchacha joven**   d. a young girl   i. **unas muchachas jóvenes**   i. some young girls
e. **el dedo pulgar**   e. the thumb   j. **los dedos pulgares**   j. the thumbs

Position of Adjectives

1. <u>Descriptive</u> adjectives stand <u>after</u> the noun they modify.

Examples:

a. **un dolor sordo**   a. a dull pain   c. **un hombre inteligente**   c. an intelligent man
b. **una roncha rojiza**   b. a reddish welt

2. <u>Limiting</u> adjectives (demonstratives, numerals, and possessives) stand <u>before</u> the noun they modify.

Examples:

a. **una píldora**   a. a (one) pill   c. **mi hijo**   c. my child
b. **esta frazada**   b. this blanket

Possessive Adjectives

1. my	1. **mi(s)**	4. our	4. **nuestro(a) (os) (as)**
2. your	2. **tu(s)**	5. their, your	5. **su(s)**
3. his, her, your	3. **su(s)**		

Demonstrative Adjectives

1. this	1. **este, esta**	4. these	4. **estos, estas**
2. that	2. **ese, esa**	5. those	5. **esos, esas**
3. that (far from the speaker)	3. **aquel, aquella**	6. those (far from the speaker)	6. **aquellos, aquellas**

Comparison of Adjectives

1. To compare adjectives use <u>más</u> before the adjective for the comparative <u>more</u> or <u>-er</u>. Use the article plus <u>más</u> before the noun for the superlative <u>most</u> or <u>-est</u>.

2. Examples:
   a. He is younger than she.   a. **El es más joven que ella.**
   b. He is the youngest in the family. b. **El es el más joven de la familia.**

Possession

1. To indicate possession in Spanish the word <u>de</u>, meaning <u>of</u>, is used. There is no apostrophe in Spanish.

2. Examples:
   a. Whose child is this?   a. **¿De quién es este(a) niño(a)?**   c. the patient's cast   c. **el yeso <u>del</u> (<u>de la</u>) paciente**
   b. Is it yours?   b. **¿Es de usted?**   d. Mary's purse   d. **la bolsa de María**

3. <u>Del</u> is one of two contractions with <u>el</u> that exists in the Spanish language. When <u>de</u> (of) precedes <u>el</u> (the) it becomes <u>del</u> (of the).
   (De + el = del.)

Personal A

1. <u>Al</u> is the other contraction in Spanish. When <u>a</u> (to, for) precedes <u>el</u> (the) it becomes <u>al</u>. (A + el = al.)

2. There is a personal <u>a</u> in Spanish that does not occur in English. Use the <u>a</u> after a verb if the direct object of the verb is a person.

3. Examples:
   a. I see John.
   b. Do you know the doctor in Emergency?
   c. I know this doctor.

   a. **Veo a Juan.**
   b. **¿Conoce usted <u>al</u> médico en la Sala de Emergencia?**
   c. **Conozco a este médico.**

Pronouns

Subject

1. I	1. **yo**	5. you (formal)	5. **usted**
2. you (familiar	2. **tú**	6. we	6. **nosotros/as**
3. he	3. **él**	7. they	7. **ellos, ellas**
4. she	4. **ella**	8. you (plural)	8. **ustedes**

Vd. or Ud.

1. <u>Vd.</u> and <u>Ud.</u> are the abbreviations in Spanish for <u>usted</u>. <u>Vds.</u> and <u>Uds.</u> are the plural abbreviations for the <u>ustedes</u> form.

2. <u>Usted</u> means <u>you</u> when speaking to one person. <u>Ustedes</u> means <u>you</u> when speaking to two or more persons.

Object (Direct)

1. me	1. **me**	4. us	4. **nos**
2. you	2. **te**	5. them, you	5. **los**
3. him, her, it, you	3. **lo, la**		

Object (Indirect)

1. me	1. **me**	4. us	4. **nos**
2. you	2. **te**	5. them, you	5. **les**
3. him, her, you	3. **le**		

Reflexive

1. myself	1. **me**	4. ourselves	4. **nos**
2. yourself	2. **te**	5. themselves, yourselves	5. **se**
3. himself, herself, yourself	3. **se**		

Object of a Preposition

1. me	1. **mí**	6. us	6. **nosotros**
2. you	2. **ti**	7. them (masculine)	7. **ellos**
3. him	3. **él**	8. them (feminine)	8. **ellas**
4. her	4. **ella**	9. you (plural)	9. **ustedes**
5. you	5. **usted**		

Note: **mí** and **ti** are combined with the preposition <u>con</u> (with):

a. with me	a. **conmigo**	b. with you	b. **contigo**

The Verb <u>To Be</u> (<u>Ser</u> and <u>Estar</u>)

<u>Ser</u> and <u>Estar</u> both mean <u>to be</u>.

Estar

1. Use <u>estar</u> for expressions of **health.**
a. How are you?	a. **¿Cómo está usted?**	b. I am not well.	b. **No estoy bien.**

2. Use <u>estar</u> for expressions of **location.**
a. Where is the pain?	a. **¿Dónde está el dolor?**	b. It's in the stomach.	b. **Está en el estómago.**

3. Use <u>estar</u> with **adjectives of condition that change.**
a. The therapist is busy.	a. **El terapista está ocupado.**	c. She is worried.	c. **Ella está preocupada.**
b. I am tired.	b. **Estoy cansado.**		

4. Use estar for the **present progressive.**

a. I am resting.   a. **Estoy descansando.**   b. They are eating.   b. **Están comiendo.**

5. Quedar is used with places only. You may also use estar.

a. Where is the clinic?   a. **¿Dónde queda la clínica?**   c. It is two blocks from here.   c. **Queda a dos cuadras de**

b. Where is the clinic?   b. **¿Dónde está la clínica?**   **aquí.**

Ser

1. Use ser for inherent characteristics—time, possession, origin, substance, and identification.

a. She is pretty.	a. **Ella es bonita.**	i. He is a doctor.	i. **El es médico.**
b. Blood is red.	b. **La sangre es roja.**	j. The patient is a carpenter.	j. **El paciente es carpintero.**
c. The room is large.	c. **El cuarto es grande.**	k. Are you Mexican?	k. **¿Es usted mexicano?**
d. We are from Mexico.	d. **Somos de México.**	l. The patient is Catholic.	l. **El/La paciente es católico/a.**
e. Whose prescription is it?	e. **¿De quién es la receta?**	m. It is necessary to rest more.	m. **Es necesario descansar más.**
f. It is John's.	f. **Es de Juan.**	n. What time is it?	n. **¿Qué hora es?**
g. The syringe is plastic.	g. **La jeringa es de plástico.**	o. It is one o'clock.	o. **Es la una.**
h. What is this? It is a glass.	h. **¿Qué es esto? Es un vaso.**	p. It is two o'clock.	p. **Son las dos.**
		q. Today is Monday.	q. **Hoy es lunes.**

Changes in Meaning

Certain adjectives change their meaning depending on whether Ser or Estar is used.

Adjectives	with ser	with estar
1. alto	1. high (tall)	1. high (location)
2. bueno	2. good (kind)	2. good (taste)
3. callado	3. quiet (disposition)	3. silent (temporarily)
4. cansado	4. boring, tiresome	4. tired (physically)
5. ciego	5. blind (permanently)	5. blind (temporarily)
6. listo	6. clever	6. ready
7. vivo	7. lively	7. alive
8. malo	8. bad (behavior)	8. ill, sick

Tense of Verbs

Simple Future

1. To indicate simple future use a form of the verb to go (IR) + a + the infinitive of the verb:

a. I am going	a. **Voy**	d. We are going	d. **Vamos**
b. You are going	b. **Vas**	e. They are going,	e. **Van**
c. He, she, you are going	c. **Va**	you (pl.) are going	

2. Examples:

   a. I'm going to examine your stomach.

   b. Are you going to return tomorrow?

   c. Are you going to take the medicine every day?

   d. We're going to go.

    a. **Le voy a examinar el estómago.**

    b. **¿Va usted a regresar mañana?**

    c. **¿Va a tomar la medicina cada día?**

    d. **Vamos a ir.**

Negation of Verbs

1. To negate in Spanish, place <u>no</u> before the verb.

2. Examples:

   a. I don't have my card.

   b. I don't go to the clinic every day.

   c. Aren't you my nurse?

    a. **No tengo mi tarjeta.**

    b. **No voy a la clínica cada día.**

    c. **¿No es usted mi enfermera?**

Questions

1. To ask a question in Spanish, place the subject of the sentence after the verb.

2. Examples:

   a. Are you the patient?

   b. Is your child sick?

   c. Is your medical card in your purse?

   d. Why did you come to the hospital?

    a. **¿Es usted la paciente?**

    b. **¿Está enfermo(a) su hijo(a)?**

    c. **¿Está su tarjeta médica en su bolsa?**

    d. **¿Por qué vino usted al hospital?**

Expressions of Obligation

HAY QUE (Should)   **TENER QUE** (To have to)   **DEBER (DE)** (Must)

These three expressions can be used before an infinitive of the verb.

You should read the instructions carefully.   Hay que leer las instrucciones con cuidado.

You have to stay in bed.   Usted tiene que quedarse en cama.

You must take this pill with milk.   Debe (de) tomar esta pastilla con leche.

Spanish Verbs and Some of Their Tenses

There are three classes of verbs in Spanish. Their infinitives end in -ar, -er or -ir. The infinitive form of the verb in Spanish is equivalent to the "to" form of the verb in English. In order to conjugate a verb in Spanish one must drop off the -ar, -er or -ir and add certain endings to indicate who is doing the action, and when it is done.

Present Tense

tomar (to take)

Singular

yo tomo (I take)

tú tomas (you take)

él toma (he takes)

ella toma (she takes)

usted toma (you take)

Plural

nosotros tomamos (we take)

*vosotros tomáis (you take)

ellos toman (they take)

ellas toman (they take)

ustedes toman (you take)

NOTE: This section will serve to introduce Spanish verbs in only five tenses. These tenses are those which will be of most frequent need in medical situations. The tenses presented here will be the Present, the Preterite, the Future, the Imperfect, and the Present Perfect. If a more thorough knowledge of verb tenses is desired, consult any acceptable text that explains Spanish language structure.

*Since the vosotros form of the verb, which is the plural of tú is not used in most countries of Latin America it will not be used after this page. Ustedes is used for the plural of you. Tú and vosotros are the familiar forms of you. The formal forms are the singular usted (abbreviation Ud. or Vd.). and the plural form ustedes (abbreviation Uds. or Vds.).

comer (to eat)

Singular	*Plural*
yo como (I eat)	**nosotros comemos** (we eat)
tú comes (you eat)	
él come (he eats)	**ellos comen** (they eat)
ella come (she eats)	**ellas comen** (they eat)
usted come (you eat)	**ustedes comen** (you eat)

sufrir (to suffer)

Singular	*Plural*
yo sufro (I suffer)	**nosotros sufrimos** (we suffer)
tú sufres (you suffer)	
él sufre (he suffers)	**ellos sufren** (they suffer)
ella sufre (she suffers)	**ellas sufren** (they suffer)
usted sufre (you suffer)	**ustedes sufren** (you suffer)

Examples of some -ar, -er, and -ir verbs which are commonly used in medicine:

analizar (to analyze)	**levantar** (to raise)	**prometer** (to promise)	**sentir** (to feel)
contestar (to answer)	**dejar** (to permit, to let)	**comprender** (to understand)	**admitir** (to admit)
soplar (to blow)	**lavar** (to wash)	**proceder** (to proceed)	**subir** (to raise, to go up)
molestar (to annoy, to bother)	**prender** (to fasten)	**meter** (to put in)	**recibir** (to receive)
fracturar (to fracture)	**leer** (to read)	**correr** (to run)	**abrir** (to open)
aumentar (to increase)	**beber** (to drink)	**cubrir** (to cover)	**discutir** (to discuss)
eliminar (to eliminate)	**doblar** (to bend)	**repetir** (to repeat)	**vivir** (to live)

Some verbs are irregular in the present tense. The most common are:

dar (to give)

doy	damos
das	
da	dan

estar (to be)

estoy	estamos
estás	
está	están

caber (to fit, to have enough room)

quepo	cabemos
cabes	
cabe	caben

caer (to fall)

caigo	caemos
caes	
cae	caen

hacer (to make, to do)

hago	hacemos
haces	
hace	hacen

ir (to go)

voy	vamos
vas	
va	van

decir (to say, to tell)

digo	decimos
dices	
dice	dicen

saber (to know)

sé	sabemos
sabes	
sabe	saben

salir (to leave, to go out)

salgo	salimos
sales	
sale	salen

ser (to be)

soy	somos
eres	
es	son

tener (to have)

tengo	tenemos
tienes	
tiene	tienen

traer (to bring)

traigo	traemos
traes	
trae	traen

poder (to be able)

puedo	podemos
puedes	
puede	pueden

poner (to put, to place)

pongo	ponemos
pones	
pone	ponen

venir (to come)

vengo	venimos
vienes	
viene	vienen

ver (to see)

veo	vemos
ves	
ve	ven

Stem-Changing Verbs

Some verbs change the stem vowel of the infinitive from <u>e</u> to <u>ie</u> or <u>o</u> to <u>ue</u> to form the present tense. A few of the most common are:

e > ie

cerrar (to close)	**pensar** (to think)
comenzar (to begin)	**querer** (to want)
despertar (to awaken)	**temblar** (to tremble)
entender (to understand)	**sentir** (to feel)
empezar (to begin)	**calentar** (to heat)

o > ue

acordar (to remember)	**mover** (to move)
recordar (to remember)	**contar** (to count)
morder (to bite)	**acostar** (to put to bed)
poder (to be able)	**morir** (to die)
dormir (to sleep)	**doler** (to hurt, ache)

These changes occur only in the <u>yo</u>, <u>tú</u>, <u>él</u> and <u>ellos</u> forms. The <u>nosotros</u> form <u>does not</u> have the vowel change.

Examples:

cerrar

cierro	cerramos
cierras	
cierra	cierran

mover

muevo	movemos
mueves	
mueve	mueven

There is a group of verbs that change the <u>e</u> in the stem to <u>i</u>. The more common ones are:

m<u>e</u>dir (to measure)   p<u>e</u>dir (to ask for, request)
g<u>e</u>mir (to groan)   rep<u>e</u>tir (to repeat)
desp<u>e</u>dir (to dismiss)   s<u>e</u>rvir (to serve)

Examples:

servir

yo sirvo	nosotros servimos	ella sirve	ellas sirven
tú sirves		usted sirve	ustedes sirven
él sirve	ellos sirven		

Preterite Tense

The preterite in Spanish is the past tense in English. The preterite indicates past, completed action.

To form the preterite of an <u>-ar</u> verb, drop off the <u>-ar</u> and add the endings to indicate the past:

tomar

yo tom<u>é</u> (I took)   nosotros tom<u>amos</u> (we took)
tú tom<u>aste</u> (you took)   ellos tom<u>aron</u> (they took)
él tom<u>ó</u> (he took)   ellas tom<u>aron</u> (they took)
ella tom<u>ó</u> (she took)   ustedes tom<u>aron</u> (you took)
usted tom<u>ó</u> (you took)

To form the preterite of an <u>-er</u> verb drop off the <u>-er</u> and add the endings to indicate the past.

comer

yo com<u>í</u> (I ate)   nosotros com<u>imos</u> (we ate)
tú com<u>iste</u> (you ate)   ellos com<u>ieron</u> (they ate)
él com<u>ió</u> (he ate)   ellas com<u>ieron</u> (they ate)
ella com<u>ió</u> (she ate)   ustedes com<u>ieron</u> (you ate)
usted com<u>ió</u> (you ate)

To form the preterite of an -ir verb drop off the -ir and add the endings that indicate the past.

sufrir

yo sufrí (I suffered)	**nosotros sufrimos** (we suffered)
tú sufriste (you suffered)	**ellos sufrieron** (they suffered)
él sufrió (he suffered)	**ellas sufrieron** (they suffered)
ella sufrió (she suffered)	**ustedes sufrieron** (you suffered)
usted sufrió (you suffered)	

Some verbs are irregular in the past tense. Examples of several of these are:

andar (to walk)	anduve, anduviste, anduvo, anduvimos, anduvieron
caber (to fit)	cupe, cupiste, cupo, cupimos, cupieron
caer (to fall)	caí, caíste, cayó, caímos, cayeron
dar (to give)	di, diste, dio, dimos, dieron
estar (to be)	estuve, estuviste, estuvo, estuvimos, estuvieron
hacer (to make, to do)	hice, hiciste, hizo, hicimos, hicieron
ir (to go)	fui, fuiste, fue, fuimos, fueron
poder (to be able)	pude, pudiste, pudo, pudimos, pudieron
poner (to put, to place)	puse, pusiste, puso, pusimos, pusieron
querer (to want)	quise, quisiste, quiso, quisimos, quisieron
saber (to know)	supe, supiste, supo, supimos, supieron
ser (to be)	fui, fuiste, fue, fuimos, fueron
venir (to come)	vine, viniste, vino, vinimos, vinieron
tener (to have)	tuve, tuviste, tuvo, tuvimos, tuvieron
traer (to bring)	traje, trajiste, trajo, trajimos, trajeron

Future Tense

To form the future tense in Spanish add the following endings to the <u>whole infinitive form</u>: -é, -ás, -á, -emos, -án.

Examples:

tomar

yo tomar<u>é</u> (I will take)	**nosotros tomar<u>emos</u>** (we will take)
tú tomar<u>ás</u> (you will take)	
él tomar<u>á</u> (he will take)	**ellos tomar<u>án</u>** (they will take)
ella tomar<u>á</u> (she will take)	**ellas tomar<u>án</u>** (they will take)
usted tomar<u>á</u> (you will take)	**ustedes tomar<u>án</u>** (you will take)

comer

yo comer<u>é</u> (I will eat)	**nosotros comer<u>emos</u>** (we will eat)
tú comer<u>ás</u> (you will eat)	
él comer<u>á</u> (he will eat)	**ellos comer<u>án</u>** (they will eat)
ella comer<u>á</u> (she will eat)	**ellas comer<u>án</u>** (they will eat)
usted comer<u>á</u> (you will eat)	**ustedes comer<u>án</u>** (you will eat)

vivir

yo vivir<u>é</u> (I will live)	**nosotros vivir<u>emos</u>** (we will live)
tú vivir<u>ás</u> (you will live)	
él vivir<u>á</u> (he will live)	**ellos vivir<u>án</u>** (they will live)
ella vivir<u>á</u> (she will live)	**ellas vivir<u>án</u>** (they will live)
usted vivir<u>á</u> (you will live)	**ustedes vivir<u>án</u>** (you will live)

Some verbs are irregular in the future tense. The endings are the same as those of the regular verbs but the stems differ. They are:

decir (to say, to tell)	diré, dirás, dirá, diremos, dirán
hacer (to make, to do)	haré, harás, hará, haremos, harán
querer (to want)	querré, querrás, querrá, querremos, querrán
caber (to fit)	cabré, cabrás, cabrá, cabremos, cabrán
poder (to be able)	podré, podrás, podrá, podremos, podrán
saber (to know)	sabré, sabrás, sabrá, sabremos, sabrán
poner (to put, to place)	pondré, pondrás, pondrá, pondremos, pondrán
salir (to leave, to go out)	saldré, saldrás, saldrá, saldremos, saldrán
tener (to have)	tendré, tendrás, tendrá, tendremos, tendrán
venir (to come)	vendré, vendrás, vendrá, vendremos, vendrán

Imperfect Tense

The imperfect tense is used to express continued or habitual past action. It is formed by dropping the -ar, -er, or -ir of the infinitive, and adding the imperfect tense endings. In this tense, the -er and -ir verbs have the same endings.

hablar (to speak)		**mover** (to move)		**vivir** (to live)	
hablaba	hablábamos	movía	movíamos	vivía	vivíamos
hablabas		movías		vivías	
hablaba	hablaban	movía	movían	vivía	vivían

There are only three irregularly-formed verbs in the imperfect tense. They are:

ir (to go)		**ser** (to be)		**ver** (to see)	
iba	íbamos	era	éramos	veía	veíamos
ibas		eras		veías	
iba	iban	era	eran	veía	veían

Present Perfect Tense

The Spanish present perfect tense is used in the same way as the English perfect tense. It is composed of the present tense of the auxiliary verb <u>haber</u> (to have), and the past participle, as in English.

The forms of the present tense of the verb <u>haber</u> are irregular. They are:

he	hemos
has	
ha	han

The past participle of the verb is formed by dropping the <u>-ar</u>, <u>-er</u>, or <u>-ir</u> of the infinitive, and adding <u>-ado</u> to <u>-ar</u> verbs; <u>-ido</u> to <u>-er</u> and <u>-ir</u> verbs.

estar (to be)		**tener** (to have)		**venir** (to come)	
he estado	hemos estado	he tenido	hemos tenido	he venido	hemos venido
has estado		has tenido		has venido	
ha estado	han estado	ha tenido	han tenido	ha venido	han venido

Note: For commonly used irregular past participles, refer to a book on Spanish language structure.

Commands

Verbs Ending in -ar		Verbs Ending in -er and -ir	
Affirmative	*Negative*	*Affirmative*	*Negative*
1. Formal (Ud., Uds.)			
Hable Ud.	**No hable Ud.**	**Beba Ud.**	**No beba Ud.**
Hablen Uds.	**No hablen Uds.**	**Beban Uds.**	**No beban Uds.**
2. Familiar (Tú)			
Habla (tú)	**No hables (tú)**	**Bebe (tú)**	**No bebas (tú)**

The formal command is formed from the first person singular of the present tense. Change the "o" to the opposite vowel. For example: **salir** = **salgo** = **salga** (Leave).

The verb form for the familiar command is the same as the third person singular of the present tense. For example: **comer** = **come (tú)**. The subject pronoun <u>tú</u> is seldom used in familiar commands. It may be added for emphasis. The plural of the familiar command is seldom used. Use the <u>Uds.</u> form for the familiar plural.

Qué and Cuál

Qué (what) is used in asking definitions. **Cuál** (which, what) is used for choice.

¿Qué es esto?	What is this?
Es un termómetro.	It is a thermometer.
¿Cuál vestido prefiere?	Which dress do you prefer?
Prefiero el rojo.	I prefer the red one.

Note: Some verbs are irregular in the commands. Some of the commands that are listed beginning on page 315 are irregular.

Impersonal Verbs

There are several verbs that are impersonal in Spanish. They cannot be conjugated like the others. Use them with the indirect pronouns before the verb.

doler (to hurt)   **gustar** (to like)   **faltar** (to need)

¿**Dónde le duele?**	Where does it hurt?
Me duele la cabeza.	My head hurts.
¿**Le gustan las comidas picantes?**	Do you like spicy meals?
Sí, me gustan.	Yes, I like them.
¿**Qué le falta?**	What do you need?
Me falta mi cepillo de dientes.	I need my toothbrush.

Hacer

1. Hacer means to make or to do.

¿**Qué hace usted?**	What are you doing?
No hago nada.	I am not doing anything.
hacer gárgaras	to gargle
hacer ejercicios	to exercise
hacer una prueba	to do a test, or run a test
hacer un puño	to make a fist
hacer una pregunta	to ask a question
hacer una visita	to make a visit

2. When used before a time expression, <u>hacer</u> means <u>ago.</u>

¿Cuándo empezó el dolor?	When did the pain begin?
¿Empezó hace dos días.	It started two days <u>ago.</u>

3. The <u>hace que</u> construction shows duration in the following pattern: **hace** + time expression + **que** = <u>has been.</u>

¿Cuánto tiempo hace que tiene este salpullido?	How long have you had this rash?
<u>Hace</u> cuatro días <u>que</u> lo tengo.	I've had it for four days. (It has been four days.)

Por and Para

Por and **para** both mean <u>for.</u>

POR

1. For the sake of
2. Because of
3. Expresses agent by which something is done
4. Means of communication or transportation
5. Exclamations
6. The object of an errand
7. In the sense that someone takes me for what I am not
8. In: the morning, afternoon, evening
9. In exchange for
10. Duration of time

PARA

1. To express purpose
2. Destination
3. Before an infinitive: in order to
4. Time limit
5. To imply a comparison
6. For what or for whom a thing is intended
7. Opinion
8. For: time in the future

Special expressions

por cierto	certainly	**por lo menos**	at least
por ejemplo	for example	**por fin**	finally
por eso	therefore	**por supuesto**	of course
por favor	please		

NUMBERS

Cardinals

NUMEROS

Cardinales

0	zero	**cero**		16	sixteen	**dieciséis**
1	one	**uno(a)**		17	seventeen	**diecisiete**
2	two	**dos**		18	eighteen	**dieciocho**
3	three	**tres**		19	nineteen	**diecinueve**
4	four	**cuatro**		20	twenty	**veinte**
5	five	**cinco**		21	twenty-one	**veintiuno**
6	six	**seis**		22	twenty-two	**veintidós**
7	seven	**siete**		23	twenty-three	**veintitrés**
8	eight	**ocho**		24	twenty-four	**vienticuatro**
9	nine	**nueve**		25	twenty-five	**veinticinco**
10	ten	**diez**		26	twenty-six	**veintiséis**
11	eleven	**once**		27	twenty-seven	**veintisiete**
12	twelve	**doce**		28	twenty-eight	**veintiocho**
13	thirteen	**trece**		29	twenty-nine	**veintinueve**
14	fourteen	**catorce**		30	thirty	**treinta**
15	fifteen	**quince**		40	forty	**cuarenta**

50	fifty	cincuenta
60	sixty	sesenta
70	seventy	setenta
80	eighty	ochenta
90	ninety	noventa
100	one hundred	cien (ciento)
101	one hundred one	ciento uno
102	one hundred two	ciento dos
103	one hundred three	ciento tres
104	one hundred four	ciento cuatro
105	one hundred five	ciento cinco
106	one hundred six	ciento seis
107	one hundred seven	ciento siete

108	one hundred eight	ciento ocho
109	one hundred nine	ciento nueve
110	one hundred ten	ciento diez
200	two hundred	doscientos
300	three hundred	trescientos
400	four hundred	cuatrocientos
500	five hundred	quinientos
600	six hundred	seiscientos
700	seven hundred	setecientos
800	eight hundred	ochocientos
900	nine hundred	novecientos
1000	one thousand	mil
1981	one thousand nine hundred eighty-one	mil novecientos ochenta y uno

Ordinals

Ordinales

1. first	1. primero
2. second	2. segundo
3. third	3. tercero
4. fourth	4. cuarto
5. fifth	5. quinto

6. sixth	6. sexto
7. seventh	7. séptimo
8. eighth	8. octavo
9. ninth	9. noveno
10. tenth	10. décimo

INTERROGATIVES

PALABRAS INTERROGATIVAS

1. How?	1. ¿Cómo?
2. How far?	2. ¿A qué distancia?
3. How often?	3. ¿Con qué frecuencia?
4. How much?	4. ¿Cuánto?
5. How many?	5. ¿Cuántos?
6. How long?	6. ¿Cuánto tiempo?
7. How many times?	7. ¿Cuántas veces?
8. What?	8. ¿Qué?
9. What else?	9. ¿Qué más?
10. What for?	10. ¿Para qué?

11. When?	11. ¿Cuándo?
12. Where?	12. ¿Dónde?
13. From where?	13. ¿De dónde?
14. To where?	14. ¿Adónde?
15. Which?	15. ¿Cuál?
16. Which (ones)?	16. ¿Cuáles?
17. Who?	17. ¿Quién?
18. Whom?	18. ¿A quién?
19. Whose?	19. ¿De quién?
20. Why?	20. ¿Por qué?

TITLES

TÍTULOS

Mr.	Señor	Miss	Señorita
Mrs.	Señora		

Family Members (Relatives)

Miembros de la Familia (Parientes)

grandfather	abuelo	son	el hijo
grandmother	abuela	daughter	la hija
mother	la madre, la mamá	children	los hijos, los niños
father	el padre, el papá	sister	la hermana
parents	los padres	brother	el hermano

cousin	el primo, la prima	husband	el esposo, el marido,
father-in-law	el suegro		"el viejo" (slang)
mother-in-law	la suegra	wife	la esposa, la mujer,
in-laws	los suegros		"la vieja" (slang)
brother-in-law	el cuñado	aunt	la tía
sister-in-law	la cuñada	uncle	el tío

Medical Personnel

Personal Médico

doctor	el doctor, el médico, la doctora	paramedic	el paramédico
		orderly	el ayudante
nurse	la enfermera, el enfermero	hospital volunteer	el voluntario, la voluntaria
therapist	el terapista, la terapista		

GREETINGS AND SOCIAL AMENITIES

SALUDOS

Good morning.	Buenos días.	Pleased to meet you.	Mucho gusto.
Good afternoon.	Buenas tardes.	How are you?	¿Cómo está usted?
Good evening.	Buenas tardes. Buenas noches.	How do you feel?	¿Cómo se siente usted?
Good night.	Buenas noches.	So, so.	Así, así. (regular)
Goodby.	Adiós.	Better than yesterday.	Mejor que ayer.
Hello.	Hola.	Please.	Por favor.
Let me introduce myself.	Permítame presentarme.	Thank you.	Gracias.
My name is _____.	Me llamo _____.	You're welcome.	De nada. Por nada.
I am _____.	Soy _____.	My deepest sympathy.	Mi sentido pésame.
What is your name?	¿Cómo se llama usted?	I am sorry.	Lo siento.

What a pity.	¡Qué lástima!	Do you want something?	¿Desea usted algo?
Congratulations.	¡Felicidades!	Come in.	Pase usted. Entre Ud.
Do you speak English?	¿Habla usted inglés?	Sit down.	Tome asiento. Siéntese.
Please speak more slowly.	Hable más despacio, por favor.	What can I do for you?	¿En qué le puedo ayudar?
What's the matter?	¿Qué le pasa?		

COMPLETIONS

anything, something	algo	less	menos
bad, badly	mal, muy mal	a lot	mucho
before	antes	more	más
better	mejor	never, ever	nunca, jamás
earlier	más temprano	now	ahora
enough	bastante, suficiente	sample, specimen	muestra
everyday	todos los días, cada día	slow	despacio
fast	rápido	soon	pronto
fever	fiebre, calentura	that	eso
here	aquí, acá	there	allá
it (not expressed as a subject)	lo	this	esto
last night	anoche	this morning	esta mañana
late	tarde	this afternoon	esta tarde
later	más tarde	today	hoy
a little	un poco—un poquito		

WEIGHTS AND MEASURES
METRIC AND UNITED STATES
EQUIVALENTS (APPROXIMATE)

Linear Measure

0.04 inch equals	1 millimeter
0.4 inch equals	1 centimeter
1 inch equals	2.54 centimeters
1 foot equals	30.48 centimeters
1 yard equals	1 meter
0.6 mile equals	1 kilometer
1 mile equals	1609 meters
1 caliber equals	.254 millimeter

Liquid Measure

1 quart equals	1 liter
1 gallon equals	3.78 liters

Weights (Avoirdupois)

.035 ounce	1 gram
1 ounce equals	28.4 grams
1 pound equals	454 grams
2.2 pounds equals	1 kilogram

Medida Linear

0.04 pulgada equivale	1 milímetro
0.4 pulgada equivale	1 centímetro
1 pulgada equivale	2.54 centímetros
1 pie equivale	30.48 centímetros
1 yarda equivale	1 metro
0.6 milla equivale	1 kilómetro
1 milla equivale	1609 metros
1 calibre equivale	.254 milímetro

Medida Líquida

1 cuarto equivale	1 litro
1 galón equivale	3.78 litros

Pesos (Avoirdupois)

.035 onza equivale	1 gramo
1 onza equivale	28.4 gramos
1 libra equivale	454 gramos
2.2 libras equivale	1 kilogramo

CENTIGRADE VS. FAHRENHEIT

To convert Centigrade temperature to Fahrenheit: multiply the Centigrade temperature by 9/5, then add 32.

To convert Fahrenheit temperature to Centigrade: subtract 32 from the Fahrenheit temperature, then multiply the remainder by 5/9.

CENTIGRADO VS. FAHRENHEIT

Para convertir la temperatura Centigrado a Fahrenheit: multiplique la temperatura Centigrado por 9/5 y añada 32.

Para convertir la temperatura Fahrenheit a Centigrado: reste 32 de la temperatura Fahrenheit y multiplique el resto por 5/9.

EXPRESSIONS OF TIME   EXPRESIONES DE TIEMPO

year	el año
month	el mes
week	la semana
day	el día
hour	la hora
minute	el minuto
second	el segundo
today	hoy
tomorrow	mañana
day after tomorrow	pasado mañana
yesterday	ayer
day before yesterday	anteayer
tonight	esta noche
last night	anoche
tomorrow morning	mañana por la mañana
tomorrow afternoon	mañana por la tarde

tomorrow evening	mañana por la noche
every morning	cada mañana, todas las mañanas
every afternoon	cada tarde, todas las tardes
every evening	todas las noches
every night	cada noche
in the morning	por la mañana
in the afternoon	por la tarde
in the evening	por la noche
at night	en la noche
all morning	toda la mañana
all afternoon	toda la tarde
all night	toda la noche
two days ago	hace dos días
three weeks ago	hace tres semanas
six years ago	hace seis años

always	siempre	before	antes
never	nunca	after	después
sometimes	algunas veces	later	más tarde
from time to time	de vez en cuando	next week	la semana próxima
now	ahora	next year	el año próximo
right now	ahora mismo	until	hasta

Time on the Clock   La Hora

To tell time in Spanish use the verb <u>SER</u> + la(s) and the number.

What time is it?	¿Qué hora es?	It is seven o'clock.	Son las siete.
It is one o'clock.	Es la una.	It is eight o'clock.	Son las ocho.
It is two o'clock.	Son las dos.	It is nine o'clock.	Son las nueve.
It is three o'clock.	Son las tres.	It is ten o'clock.	Son las diez.
It is four o'clock.	Son las cuatro.	It is eleven o'clock.	Son las once.
It is five o'clock.	Son las cinco.	It is twelve o'clock.	Son las doce.
It is six o'clock.	Son las seis.		

Use "Media" for "30" or half past the hour.

| It is 3:30. | Son las tres y media. |

a.m. = **de la mañana**
p.m. = **de la tarde (till 6 o'clock)**
p.m. = **de la noche (from 6 till midnight)**

On the right side of the clock use "y" when expressing minutes:

| It is ten after one. | Es la una y diez. | It is three fifteen. | Son las tres y quince. |
| It is two fifteen. | Son las dos y cuarto. | It is three thirty. | Son las tres y media. |

On the left side of the clock use "**menos**" or "**falta(n)**."

| It is twenty to two. | **Son las dos menos veinte.** | It is five to eight. | **Son las ocho menos cinco.** |
| It is twenty to two. | **Faltan veinte para las dos.** | It is five to eight. | **Faltan cinco para las ocho.** |

Time expressions:

At what time?	**¿A qué hora?**	early	**temprano**
At eight o'clock.	**A las ocho.**	late	**tarde**
At noon.	**Al mediodía.**	on time	**a tiempo**
At midnight.	**A la medianoche.**		

USEFUL WORDS AND PHRASES

PALABRAS Y FRASES ÚTILES

after	**después**	I understand.	**Entiendo. Comprendo.**
also	**también**	I'd like	**Quisiera**
and	**y**	in, on	**en**
at	**a, en**	inside	**dentro, adentro**
before	**antes**	Is there/Are there?	**¿Hay?**
Can I have?	**¿Puedo tener?**	Is it?	**¿Es? ¿Está?**
Can you help me?	**¿Puede ayudarme?**	it is	**es/está**
Can you show me?	**¿Puede enseñarme?**	it isn't	**no es/está**
Can you tell me?	**¿Puede decirme?**	I want	**Quiero**
down	**abajo**	Just a minute.	**Un momento**
during	**durante**	none	**ninguno**
from	**desde, de**	nor	**ni**
I don't understand.	**No entiendo. No comprendo.**	not	**no**
I need	**necesito**	nothing	**nada**

on	sobre	through	**a través de**
or	o	to	**a, para**
outside	**fuera, afuera**	too much	**demasiado**
perhaps	**tal vez, quizás**	toward	**hacia**
please bring me	**tráigame, por favor**	until	**hasta**
Please, give it to me.	**Démelo, por favor.**	up	**arriba**
please give me	**favor de darme, por favor**	very	**muy**
	déme	well	**bien**
soon	**pronto**	with	**con**
there is/there are	**hay**	without	**sin**
there isn't/there aren't	**no hay**		

Key Commands

Mandatos Importantes

Advise, inform	**Avise**	Close	**Cierre**
Be careful	**Tenga cuidado**	Come in	**Adelante, pase, entre**
Be quiet	**Cálmese, cállese**	Danger	**Peligro**
Bend	**Doble**	Dissolve	**Disuelva**
Blow	**Sople**	Drain	**Desagüe**
Breathe	**Respire**	Drink	**Tome, Beba**
Bring	**Traiga**	Eat	**Coma**
Call	**Llame**	Exhale	**Exhale**
Calm down	**Cálmese**	Extend	**Extienda**
Change	**Cambie**	Follow (me)	**Siga, sígame**
Chew	**Mastique**	Get up	**Levántese**
Clean	**Limpie**	Give me	**Déme**
Clear	**Despeje**	Go	**Vaya**

Grab	Agarre
Help	Ayude
Hold (breath)	Mantenga, Sostenga
Hold (onto something)	Agarre, Tenga
Hop	Salte
Induce vomiting	Induzca vómitos
Inhale	Inhale
Keep	Mantenga
Leave me	Déjeme
Lie down	Acuéstese
Lift	Levante
Look for	Busque
Make	Haga
Mix	Mezcle
Move	Mueva
Move bowels	Obre, Mueva el vientre, "haga caca" (coll.)
Open	Abra
Place	Ponga
Point	Señale
Press	Apriete, Presione
Pull	Jale, Tire
Push	Empuje
Put	Ponga
Relax	Relájese
Remove	Quite
Repeat	Repita "¿Mande?" (coll.)
Rest	Descanse
Return	Regrese
Save	Guarde
Say	Diga
Sign here	Firme aquí
Sit down	Siéntese
Spit	Escupa
Stand up	Párese, Levántese
Stay	Quédese, Espérese
Stay quiet	Esté tranquilo
Step	Tome paso
Stop	Pare, Deje
Straighten	Enderece
Squeeze	Apriete
Swallow	Trague, Pase
Take	Tome
Take off	Quítese
Tell me	Dígame
Tense (make tense)	Apriete
Touch	Toque
Turn	Voltéese
Urinate	Orine
Wait	Espere
Wash	Lave
Watch	Mire

Familiar Commands (Irregular)*   ## Mandatos Familiares

	Infinitive	Command	Negative Command
to be	ser	sé	no seas
to do or make	hacer	haz	no hagas
to come	venir	ven	no vengas
to go	ir	ve	no vayas
to have	tener	ten	no tengas
to leave	salir	sal	no salgas
to put or place	poner	pon	no pongas
to tell	decir	di	no digas

CLOTHING   ## LA ROPA

bathing suit	el traje de baño	coat	el abrigo
bathrobe	la bata (de baño)	collar	el cuello
belt	el cinturón	corset	el corsé
blouse	la blusa	diaper	el pañal
blue jeans	los pantalones vaqueros	dress	el vestido
boot	la bota	hat	el sombrero
brassiere	el sostén, el portabustos	heel	el tacón
button	el botón	low heels	los tacones bajos
cap	la gorra	high heels	los tacones altos

*Use only with children or adults that you know very well (familiar friends).

hose	las medias	shorts (men's)	los calzones, los calzoncillos
jacket	la chaqueta	skirt	la falda, la pollera
light weight (light clothes)	ligero (la ropa ligera)	sleeve	la manga
nightgown (gown—hospital)	el camisón de dormir (camisón)	long	larga
		short	corta
oxfords	los zapatos bajos	slipper	la zapatilla, la chancleta
pajamas	las pijamas	sneakers	los zapatos de goma
panties	las pantaletas	sock(s)	el calcetín, los calcetines
pants	los pantalones	stockings	las medias
rubber pants	los pantalones plásticos	suit	el traje
sandals	las sandalias	sweater	el suéter
scarf	la bufanda	tie	la corbata
shirt	la camisa	trousers	los pantalones
undershirt	la camiseta	underwear	la ropa interior
T-shirt	la camiseta	vest	el chaleco
shoe	el zapato		

JEWELRY AND OTHER PERSONAL ARTICLES
LAS JOYAS Y OTROS ARTÍCULOS PERSONALES

bobby pin, hair pin	la horquilla	hair brush	el cepillo para el pelo
bracelet	la pulsera	lipstick	la pintura para labios, el lápiz labi
contact lenses	los lentes de contacto	necklace	el collar
curlers	los rizadores, los rollos	purse	la bolsa
earring	el arete	razor	la máquina de afeitar
glasses	los anteojos, las gafas, los lentes	ring	el anillo
		shampoo	el champú

tampon	el tampón, tapón	tweezers	las pinzas
toothbrush	el cepillo de dientes	wallet	la cartera
toothpaste	la pasta dental	watch	el reloj de pulsera

Some Key Commands Using Articles of Clothing and Jewelry

1. Drop your pants.	1. **Bájese los pantalones.**	7. Dress the child.	7. **Vista al/a la niño(a).**
2. Strip to the waist.	2. **Desvístase hasta la cintura.**	8. Take off the baby's shoes and socks.	8. **Quítele al/a la bebé los zapatos y los calcetines.**
3. Take off your shirt.	3. **Quítese la camisa.**	9. Get dressed now.	9. **Póngase toda la ropa ahora.**
4. Take off your blouse.	4. **Quítese la blusa.**	10. Take off all your clothes.	10. **Quítese toda la ropa.**
5. Take off your shoes.	5. **Quítese los zapatos.**	11. Put on this gown.	11. **Póngase este camisón.**
6. Remove all your jewelry.	6. **Quítese todas las alhajas.**		

LOCATIONS   SITIOS

administration	la administración	east	el este
admissions	la sala de admisión	elevator	el ascensor, el elevador
bathroom (restroom)	el baño, el cuarto de baño	emergency room	la sala de emergencia
cafeteria	la cafetería	entrance	la entrada
cardiology	la sección de cardiología	exit	la salida
cashier	la caja	gift and flower shop	la tienda de regalos y flores
chapel	la capilla	hallway	el pasillo
corridor	el corredor	hospital	el hospital
contagious diseases	la sección de enfermedades contagiosas	information center (receptionist)	el centro de información (el (la) recepcionista)

intensive care	la sección de cuidado intensivo	orthopedics	la sección de ortopedia
laboratory	el laboratorio	pediatrics	la sección de pediatría
north	el norte	pharmacy	la farmacia
nuclear medicine	la sección de medicina nuclear	psychology	la sección de psiquiatría
nurses station	la estación de las enfermeras	public telephone	el teléfono público
OB-GYN	la sección de obstetricia y ginecología	south	el sur
		stairway	la escalera
operating room	la sala de operaciones	telephone	el teléfono
ophthalmology	la oftalmología	waiting room	la sala de espera
		ward	la sala de enfermos
		water fountain	el agua (el surtidor)

GLOSSARY OF TERMS   GLOSARIO DE TÉRMINOS

Spanish to English

afta, thrush or monoliasis
agudo, sharp (pain) or synonym for acute
ampolla, blister
asma, asthma
astilla, splinter
borracho, drunk
bulto, bump or lump
calambres, cramps
callo, callus
carbunclo, carbuncle

cardenal, bruise, bump
carga, commonly used slang for heroin
caspa, dandruff
catarata, cataract
cicatriz, scar
ciego, blind
circuncisión, circumcision
cirrosis, cirrhosis
cita, appointment
cojo, lame

cólico, colic
coma, coma
conjuntivitis (una infeccion del ojo), conjunctivitis
contagioso, contagious
costra, scab (of wound)
crónico, chronic
chancro, chancre
chichón, lump or bump
debilidad, weakness
deformidad, deformity

delirio, delirium
dermatitis, dermatitis
descongestivo, decongestant
deslocación, dislocation
desnutrición, malnutrition
diabetes, diabetes
dilatación, dilatation
disco, disc (**disco desplazado,** slipped disc)
diurético, diuretic
disentería, dysentery

drogas, drugs (generally referring to illegal drugs: **drogas alucinogénicas)**
eczema, eczema
edema, edema
empacho, digestive disturbance often linked to behavior or emotions (Mexican folk medicine term)
enema, enema
eructar, to burp
erupción, eruption
escalofrío, chill
escoliosis, scoliosis
espasmo, spasm
esputo, sputum, also spit, saliva
esquizofrenia, schizophrenia
estupefacientes, hallucinogenic drugs
esteroides, steroids
expectoración, expectoration
fibroma, fibroma
físico, physical
fisioterapia, physical therapy
fístula, fistula
fisura, fissure
fractura, fracture
frecuencia, frequency

gastritis, gastritis
gonorrea, gonorrhea
grave, serious, grave
gripe, flu, grippe
hemofilia, hemophilia
hemorragia, hemorrhage
hepatitis, hepatitis
hernia, hernia
herpes, herpes
hinchazón, swelling
hipertensión, hypertension
histeria, hysteria
hormona, hormone
infección, infection
infestado, infested
influenza, influenza, flu
inmunización, intermittent
intermitente, intermittent
jarabe, syrup (cough)
laringitis, laryngitis
leucemia, leukemia
lumbago, lumbago
malaria, malaria
menopausia, menopause
menstruación, menstruation (more commonly referred to as **la regla)**
miedo, fear
migraña, migraine

mononucleosis, mononucleosis
mordedura, bite
mudo, mute
nasal, nasal
náusea, nausea
nervioso, nervous
neurosis, neurosis
neurótico, neurotic
obeso, obese
palpitación, palpitation
PAP, pap smear
parálisis, paralysis
PCP, PCP
pedo, fart (slang)
pelagra, pelagra
placenta, placenta
polio, polio
prematuro, premature
prolapso, prolapse
proteína, protein
psicosis, psychosis
pulmonía, pneumonia
pulsación, pulsation
pulso, pulse
purga, purge
pus, pus
quemadura, burn
rabia, rabies
rasguño, scratch

recto, rectum
regla, menstrual period
retorcijones, cramps, muscle cramps
Rh factor, Rh factor
roncha, hives, or welt-like rash or swelling
roséola, roseola
rubéola, rubella
sacar aire, to burp
sacar leche del pecho, to express breast milk
salpullido, rash
sensación, sensation
severo, severe
sífilis, syphilis
síntoma, symptom
sofocación, suffocation
sordo, deaf
suero, serum
suicidio, suicide
supositorio, suppository
susto, extreme fear and depression sometimes accompanied by vague ill health (a Mexican folk health term, very commonly used to describe emotional illness)
temblor, tremor, trembling

temperatura, temperature
tendón, tendon
tensión, tension
termómetro, thermometer
tétanos, tetanus
tetraciclina, tetraclene
tifus, typhus
tonsilitis, tonsilitis
torcedura, sprain
torcido, sprained
tos, cough
tranquilizante, tranquilizer
tumor, tumor

úlcera, ulcer
ungüento, ointment
uñero, ingrown toenail
vacuna, vaccine
vacunación, vaccination
vagina, vagina
varicela, chickenpox
vasectomía, vasectomy
vejiga, bladder
venas varicosas, varicose
  veins
venda, bandage
veneno, poison

vergüenza, shame or embarrassment, expressed by many
  Spanish speaking people con-
  cerning V.D. and/or their
  genitals
verdugón, welt (large)
vesícula biliar, gall bladder
víctima, victim
viento, air, wind as in passing
  gas, flatulate
virus, virus
vista, vision
vista doble, double vision

vista nublada, cloudy vision
vitaminas, vitamins
vómitos, vomit
hiedra venenosa, poison ivy
  (oak)
yerba, herb
yerba buena, mint, often given
  as a tea for many things from
  nausea to colic and other
  digestive troubles
yeso, plaster cast
zumbidos, tinnitus, buzzing
  noises in the ear

English to Spanish

acute, **agudo**
appointment, **cita**
asthma, **asma**
bandage, **venda**
bite, **mordedura, mordida**
  (animal or human),
  piquete (of insect)
bladder, **vejiga**
blind, **ciego**
blister, **ampolla**
blurred, **nublado**
bruise, **cardenal (moretón)**

bump, **bulto, chichón**
burn, **quemadura**
burp, **eructar, sacar aire**
buzzing sound in ears,
  zumbidos
callus, **callo carbuncle,**
  carbunclo
cast, **yeso**
cataract, **catarato**
chancre, **chancro**
chills, **escalofríos**
chronic, **crónico**

circumcision, **circuncisión**
cirrhosis, **cirrosis**
colic, **cólico**
colitis, **colitis**
coma, **coma**
conjunctivitis, **conjuntivitis**
  (una infección del ojo,
  pink eye)
cough, **tos**
cramps, **calambres** (menstrual
  or stomach), **retorcijones**
  (muscle cramps)

crippled, **cojo**
dandruff, **caspa**
deaf, **sordo**
decongestant, **descongestivo**
deformity, **deformidad**
delirious, **delirio**
dermatitis, **dermatitis**
diabetes, **diabetes**
digestive disturbances, **dolor**
  de estómago, empacho
dilatation, **dilatación**
disc, **disco**

dislocation, **deslocación**
diuretic, **diurético**
double vision, **vista doble**
drugs, **drogas**
drunk, **borracho**
dysentery, **disentería**
eczema, **eczema**
edema, **edema**
embarrassment, **vergüenza**
enema, **enema**
eruption, **erupción**
expectoration, **expectoración**
express (as in breast milk),
   sacar (leche del pecho)
fart, **pedo** (slang, and somewhat improper although
   commonly used)
fat, **gordo, obeso**
fear, **miedo, susto**
fibroma, **fibroma**
fissure, **fisura**
fistula, **fístula**
flatulence, **viento, pasar gas**
flu, **influenza, gripe**
gallbladder, **vesícula biliar**
gas, **gas, pedo** (slang)
gastritis, **gastritis**
gonorrhea, **gonorrea**

hallucinogenic drugs,
   estupefacientes, drogas
   alucinogénicas
hemophilia, **hemofilia**
hemorrhage, **hemorragia**
hepatitis, **hepatitis**
heroin, **heroína, carga**
herpes, **herpes**
hives, **ronchas**
hormones, **hormonas**
hypertension, **hipertensión**
hysteria, **histeria**
immunization, **inmunización**
infection, **infección**
infested, **infestado**
influenza, **influenza, gripe**
ingrown toenail, **uñero**
intermittent, **intermitente**
lame, **cojo**
laryngitis, **laringitis**
leukemia, **leucemia**
lumbago, **lumbago**
lump, **bulto, chichón**
malaria, **malaria**
malnutrition, **desnutrición,**
   malnutrición
menopause, **menopausia**
menstruation, **menstruación,**
   regla

migraine, **migraña, jaqueca**
mint (herb), **yerba buena**
monoliasis (AKA thrush), **afta**
mononucleosis, **mononucleosis**
mute, **mudo**
nasal, **nasal**
nausea, **náusea**
nervous, **nervioso**
neurosis, **neurosis**
neurotic, **neurótico**
obese, **obeso**
ointment, **ungüento**
palpitation, **palpitación**
Pap smear, **PAP, prueba de PAP**
paralysis, **parálisis**
PCP, **PCP**
pelagra, **pelagra**
period, **regla**
phlegm, **gargajo, flema**
physical, **físico**
physical therapy, **fisioterapia**
placenta, **placenta**
pneumonia, **pulmonía**
   neumonía
poison, **veneno**
poison ivy, **hiedra venenosa**
poisonous, **venenoso**
premature, **prematuro**
prolapse, **prolapso**

protein, **proteína**
psychosis, **psicosis**
pulsation, **pulsación**
pulse, **pulso** (rapid pulse,
   pulso rápido; slow pulse,
   pulso lento)
purge, **purga**
pus, **pus**
rabies, **rabia**
rash, **salpullido**
rectum, **recto**
Rh factor, **factor de Rh,**
   Rh factor (negativo/positivo)
roseola, **roséola**
rubella, **rubéola**
saliva, **esputo, saliva**
scar, **cicatriz**
schizophrenia, **esquizofrenia**
scratch, **rasguño**
sensation, **sensación**
serum, **suero**
severe, **severo, grave, fuerte**
shame, **vergüenza**
sharp, **agudo**
sharp-pointed, **puntiagudo**
spasm, **espasmo**
splinter, **astilla**
sprain, **torcedura**
sprained, **torcido**

sputum, **esputo**
steroids, **esteroides**
suffocation, **sofocación**
suicide, **suicidio**
suppository, **supositorio**
swelling, **hinchazón**
symptoms, **síntomas**
syphilis, **sífilis**
syrup, jarabe

temperature, **temperatura**
tendon, **tendón**
tension, **tensión**
tetanus, **tétano(s)**
tetracyclene, **tetraciclina**
thermometer, **termómetro**
thrush, **afta**
tinnitus, **zumbidos**
tonsilitis, **tonsilitis**

tranquilizer, **tranquilizante**
trembling, tremor, **temblor**
tumor, **tumor**
typhus, **tifus**
ulcer, **úlcera**
vaccination, **vacunación,
    vacuna**
vagina, **vagina**
varicose veins, **venas varicosas**
vasectomy, **vasectomía**

victim, **víctima**
virus, **virus**
vision, **vista**
    double vision, **vista doble**
    blurred vision, **vista nublada**
vitamins, **vitaminas**
vomit, **vómitos**
wart, **verruga**
weakness, **debilidad**
welt, **roncha, verdugón**

INSTANT ACCESS